Looking at *Persians*

Also available from Bloomsbury

Looking at Agamemnon, edited by David Stuttard
Looking at Ajax, edited by David Stuttard
Looking at Antigone, edited by David Stuttard
Looking at Bacchae, edited by David Stuttard
Looking at Lysistrata, edited by David Stuttard
Looking at Medea, edited by David Stuttard

Looking at *Persians*

Edited by David Stuttard

BLOOMSBURY ACADEMIC
LONDON • NEW YORK • OXFORD • NEW DELHI • SYDNEY

BLOOMSBURY ACADEMIC
Bloomsbury Publishing Plc
50 Bedford Square, London, WC1B 3DP, UK
1385 Broadway, New York, NY 10018, USA
29 Earlsfort Terrace, Dublin 2, Ireland

BLOOMSBURY, BLOOMSBURY ACADEMIC and the Diana logo are trademarks of Bloomsbury Publishing Plc

First published in Great Britain 2023
Paperback edition published 2024

Copyright © David Stuttard & Contributors, 2023

David Stuttard has asserted his right under the Copyright, Designs and Patents Act, 1988, to be identified as Author of this work.

Cover design: Terry Woodley
Cover image © Terracotta *kylix* eye-cup (drinking cup) *c.* 520 BC, Greece. Fletcher Fund, 1956/The Metropolitan Museum of Art.

All rights reserved. No part of this publication may be reproduced or transmitted in any form or by any means, electronic or mechanical, including photocopying, recording, or any information storage or retrieval system, without prior permission in writing from the publishers.

Bloomsbury Publishing Plc does not have any control over, or responsibility for, any third-party websites referred to or in this book. All internet addresses given in this book were correct at the time of going to press. The author and publisher regret any inconvenience caused if addresses have changed or sites have ceased to exist, but can accept no responsibility for any such changes.

A catalogue record for this book is available from the British Library.

Library of Congress Cataloging-in-Publication Data
Names: Stuttard, David, editor, translator. | Aeschylus. Persae. English (Stuttard)
Title: Looking at Persians / David Stuttard.
Description: London ; New York : Bloomsbury Academic, 2022. | Includes bibliographical references and index.
Identifiers: LCCN 2022021824 | ISBN 9781350227927 (hardback) | ISBN 9781350227965 (paperback) | ISBN 9781350227934 (ebook) | ISBN 9781350227941 (epub) | ISBN 9781350227958
Subjects: LCSH: Aeschylus. Persae. | Aeschylus–Themes, motives. | Greek drama (Tragedy–History and criticism. | Literature and history–Greece.
Classification: LCC PA3825.P3 L66 2022 | DDC 882/.01—dc23/eng/20220525
LC record available at https://lccn.loc.gov/2022021824

ISBN:	HB:	978-1-3502-2792-7
	PB:	978-1-3502-2796-5
	ePDF:	978-1-3502-2793-4
	eBook:	978-1-3502-2794-1

Typeset by RefineCatch Limited, Bungay, Suffolk

To find out more about our authors and books visit www.bloomsbury.com and sign up for our newsletters.

Contents

List of Contributors ... vi
Foreword ... vii

Introduction: *Persians* in Context   *David Stuttard* ... 1

1   Persians on Stage   *Paul Cartledge* ... 15
2   Athens and Persia, 472 BCE   *Lloyd Llewellyn-Jones* ... 27
3   *Persians'* First Audience   *Robert Garland* ... 45
4   Imperial Stirrings in Aeschylus' *Persians*   *Sophie Mills* ... 59
5   Homeric Echoes on the Battlefield of *Persians*   *Laura Swift* ... 73
6   Individual and Collective in *Persians*   *Michael Carroll* ... 85
7   Land, Sea and Freedom: The Force of Nature in Aeschylus' *Persians*   *Rush Rehm* ... 99
8   The Persians Love their Children, too: Common Humanity in *Persians*   *Alan H. Sommerstein* ... 115
9   Atossa   *Hanna M. Roisman* ... 129
10 Theatrical Ghosts in *Persians* and Elsewhere   *Anna Uhlig* ... 151
11 Words and Pictures   *Carmel McCallum Barry* ... 163
12 National Theatre Wales: *The Persians* (2010)   *Mike Pearson* ... 177

Aeschylus' *Persians*   translated by *David Stuttard* ... 189

Bibliography ... 245
Index ... 255

Contributors

Michael Carroll is Lecturer in Greek Literature at the University of St Andrews.

Paul Cartledge is A. G. Leventis Senior Research Fellow, Clare College, Cambridge and A. G. Leventis Professor of Greek Culture emeritus, University of Cambridge.

Robert Garland is Roy D. and Margaret B. Wooster Emeritus Professor of Classics, Colgate University.

Lloyd Llewellyn-Jones is Professor in Ancient History at Cardiff University.

Carmel McCallum Barry is former Lecturer in Classics, University College, Cork.

Sophie Mills is Professor of Ancient Mediterranean Studies University of North Carolina Asheville.

Mike Pearson was Professor Emeritus of Performance Studies at Aberystwyth University and an Honorary Professor at Exeter University.

Rush Rehm is Professor of Theatre and Classics Emeritus at Stanford University.

Hanna Roisman is Arnold Bernhard Professor of Arts and Humanities, Emerita, Department of Classics, Colby College.

Alan H. Sommerstein is Emeritus Professor of Greek, University of Nottingham.

David Stuttard is a freelance writer, historian and theatre director, and Fellow of Goodenough College, London.

Laura Swift is Fellow and Tutor in Classics at Magdalen College, Oxford, and Associate Professor of Greek at the University of Oxford.

Anna Uhlig is Associate Professor of Classics at the University of California, Davis.

Foreword

Aeschylus' *Persians* is unique. The earliest surviving Greek tragedy, it is also the only one not to be set in the world of mythology. Indeed, the real historical facts around which it is constructed – the Persian Wars and Xerxes' invasion of the Greek mainland in 480 BC – occurred just under eight years before the first performance (in March or April 472 BC), and most of the audience and performers had fought in the Battle of Salamis, a description of which forms a central part of the drama. Nonetheless, in all other respects, *Persians* adheres to patterns with which we are familiar from other Athenian tragedies.

This collection of essays begins with assessments of *Persians*' place in history (including its context and the effect it may have had on its first audience) before considering some of the issues raised by the play, highlighting its main character, Atossa, the chorus, and the compelling necromancy scene, and ending with a director's view of an important modern production.

The volume concludes with my own translation of the play. Written (like the rest of the book) during the Covid-19 pandemic lockdown, this is the first translation in the *Looking at*... series which at the time of writing is yet to be performed. The challenges of translating Aeschylus are many, and I refer readers to my introduction to *Looking at Agamemnon* for a more detailed consideration. Suffice to say here, however, that his style is dense, sometimes ambiguous and on occasion not easily comprehensible, and that rendering his poetry into English can require often difficult choices, with which others may not always fully agree. For this reason, while suggesting to contributors that they use my translation wherever possible, I have been more than happy for them to use their own or others'. Readers will notice the occasional unintelligible outburst (printed in italics) such as *é-e*, *aiai* and *otototoi*. Simply transliterated, these represent incoherent groans or exclamations, as meaningless in Greek as they are in English, but nonetheless an important part of the text, indicating heightened emotion.

Those wishing to use the translation for productions of their own should contact me through my website, www.davidstuttard.com, where applications for performance should be made before the commencement of any rehearsals.

Finally, I would like to thank all those who have been involved in the production of this book, especially the twelve contributors, who, despite the impact of the pandemic and the many upheavals to which it has given rise, have been so generous with their time. It has been a pleasure to work with every one of them. At Bloomsbury, my thanks go to the incomparable Alice

Wright, who commissioned this volume, and her assistant Lily Mac Mahon, who oversaw its development with the wisdom of Athena and the patience of a saint. Thanks, too, to Merv Honeywood and all at RefineCatch who oversaw its layout, and especially to Roza I. M. El-Eini, who edited the text, and to Terry Woodley, who designed the stunningly appropriate cover – triremes (reminding us of Salamis); a hoplite (Aeschylus himself fought the Persians as a hoplite); and gigantic eyes (ideal for a *Looking at* volume): what more could anyone ask for?

Last but definitely not least, a massive thank you to the home team: my wife Emily Jane, without whose support I would find myself as adrift as Xerxes at the end of *Persians*; and our two cats, Stanley and Oliver, who, like the Great King viewing the Battle of Salamis from Mount Aegaleos, prefer to watch while others do the work.

Post Script

As this volume entered its final stages of production, we were saddened to learn of the death of one of its contributors, Mike Pearson. A towering figure in the world of theatre and scholarship, he will be sorely missed. This book is dedicated to his memory.

Introduction: *Persians* in Context

David Stuttard

Persians is the earliest fully extant Greek drama. It is also the only surviving tragedy to explore a real historical situation, the defeat of the huge invasion force which Persia's Great King Xshayarashā (in Greek and hereafter in this introduction, Xerxes) led against mainland Greece in 480 BC, an episode that touched the lives of everyone present at the first performance just eight years later. So, to appreciate *Persians* and the impact that Aeschylus, its author, may have intended, we must begin by looking at its historical and cultural context. While several contributors to this volume examine this in their chapters, it is so crucial to our understanding that it is worth briefly covering the ground here, too. We shall then consider the play in its dramatic context before touching on revivals both by Aeschylus and in more modern times.

Historical context

Democratic Athenians' relationship with the Persians (or Medes as they also called them) was always edgy. In 507/6 BC, threatened by other Greek states, they had toyed with allying with Persia, and Athenian ambassadors went so far as to agree to offer amphoras of earth and water, signs of submission. However, when Athens' popular Assembly, keen to preserve hard-won political autonomy, reneged on the deal the then Persian Great King Darius (Dārayavaush) interpreted their vote as a sign of duplicity if not rebellion.

Then in 499 BC there was a real rebellion. Greek cities on the west coast of Asia Minor had been subsumed into Persia's empire, and they now wanted to be free. Athens supported this Ionian Revolt, but a joint attack on Persia's provincial capital at Sardis achieved little except the (accidental) burning of the Temple of Cybele, the Anatolian equivalent of Greek Artemis. Athenians played no further role in the revolt, so when it ended in 494 BC with the Persian sack of the wealthy Ionian Greek city, Miletus, the slaughter of its men and the enslavement of its women and children, they may have felt some sense of guilt. Certainly, when Athens' leading tragedian, Phrynichus, staged his *Capture of Miletus* shortly afterwards, the audience fined him, and forbade its future staging, since 'it caused them to remember their own problems'.[1]

And problems they had aplenty. In 490 BC, Darius' fleet swept across the Aegean, burning cities and enslaving populations. But at Marathon on the east coast of Athens' territory, Attica, the Persians were defeated by a heavily outnumbered Athenian (and Plataean) army. Yet victory was bittersweet. Almost two hundred Athenians had fallen, among them Aeschylus' brother. As for Aeschylus himself, he was proud of his own role in the battle. Years later, his epitaph would boast how, 'the groves of Marathon tell of his courage, and the long-haired Medes know it well'.

Ten years later, in 480 BC, with Darius now dead, his son Xerxes led a new expedition into Greece (the subject matter of our play), crossing the Hellespont on pontoon bridges, while his navy shadowed him by sea. The Persians seemed unstoppable. When they smashed their way through the pass at Thermopylae, the allied Greek fleet which had been stationed at nearby Artemision (in northern Euboea), fled back to Salamis, an island off Attica's south coast, now home to countless Athenian refugees – for Attica had been evacuated. Its people no longer hoped to defend their land: whatever hope they had lay with their navy.

While the allied fleet was commanded by a Spartan admiral, at its heart were 200 Athenian triremes, state-of-the-art warships financed from revenue from a seam of silver discovered three years earlier at Laurium in Attica. As our Messenger tells Atossa: 'They have a silver wellspring. Their very land's a treasure trove' (238).

Fitted with a deadly bronze beak, each trireme was powered by 170 oarsmen, trained to ram the enemy at speed, while marines on deck hurled javelins into stricken ships or, on occasion, boarded them. With each crew totalling 200, Athens' fleet required 40,000 personnel, possibly every citizen of fighting age. While land battles were won mainly by the wealthy who could afford armour, naval warfare was intensely democratic: all Athenian males must play their part.

When the Persians entered Attica, they took revenge for Sardis by burning all its temples, including those on Athens' Acropolis. The psychological impact on the Athenians is almost unimaginable. Aeschylus has Darius' ghost describe the vandalism:

> When they got to Greece, they felt no compunction whatsoever about looting ancient wooden statues of the gods or torching temples. Altars have been smashed. Statues of divinities have been torn down from plinths and shattered.
>
> 809–13

Aeschylus may have seen this as a turning point, the moment when the Persians' fate was sealed. In the very next line he writes, 'Since [the Persians] acted so outrageously they are suffering no less outrageously in turn.'

Meanwhile, with the Greek fleet nervously readying to abandon Salamis for the Isthmus of Corinth, Athens' admiral Themistocles tricked Xerxes into fighting. While the audience knew this, Aeschylus never names Themistocles (or any individual Greek). He is simply 'a Greek man – from the Athenian army' (355). What is important is not Themistocles' individuality, but his Greek ethnicity and his Athenian identity. Moreover, a few lines later by linking 'the Greek man's cunning' to 'the gods' resentment' (362), Aeschylus suggests he is an agent of the gods.

Themistocles told Xerxes that the Greeks would try to sail from Salamis that night: if the Persians surprised them unawares, they would defeat them. The Messenger's first speech describes what happened next. All night Xerxes' fleet patrolled the exits from the Straits of Salamis. Only at dawn did they realize they had been duped. Exhausted, they heard the Greek war cry ring out as Greek triremes swung into action. According to one source, the first to attack was captained by another of Aeschylus' brothers, Ameinias.[2]

Aeschylus himself probably fought at Salamis, either as a marine or as a hoplite attacking Psyttaleia, a little 'island, sacred to the god Pan' (448–9). In *Persians* he describes this very attack:

> Then – in the end – [the Athenians] with one long endless roar rushed at [the Persians], cut them down, kept on hacking at their limbs and butchering those poor unfortunates, 'till every one of them was dead.
>
> 462–4

Although seen from the enemy Persian point of view, Aeschylus' account of the battle is the closest we have to an eyewitness report. While we cannot judge its accuracy, we do know that Aeschylus is guilty of 'fake news' – or dramatic invention – in his description of subsequent events. His fleet decimated, and with autumn looming, Xerxes left a body of crack troops to overwinter in Macedonia (and conclude what most still believed would be the defeat of Greece the next year), while he returned with the rest of his men to Asia. While his march home may have been plagued by logistical problems, it was far from the disastrous rout imagined by Aeschylus, and he stayed in Sardis for much of the next year. When he did return to Susa, his carefully choreographed reception was undoubtedly very different to how it is imagined in *Persians*.[3]

In summer 479 BC, Greek allies won a decisive victory at Plataea, an event which (with the benefit of just a little hindsight) Darius' ghost predicts in *Persians*:

> The oozing mess of blood spilled at Plataea by Greek spears will prove so prodigious that the piles of corpses will be for men a silent witness – even to the third generation – that they must not think too big.
>
> 816–20

Once more, Aeschylus takes the opportunity to suggest divine intervention and draw a moral lesson: 'When hubris flowers, it bears rich fruit – blind recklessness, a bumper harvest thick with tears' (821–2).

Over the next few years, Greeks 'liberated' most of the territory once ruled by Persia that the chorus lists in 864–96 as 'all the cities that [Darius] captured'. But by now Sparta had taken a back seat. Athens with her alliance, the Delian League, was spearheading the fightback, and beginning to claim victory over Persia as her own. It is to the period of that propaganda war that our play belongs. But *Persians* is not simply a piece of jingoism. Why? Before addressing this question, we must first consider *Persians* within the context of its wider tetralogy.

Persians and its tetralogy

Athenian drama was competitive. Over three days at each annual City Dionysia (festival of Dionysus), three rival writers each produced a tetralogy (three tragedies and a satyr play, named from its playful chorus of half-human half-horse creatures, which pricked the tragedies' solemnity), and a prize was awarded to the best playwright.

Persians was possibly the middle tragedy of Aeschylus' tetralogy of 472 BC, sandwiched between *Phineus* and *Glaucus*, with the satyr play, *Prometheus*. Save for a few lines, these other plays are lost, and no ancient 'hypothesis' (or précis) survives. But since most Aeschylean trilogies explored different episodes from the same larger story (for example, *Oresteia*, unravelling the effect of a curse over several generations), some scholars believe that the entire trilogy dealt somehow with either the Persian Wars or a struggle between Europe and Asia.

According to this thesis, *Phineus*, which may have been set near the Bosporus, may have dramatized an episode from the voyage of the Argonauts (note the ship theme), 'regarded by the Persians as an invasion of Asia by Europe, to be repaid in course of time by the invasion of Europe by Asia under the Persians'.[4] Perhaps too, since Phineus was a seer, it included a prophecy about Darius' expedition against Scythia in 513 BC.

Regarding *Glaucus* our speculations are complicated by the fact that Aeschylus wrote two plays of that name, and it is not always clear which surviving fragments belong to which drama.⁵ We know nothing of the plot, but one tradition suggests that Glaucus built the Argo – a link, perhaps, with *Phineus* and ships. Also, *Glaucus* may have been set near Plataea, and perhaps concluded with Glaucus prophesying about both the Greek victory there and the Sicilian Greeks' defeat of Carthaginians at the Battle of Himera (traditionally fought on the same day as Salamis). Since Carthage was founded from Phoenician Tyre, Carthaginians could be regarded as Asiatic, which reinforces the suggested Europe–Asia theme. *Glaucus* may have ended with 'some prophecies on the future of Greece followed by choral jubilations over the victory (contrast the dirge that concludes the *Persae*)'.⁶

There is a suggestion, too, that the satyr play, *Prometheus*, may have celebrated the purification of Greek altars whose fires were rekindled following the Persian Wars.

Readers will observe how often the words 'may' and 'perhaps' appear in preceding paragraphs. So much is speculation. The tetralogy may not have been thematically connected at all. But discussing it even briefly does remind us of an important known unknown: we simply do not know the wider dramatic context of *Persians*. Like *Choephoroi* in *Oresteia*, it probably marked neither the beginning nor the end of the day's theatrical experience and, without possessing the accompanying dramas, we cannot fully appreciate its role within the tetralogy.

Persians: A celebration of victory?

For many today, the idea of a victorious community joining in grief for its fallen enemy is almost unthinkable. In 1982, the UK's Archbishop of Canterbury, Robert Runcie, 'was attacked by the government and tabloid press for his sermon praying for the dead of both sides after the Falklands war (*sic*)'.⁷ Yet in *Persians*, Aeschylus invites fellow Athenians to empathize with the suffering of an enemy in a war not on the other side of the world but on their own soil – a war, in which homes and temples were destroyed and many citizens were killed or badly maimed. Perhaps even more surprisingly, just eight years after Athens' sack Athenians awarded him first prize at the City Dionysia. Why might this be so?

Of course, *Persians* contains occasional patriotic outbursts. Certain lines still meet with spontaneous applause from Greek audiences. During the Epidavros Festival production of 2020, the chorus' comments on Athenian democracy, 'They are not slaves of any man – nor vassals either' (242), together with the war cry, 'Forward, Greeks! Set free your fatherland!' (402), were clapped enthusiastically. Probably the first audience applauded, too, while other lines such as 'The gods protect the city of Athena' (347) may have encouraged similar reactions.

But for *Persians* to work as drama, despite such dog-whistle jingoism, the audience must see in it something more profound – and if we examine both its structure and its overarching concept of morality, we can see that in almost every respect this most unusual of plays follows many conventions familiar from other Greek tragedies, not least Aeschylus' own *Oresteia* (consisting of *Agamemnon*, *Choephoroi* and *Eumenides*).

Both *Persians* and *Agamemnon* are 'nostos' ('return') plays, exploring the homecoming of a powerful king and his army. Both begin ominously ('concerning their return [nostos] / however / (his – / the king's – / his richly kitted army's) / i feel / extreme foreboding / a premonition of disaster', *Persians* 8–10) – as their chorus recalls preparations for war. In both a messenger brings news of disaster to a queen – in *Agamemnon* following a storm at sea; in *Persians* following defeat and natural disaster. In *Choephoroi* and *Persians*, a queen sends offerings to her dead husband's tomb, while the chorus engages in necromancy. In *Eumenides* and *Persians*, a ghost appears. In *Agamemnon* and *Persians*, a king's homecoming is dangerous: Agamemnon, killed by his wife; Xerxes apparently shunned by his mother, dishonoured by his court, and facing an uncertain future – 'what will happen to me now, now that all this has happened?' (912) – while facing the possibility that 'the peoples of / the land of asia / will not remain for long now / under persian rule' (584–5).

In both dramas, gods play a major role, punishing the king for overstepping moral bounds in his lust for victory: Agamemnon sacrifices his daughter for a fair voyage, although he knows that in consequence his 'demon will destroy' him; Xerxes bridges the Hellespont because 'some *thing* from the spirit world usurped his mind ... some powerful spirit came on him and stopped him thinking clearly; and now we see how it all ended, the whole catastrophe he set in motion' (724–7). Moreover, both kings are punished for sacrilege: Agamemnon for destroying Troy's temples, Xerxes for destroying Athens'.

The idea of divine retribution permeates *Persians*. Até, the spirit of infatuation which leads to human downfall, bookends the play. In the parodos (the choral entrance song), the chorus tells how 'so attentive to our wants / [she] lures mankind deep / inside her snare / and no-one can escape / unbroken' (111–14), while towards the end of the play they reflect, 'you / gods / you / demons / you / clamped us with / catastrophe / so unexpected yet / so glaring / like the glance of / até / goddess of infatuation' (1005–7). Elsewhere, a demon (in Greek, *daimon*, a divine but not necessarily malevolent spirit) is blamed for Persia's defeat, while the messenger declares that 'it was some divine agency that tipped the scales and wrecked our army' (345).

Like other Greek tragedies, then, the action of *Persians* takes place on a more than human level, and it is partly by equating recent events with mythology, by treating Xerxes and the Persian Wars as he will later treat Agamemnon and the Trojan War, by using heightened imagery and language, that Aeschylus transforms lived experience into sacred drama, elevating his subject matter, avoiding cheap jingoism (on the whole) and inviting his audience to reflect on what victory teaches them about their own humanity, a humanity they share with the Persians. The chorus sums this up perfectly. Immediately having proclaimed that 'athens is abhorrent / to her enemies' (cue audience applause?), they add:

and we
we must remember
    persian wives
        widowed
    persian mothers
        robbed of their dead sons

286–9

Indeed, Aeschylus stresses this shared humanity. Atossa's dream imagines the two sides in the Persian Wars as 'two sisters of one family' (185), who live in Greece and Asia not because they are fundamentally different (they are not) but simply by chance. Gods' laws govern Greeks and Persians alike. Excess is wrong, whether it involves excessive wealth (a cause of downfall in both *Persians* and *Agamemnon*) or excessive triumphalism. To retain our humanity and avoid the gods' anger we must temper that excess. Our play lets us do exactly that. Moreover, it reminds Athenians, now enjoying the upper hand in dealings with both Persians and fellow Greeks, that they must continue to temper it.

Persians was not the only historical (or more accurately 'contemporary') tragedy to ask an Athenian audience to empathize with a defeated enemy. In 476 BC, Phrynichus' *Phoenician Women* had already explored the impact of Salamis on Persians back home. Given that his *Capture of Miletus* provoked a hefty fine, Phrynichus must have carefully considered the risks involved in inviting Athenians to share their enemy's grief, but the play was such a success that one fifth-century AD scholar tells us that Aeschylus' *Persians* was *adapted* from Phrynichus' *Phoenician Women*.[8]

It opened with a eunuch, who has just heard of Xerxes' defeat, arranging chairs for speakers in the Persian Council (perhaps a semi-chorus: the main chorus were Phoenician Women). Stripped of uncertainty regarding the invasion's success and with no hopes left to be dashed by the announcement of defeat, the play is likely to have been heavy on lament. Surviving fragments include a description of the fleet setting sail ('leaving the city of Sidon, and Arados, glistening with dew', fragment. 9), the Battle of Salamis ('men were slaughtered until evening fell', fragment 10a)[9] and the impact of defeat on the eponymous Phoenician women ('singing threnodies accompanied by plucking harps', fragment 11).[10] Perhaps the most popular line was 'all these are Persian possessions, but the Persians themselves have long ago departed' (fragment 8), which may have referred to either the immediate setting (the Council Chamber), or Greek cities in Ionia, from which Athenians were already expelling Persian garrisons and governors (cf. *Persians* 864–6). Like *Persians*, *Phoenician Women* probably trod a narrow line between pride in victory and empathy for the enemy bereaved.

We do not know what part gods played in Phrynichus' treatment, but many of Aeschylus' near contemporaries shared his vision of a world where Persian hubris meets divine punishment, not least the historian Herodotus, who like Aeschylus often hints that 'the very land is on the side of Greece' (792). Yet, neither Aeschylus nor Herodotus (nor Homer before them) are xenophobes. Foreigners may be clumped together as 'barbarians' (Aeschylus' Persians even refer to themselves as such); they may have different customs; some may be braver or more cowardly than others; but in the end it is the soil from which people spring and the land whereon they live that shape them most. Otherwise, we are mostly all the same.[11]

So, while, as the only extant contemporary Greek drama, *Persians* is unique, it is wholly representative of Athenian tragedy, whose protagonists – no matter if we love or loathe them, be they mythological or the Great King of Persia – are human beings like us, subject to more powerful cosmic rules, prone to reversals and capable of deep emotion, and by recognizing this we recognize our own humanity. Later playwrights recognized this, too. Euripides' tragedies sing with sorrow for defeated barbarian enemies, not least those about the fall of Troy and the fate of its queen, Hecuba. 'What's Hecuba to him, or he to Hecuba, that he should weep for her?' asks Hamlet.[12] Like Shakespeare and Aeschylus, Euripides knew the answer: like him, she is a human being.

Staging Greek tragedy

Persians was first staged *al fresco* on the southern slopes of the Athenian Acropolis in the Theatre of Dionysus. In 472 BC, this consisted of a rectangular 'theatron' (auditorium) where the audience – upwards of 4,000 strong, and probably all male – sat on the ground or wooden bleachers around three sides of a rectangular flat 'orchestra' (dance floor) behind which (on the fourth side) rose the '*skēnē*', perhaps a simple curtain, a temporary wooden structure or – as the name suggests – a tent. A later Greek tradition maintained that it was Xerxes' own tent, looted from the battlefield of Plataea, a romantic notion which, if true, would have added piquancy to the staging of *Persians*, but which is almost certainly erroneous.

Athenian drama was sacred to Dionysus, god of wine, burgeoning nature and transformation. Like most extant tragedies, *Persians* was performed as part of an annual festival, the City (or Great) Dionysia, held close to the Spring equinox, and established either around 534 BC or following the introduction of democracy around 507 BC. Early drama appears to have evolved from choral performances – that is, performances by a group of men involving movement and singing to the accompaniment of a wind instrument, the aulos – and the chorus plays a vital role in every Aeschylean tragedy.

Early tragedies involved just one actor interacting with the chorus (though the chorus-leader sometimes performed solo lines), but Aeschylus is said to have introduced a second actor, a major development, which enabled greater dramatic flexibility. In 472 BC, the chorus consisted of twelve men, who probably rehearsed throughout the preceding winter. In *Persians*, they took the role of Persian (male) elders, though in other Aeschylean tragedies they played female Egyptian refugees (*Suppliants*) and demonic Furies (*Eumenides*). All performers were masked, and vase paintings suggest that the chorus' masks were identical, encouraging audiences to view them not as individuals but as anonymous members of a wider group. Solo actors (who might play multiple roles within the same play) wore masks, too, which were probably more individualized.

Most performers in *Persians* are likely to have been sumptuously costumed not least because (tradition suggests) the production was financed by an ambitious 'choregus' (backer), keen to make his mark and earn a reputation – a wealthy young aristocrat called Pericles. The text gives pointers regarding these costumes. Darius wears yellow slippers and a tiara (a Persian royal crown). Athenians probably knew that Persian Great Kings never appeared in public unless elaborately dressed in rich ceremonial clothing, and some audience members may actually have glimpsed Xerxes from afar as he sat on the hillside overlooking Salamis to watch the battle. If so, the visual impact of his homecoming in rags must have been doubly powerful, even if it bore no relation to historical reality: the ragged living Xerxes entering so soon after the splendidly attired ghost of Darius has exited makes for a striking contrast, emphasizing the depths to which Persia has sunk.

Equally provocative must have been the sight of the chorus prostrating themselves before Atossa. Greeks thought this Persian custom (which they called *proskynesis*) sacrilegious, since they themselves performed it only before gods' statues, and they believed (wrongly) that Persians considered their king to be divine. Indeed, such was Greek resentment of *proskynesis* that Alexander the Great's Greek soldiers would later become mutinous when he asked them to prostrate themselves before him. In actions as in dress, then, Aeschylus reinforces his characters' foreignness (while preserving their humanity).

It is possible that in the first performance Aeschylus himself played Xerxes and Atossa, since in this period dramatists acted in their own plays as well as being their own directors and composers. Music, too, played a major role. Choral odes (or stasima) were sung, as were solo passages of heightened emotion, and Aeschylus' music for *Persians* was probably deliberately orientalizing, adding an extra layer of supposed 'authenticity'. (In the accompanying translation, changes in layout indicate where these musical passages occur.)

Little about Greek performance was naturalistic. Masks, as well as the demands of outside performance, probably forced lines to be delivered 'up and out', directly to the audience, while the need to be clearly heard must have meant that the chorus – far from dancing energetically – may have performed relatively sedate steps, confining most movement to their upper bodies.

Despite these restrictions, tragedies were clearly both emotionally enthralling and visually spectacular. Atossa's first appearance on a horse-drawn vehicle was accompanied by pomp and ceremony (as she tells us during her more restrained second entrance); the contrast to Xerxes' return, in a curtained carriage, in rags cannot have been greater; and, placed between these two extremes, one of *Persians'* many *coups de théâtre*, the necromancy scene, was no doubt spine-tingling. Aeschylus suggests that the chorus scratch the earth as they coax Darius from the underworld, perhaps gyrating as they intersperse their words with inarticulate cries (*e-é*; *aiai*). The dead king's epiphany must have been memorable, but how the effect was managed we simply do not know.

Persians: Afterlife

Persians was an immediate success. Shortly after its first performance, Hieron, brother of Gelon, the victor of Himera, invited Aeschylus to take it (alone or with the complete tetralogy?) to Sicily. Oddly, the fact that Hieron was a ruthless tyrant did not seem to worry Aeschylus overmuch (but *Persians'* praise of democracy did not appear to worry Hieron), and Aeschylus later wrote another quasi-historical drama, *Women of Aetna*, celebrating Hieron's forcible relocation of the populations of several Sicilian cities to Catania, before returning to the island at least once and dying there of natural causes in 456 BC.

Fifty years later, in 405 BC, *Persians* was so well known that Aristophanes could reference it in *Frogs*, where he has the dead Aeschylus debate with Dionysus in the underworld:

Aeschylus ... Then in *Persians* I instructed my actors – and my audience – always to defeat the enemy; I wreathed their finest hour in honour.

Dionysus I definitely cheered when I learned about the dead Darius, and at once the chorus beat their hands together, shouting '*i-au-oi*'.[13]

Like the rest of *Frogs*, this scene is comedic, so we should not imagine that the stage-Aeschylus' speech reflects the real Aeschylus' intent. However, Dionysus' description of the staging with its inarticulate cries is probably based on a recent revival.

One of just seven Aeschylean tragedies deliberately preserved throughout antiquity (actually, just six – *Prometheus Bound* is falsely attributed), *Persians* was understandably popular during Greece's struggles against Ottoman Turkey, and in the twentieth and twenty-first centuries it has enjoyed productions too numerous to discuss here. Suffice to say that they have generally fallen into one of two broad categories: those which emphasize the play's timelessness and those that try to shoehorn it into a modern context to make a political point.[14]

One example of the latter was Peter Sellars' 1993 version staged at venues including the Edinburgh and Salzburg festivals. An adaptation by Robert Auletta, using a chorus of three and with oud music composed and performed by Hamza El Din, its context was the Gulf War of 1990–1, with the 'invading' US army standing in for the original Persians. Iraq provided inspiration for another US production, this time by the National Actors Theater in New York, staged in 2003 in a version by Ellen McLaughlin directed by Ethan McSweeny in response to George W. Bush's invasion of the country the previous year.

Responses to both were mixed. While many found Sellars' production gripping, the *Los Angeles Times* theatre critic opined that 'the analogy doesn't work', calling it a 'misfired exercise in misplaced activism'. On the other hand, although theatre critic, Elysse Sommer, did not regard *Persians* as 'one of the top-drawer Greek dramas', she believed that MacSweeny's *Persians* (with a chorus of seven and 'very effective musical elements') encapsulated the essence of Aeschylus' original, concluding that 'its history lesson about power and its misuse is also the stuff of high drama – especially as executed here'.[15]

In truth, although timeless in its scope, Aeschylus' *Persians* is rooted in one particular war. Attempts to make the Persian War stand in for a specific other risk compromising either text or production. Dimitrios Ligdanis knew this when he directed his powerful version at the 2020 Epidavros Festival with Lydia Koniordou giving a devastatingly intense performance as Atossa for what was billed as a celebration of the 2,500th anniversary of Salamis (though it was but the 2,499th). Stripped of excessive modern allusion and featuring a muscular delivery by the chorus of twelve, it was broadcast live worldwide on 25 July, inspiring the *New York Times* critic Elisabeth Vincentelli to observe, 'the four lead actors essentially deliver arias, achieving an incantatory power that feels otherworldly. We never forget, though, that the play is rooted in emotions that are all too human.'[16]

Perhaps most telling of all is a serving soldier's reaction to the production discussed in our final chapter. In 2010, Mike Pearson directed *The Persians* for the National Theatre Wales, immersing his audience in an alien war-torn environment – a training camp, where armed forces rehearse for urban warfare. Like Ligdanis at Epidavros, he explored the impact of war in general. The *Guardian* review concluded with a neat summation: 'Aeschylus fought the Persians and his play has variously been read as a critique of war, a celebration of victory, a mockery of defeated enemy. The training camp's commander, who praised this production highly, had an alternative view: "We recognise it. We learn from the mistakes."'[17]

Notes

1 Herodotus 6.21.
2 *Life of Aeschylus* 4: but Athenian brothers belonged to the same deme (a grouping determined by geography) and given that Ameinias' deme was different from Aeschylus', their consanguinity is unlikely.
3 Logistical problems: Herodotus 8.115.
4 Broadhead (1960), lv. See also Wright (2019), 60–1.
5 See Wright (2019), 25–6.
6 Broadhead (1960), lvii.
7 Bates (2000).
8 Glaucus of Rhegium, quoted in Wright (2016), 24. See, too, my discussion of *Phoenician Women* and *Persians* in *Phoenix* (2021), 206–8. The fragments of Phrynichus are gathered (and numbered) in Kannicht, Snell and Radt (1971–2004).
9 Compare *Persians*: 'Screams and groaning blanketed the surface of the sea until black night came down and hid it all from view' (426–8).

10 Compare *Persians*: 'in marriage beds / wives weep / with longing / for their husbands' (123–4).
11 Soil and land: Herodotus 9.122.
12 Shakespeare, *Hamlet*, Act II, Scene 2.
13 Aristophanes, *Frogs* 1026–9.
14 *Persians* and Greek struggles with Ottoman Turkey: see Nevin (2022), 178 with references.
15 S. Drake's *Los Angeles Times* review of Peter Sellars' production, at: https://www.latimes.com/archives/la-xpm-1993-10-02-ca-41199-story.html (accessed 3 February 2022). E. Sommer's *Curtainup* review of National Actors Theater's production, at: http://www.curtainup.com/persians.html (accessed 03/02/33). A list of productions between 1571 and 2010 is contained on the website of The Archive of Performances of Greek and Roman Drama (APGRD): http://www.apgrd.ox.ac.uk/productions/canonical-plays/persai-persians/590 (accessed 3 February 2022).
16 E. Vincentelli's review of the 2020 Epidavros production in the *New York Times*, at: https://www.nytimes.com/2020/07/26/theater/the-persians-review-aeschylus.html (accessed 3 February 2022).
17 C. Brennan's review of the National Theatre of Wales' production in *The Guardian*, at: https://www.theguardian.com/stage/2010/aug/15/the-persians-national-theatre-wales (accessed 3 February 2022).

1

Persians on Stage

Paul Cartledge

'... And the long-haired Mede knew too ...' So ends the possibly self-penned epitaph of Aeschylus son of Euphorion of the deme Eleusis, who died not in his native Attica but at wheat-bearing Gela in Sicily in 456 BCE.[1] He was the first truly great tragic poet of Athens and Greece, canonized as such by the Athenians themselves towards the end of the fourth century.[2] The earliest of his six or seven (the authorship of *Prometheus Bound* is contested)[3] tragedies to survive – in a form that putatively approximates closely to the text as originally enacted – was staged at the annual Athenian Great / City Dionysia festival in spring (March/April) 472 BCE. As was customary, it was one of his three tragedies then performed, and its title is *Persians*.[4]

'Mede(s)' – or 'Persians'? Though related, the Medes of what is now northern Iran and the Persians of southern Iran were in fact distinct peoples, with distinct customs (e.g. the *magoi* priests were originally priests of the Medes) and distinct attributes, e.g. of dress, as depicted on the Apadana ceremonial palace stairway at the Achaemenid Persian capital that the Greeks in a typical appropriation renamed 'Persepolis' or 'City of the Persians'.[5] Likewise, the Greeks in their classically ethnocentric way refused to mark the difference between Medes and Persians consistently in their unofficial everyday nomenclature. Instead, they applied the term 'Mede' generically to include both peoples, as in the Aeschylean epitaph above, although they knew the difference and distinction full well, and never spoke of the Great King of Persia as a 'Mede'.[6] Aeschylus knew what he was doing in calling his play 'Persians', as did Herodotus when referring to what we call the Persian Wars as *ta mêdika*, 'the Median things'.

As has been very well brought out in previous scholarship, such diminishing, indeed sometimes denigrating, ethnocentrism was by no means confined to the Greeks' attitudes towards Iranians. Indeed, it was a fundamental move of cultural self-definition for them to divide up the entire human race in a polar, binary, antithetical way: Hellenes and – or, rather, as opposed to – 'barbarians'.[7] The ultimate basis of that bifurcation was linguistic/onomatopoeic: 'bar-bar' sounds are unintelligible sounds, mere noises; and the distinction was put into common Hellenic circulation very early on indeed, since 'barbarophônoi' –

bar-bar-sounding – Carians appear already in the *Iliad* (2.867) probably not later than 650 BCE.[8] However, what might at first have appeared to be a (merely) descriptive term of difference/distinction could not remain so, once relations between Greeks/Hellenes and non-Greeks had taken a hostile, military-political turn as they did from the mid-sixth century BCE.

Herodotus, himself a privileged witness hailing from mixed Hellenic-barbarian/Greek-Carian Halicarnassus, compiled his *Histories* during the third quarter of the fifth century BCE in broad terms. He unhesitatingly points the finger at King Croesus of Lydia (reigned *c.* 560–545) as the first barbarian within known, accessible historical space and time to have subjugated Greeks (1.5). Croesus and his mini-empire were in their turn conquered and absorbed by (mixed Persian-Median) Great King Cyrus II of Persia, founder of the Achaemenid Persian (never 'Median') Empire that flourished as a major Middle Eastern player between about 550 and 330 BCE.[9] It was of the essence of Herodotus' pioneering historiographical project to describe and above all explain how and why this empire had come not only to subjugate and rule many Greeks of Asia and then – rather fewer – of north Africa and northern Greek Europe but also to attempt to subjugate all mainland and Aegean Greece.[10]

That project, inherited from his father, Great King Darius I, and doubtless enhanced, had been undertaken in 480–479 BCE by Xerxes (as the Greeks transcribed a name that in Old Persian sounded something like Khshayathra). It had been a resounding failure – for complex reasons that are beyond the scope of this essay to explore.[11] And not the least of Xerxes' failures – Herodotus controversially concluded that it was his greatest and most decisive (7.139) – was the naval Battle of Salamis in August–September 480 BCE.[12] It was that battle which was the original inspiration and dramatic context of Aeschylus' *Persians*, which we may assume that he began seriously to compose in or before summer 473, some seven years after the battle itself.

Aeschylus' life (*c.* 525–456?), however, is not at all well known – biography was not yet then a distinct Greek literary genre. So, although we know with certainty from his epitaph that Aeschylus was a veteran of the famous land battle of Marathon (490 BCE), we cannot say for certain even that he was an active participant at Salamis ten years later. It is, however, a plausible hypothesis that he was, though – by then aged about forty-five – more likely as a supporting land fighter than as a frontline sailor.[13]

The Greeks and especially the Athenians engaged with their 'barbarian' foes in manifold complex ways. There were indeed Athenians who – at least according to their political enemies – were so well disposed towards the Persians that they could be accused of and even legally condemned for the heinous crime of 'medism' (note again the derogatory use of 'Mede'), that is, for somehow politically favouring or taking the side of the Persians, a form of high treason.[14] Far less objectionable were cultural borrowings, even appropriations, some of which might even fall within the sphere of official policy, such as the remarkable building constructed at the foot of the Athenian Acropolis in the mid-fifth century and known as the Odeion or 'Singing Hall'.[15] Somewhere between those influences that were generally deemed to be malign and those that were generally considered benign fell creative representations of Persia and Persians both visual (e.g. vase paintings)[16] and audio-visual. In the latter category, pride of place must be accorded to Athenian tragic drama. This chapter will therefore explore Athenian tragic representations of Persians on stage and, correlatively, Persian representations of Athenian tragedy from Phrynichus' lost *Capture of Miletus* and Aeschylus' *Persians* to Abdollah Kowsari's translations into Persian of five tragedies by Euripides. The Persian mirror may distort but it also reflects, deeply.

Phrynichus had a long and original if chequered career as a tragic dramatist, stretching it is thought from about 510 BCE to at least 476. If he did indeed exhibit as early as 510, that would have been at the very end of the reign of tyrant Hippias (*c.* 527–510) and well before Athens experienced the democratic or proto-democratic reform attributed to the senior aristocrat Cleisthenes in *c.* 508/7. Since theatre at Athens was a form of politics, it has been argued, plausibly, that a major theatrical reform followed suit quite shortly thereafter, perhaps around 500 BCE, whereby the annual Great or City Dionysia festival was reorganized as a festival of tragedy-plus-satyr drama, on a democratic or proto-democratic basis.[17] Just seven years or so later, Phrynichus found himself in the eye of a classic democratic storm.

The maiden democracy in its concern for security and from a keenness to avoid multiplying enemies seems to have humbled itself initially before the Great King of Persia, Darius I, paying him the formal tokens of submission in the shape of 'earth and water'.[18] But seeing off a threatened Spartan invasion followed by military success against its immediate neighbours in 506 apparently encouraged a change of heart and a more or less immediate repudiation of its formal Persian subservience.[19] At all events, when a ruler of Miletus, a major Anatolian Greek city subjected to Persia, came calling for assistance in making a revolt in 500, the Athenian people voted to give aid and followed up their words with deeds: they not only sent a score of ships in support but even marched inland to torch the nearest Persian vice-regal capital, Sardis in Lydia, in 498. Four years or so later, however, in 494, the so-called 'Ionian Revolt' was finally and decisively crushed by the Persians after a major naval battle fought near an island (Lade) just off Miletus.[20]

Our major source for this revolt, and therefore for the Athenians' involvement, is another Anatolian Greek, Herodotus, himself probably born a Persian subject who made himself into the historian of why Greeks and Persians had come to be involved in a series of hostile encounters going back as far as the 540s, but more especially in a deadly two-year struggle (480–479) on either side of the Aegean for the liberty of mainland Greece from Persian domination, and of why the resisting Greeks had unexpectedly won. Herodotus thus relates the Battle of Lade and, more relevantly for us, its consequences for the city of Miletus and its Athenian ally.

Quite soon after their naval victory, the Persians meted out extreme punishment to the rebels of Miletus, selling the women and children into slavery, forcibly transporting those male citizens they had not killed to the deeply alien shores of the Persian Gulf and effectively annihilating the physical city. Probably not long after that, Phrynichus responded to a real-world tragedy that had affected many Athenians deeply with a tragic drama entitled *Miletou Halôsis* or 'The Capture of Miletus' that also affected them very strongly. 'Capture' in the circumstances was a considerable euphemism, perhaps designed not to arouse the suspicion or veto of the Athenian official responsible for choosing which plays and playwrights were to feature in the next Great Dionysia. However, although no text of the play has survived, Herodotus (6.21) bears witness that either the subject matter of the play or its treatment proved so affecting for many or most of the Athenians in the audience that – no doubt at or after the Assembly meeting that regularly followed the Great Dionysia – Phrynichus was fined the huge sum of six talents (at least a couple of small fortunes) precisely for reminding the Athenians of their own sorrows.

One might have predicted that that would have put paid to Phrynichus' career altogether, but in 476[21] he was once more 'given a chorus' at the Great Dionysia, and again for a play with a Persian theme, this time entitled the *Phoenissae* or 'Women of Phoenicia'. But by 476, the political context of the performance was radically different from that of the late 490s: the Persians had been beaten, first at Marathon in 490 and then from the Athenian point of view most signally in the naval battle off Salamis in 480; and the hero of that latter battle, Themistocles, just happened also to be Phrynichus' *chorêgos* or financial sponsor. Phrynichus duly won first prize with a play whose eponymous chorus, probably of Phoenician widows or slaves at a Persian court, emphasized the weeping and wailing and gnashing of teeth that the Salamis victory caused to Darius I's son and successor, Great King Xerxes.[22] Their lament was music to the Athenian audience's ears, but for sponsor Themistocles we can see with hindsight that it marked pretty much the summit of his popularity with the Athenian *demos* (masses).

To them, Persia was and would for the foreseeable future remain public enemy number one, but in the eyes of Themistocles the Athenians and their newly reinvigorated and recalibrated democracy had an even more formidable enemy to counter much nearer to home: resolutely anti-democratic Sparta. Themistocles seems to have taken no part in the foundation in 478/7 or early activities of the Athenians' anti-Persian alliance that we know as the Delian League.[23] By 473/2, Themistocles' star had so far fallen that at least two Athenians believed he needed a massive propaganda boost, and in a very public, political space. Those two Athenians were tragic playwright Aeschylus, by then aged just over 50 and a veteran of Marathon and possibly also of Salamis, and his financial sponsor, a very young (only 20 or so) Pericles son of Xanthippus, a descendant of reformer Cleisthenes on his mother's side.

So it was that for the Great Dionysia festival of 472 Aeschylus was 'granted a chorus' by the Archon Eponymos, for a tetralogy (three tragedies plus, as a relieving coda, a satyr-drama) that included *Persai* or 'Persians'. Of course, there was more, much more, to *Persians* (note – not 'Medes') than just propagandizing for Themistocles, as this collection amply demonstrates; this was by no means only an incidental or minor motif or motive. Of course, it is conceivable that there was an informal convention or taboo against naming living Greek individuals in a tragedy, at any rate for party political purposes; indeed, such was the apparent taboo on everyday, real-life political scenarios after the Phrynichus debacle that there are hardly any other known Athenian tragedies on near contemporary as opposed to mythic themes besides the three discussed here. But by the same token there can be now, as there could have been in 472, absolutely no doubt who was the – unspoken – hero on the loyalist Greek side, although it cannot be assumed further that Aeschylus and his youthful sponsor were so to speak on the same page politically and ideologically. Their visions of what a post-Salamis *demokratia* could or should mean might have been quite divergent then, as they very likely were in 458, the occasion of Aeschylus' *Oresteia* trilogy.[24]

In 'bigging up' the achievement of Themistocles, Aeschylus was pretty much following the lead of Phrynichus' *Phoenissae*, but in one other, fundamental respect it would appear that the two dramatists differed from each other quite radically in their treatments. Phrynichus had every reason for not only wanting his mainly Athenian audience to appreciate the depth of the Persians' suffering but also seeking to as it were rub it in, to make them glory in it, as something totally deserved. By contrast, what has often struck more recent commentators on *Persai* is the apparent sympathy which Aeschylus either consciously aimed to or at least was seemingly able to elicit and evoke from the audience for the defeated Persians. Here was a people who – as Herodotus later confirmed, no doubt influenced at least in part by the Aeschylean portrait of Xerxes – had been grossly misled (in every sense) by their power-crazed, sacrilegious, autocratic ruler.[25]

Indeed, such was Aeschylus' apparent sympathy for the defeated Persians that many commentators tended to overlook or underplay another key feature – and, surely, a key ideological motivation – of the play, one that was first drawn attention to, if in a very one-sided and unhistorical way, by Edward Said, who saw *Persians* as the fount and origin of 'orientalism' in its decidedly negative signification.[26] This binary, polar opposition of Greek (and especially Athenian) and Persian culture was then fully and historically explicated in the work of Edith Hall. In an exemplary chapter of a book devoted to how a Greek perception of barbarian identity was 'invented' through Athenian dramatic representations in tragedy she revealed that, however pitiable the Persians might have been as human beings suffering bereavement, as members of a profoundly anti-democratic, anti-political society they were not to be pitied at all by an audience of radical democrats living in a participatory, face-to-face, civic-democratic republic.[27]

Of all the political qualities that the Persians systematically lacked, and the lack of which Aeschylus highlighted, perhaps the single most important absence was that of the peculiarly democratic notion of responsibility or accountability.[28] It is therefore, I believe, no accident that Herodotus, when compiling the western world's earliest extant example of political theory (3.80–2), regarded accountability of all officials, however selected for office, as one of the three cardinal features of what he chose to call *isonomia*, a precursor of and surrogate for the term *demokratia* (3.80).[29] Herodotus, oddly at first sight, placed this theoretical exercise in the mouths of three Persian aristocrats, precisely the sort of people who would in actual historical fact have been unable to contemplate living in any other than a despotic, autocratic political order. But on reflection, one of the points of having that Debate be a Persian Debate was surely that the three speakers rejected the proto-democratic views of the first speaker, Otanes, and agreed to stick with the autocratic, anti-democratic vision of the third, the man who in actual reality did indeed become Persian Great King, Darius I. He was accountable to no man, and if accountable at all only to supreme deity Ahura Mazda.[30]

Almost exactly contemporary, I believe, if not coterminous with Herodotus' working life was the construction of the Parthenon and its chryselephantine Athena Parthenos up on the Athenian Acropolis (447–432). That extraordinary building clearly was a central part of the Athenians' claim to have 'saved' Hellas in 480–479 and to be the current champions of Hellenic freedom in the post-war decades, and as such it was an intrinsically anti-Persian monument.[31] But closer to our dramatic-theatrical perspective and indeed directly connected to the Theatre of Dionysus at the foot of the Acropolis was another quite nonstandard building with the construction of which Pericles appears to have been rather intimately associated. Quite likely the Odeion or Odeum (Singing Hall) was directly inspired in form by the Apadana or Great Audience Hall of Persepolis; at all events, it was clearly a direct public response of Athens to the Achaemenid Persian Empire. It was here that henceforth occurred the Proagon – the day's ceremonies immediately preceding the Great / City Dionysia at which the chosen playwrights advertised their forthcoming wares.[32]

So far as can be seen, tragedians did not share the taste for *Perserie* and other Persian-inspired material-cultural adaptations or imitations that appear to have gripped many Athenians in the second half of the fifth century BCE, a 'cultural receptivity' that forms the main theme and thesis of Miller 1997. Athenian Old Comic poets were less bashful. For instance, the title character of Eupolis' 421 BCE *Marikas*, a surrogate for leading politician Hyperbolus, was arguably given a Persian-derived name, to heap ignominy on insult. Then, right at the end of the Atheno-Peloponnesian War, won by Sparta thanks largely to massive Persian financial aid, Dionysus himself is made actually to refer to Aeschylus' *Persians*, if in an unfortunately unclear way, in Aristophanes' prize-winning and much lauded *Frogs* (1028-9) of 405.

Probably somewhere between *Marikas* and *Frogs* came Timotheus of Miletus' experimental *Persai*. This was not a play for a cast and chorus, but a solo composition performed on the *kithara* (lyre), but the reason for including mention and brief discussion here is that it is a key and indeed one of the few extant instances of the more or less direct ancient reception of Aeschylus' homonymous play. As Bridges (2015: 37–43) has well observed, there are some striking differences between the two treatments as regards the character Xerxes: above all, there seems to be no suggestion in the extant Timotheus nome, as there is in *Persians*, that Xerxes might even have considered accepting any personal responsibility for the Salamis debacle. By contrast, Timotheus was at one with his tragic forerunner and inspiration in depicting a melodramatic Xerxes character, one that 'allowed them to create arresting theatrical performances' and a 'vision of the Persian king as a shadow of his former self' that are 'the tragic theatre's bequest to posterity' (ibid., 43). Timotheus' Milesian origin will not have been irrelevant. By the time of his *Persai*, his native city had been resettled after the urbicide of 494 and found itself again in the eye of the East–West storm.

Coda

Talking of posterity: Whether or not a Persian victory at Salamis would have meant the end of the possibility of ancient Greece as a cultural ancestor of the West is open to continuing question (Harrison 2011: 125). But it would certainly have precluded the composition, performance and so reception of Aeschylus' *Persians*. This is not the place to enter into anything like a detailed survey of the modern – mainly (but not only – see below) Western – reception of Aeschylus' *Persians*.[33] But there is one notable facet of its dramatic, theatrical and especially operatic reception that deserves special mention, what Stoneman (2015: 222) has memorably dubbed an 'avalanche of Italian Persica'.[34] Handel's 1738 opera seria *Serse* is perhaps the most famous example. Instead, I shall in conclusion take a rather different tack.

In 2016, Abdollah Kowsari brought out verse translations into Persian of five tragedies by Euripides, acknowledging as his inspiration his fellow Iranian intellectual Shahrokh Meskoub (1924–2006), who had translated a play of Aeschylus. Not *Persians*, however, but the Aeschylean *Prometheus Bound* (1963), the tyrannous theme of which perhaps seemed more apropos in the age of the last Shah. At last, though, in 1998, an Iranian translation of *Persians* was published, done by Fuad Rouhani, who, so far from being a 'mere' academic, was a former Secretary-General of OPEC. This did not escape the eagle eye of Edith Hall (2007: 196), who mused pointedly: 'It is tempting to speculate on how long it will take for his translation of Aeschylus' *Persians* to find a performance in his own country, and on what type of interpretation it might be given.'

Tempting, indeed, but I suspect it will not be in my lifetime at least ... By contrast, Aeschylus' *Persians* is enjoying something of a – dare I say? – Indian summer. On 25 July 2020, a bilingual (modern and ancient Greek) and subtitled production by the Hellenic National Theatre was performed at, and livestreamed from, the fourth-century BCE theatre of Epidaurus to mark the 2500th anniversary of the Battle of Salamis. In this latter respect, however, the producers had jumped the gun – though they were far from alone in so doing: the actual 2500th anniversary fell not in 2020 but in 2021, there being no BCE or CE '0'. Clearly, anniversaries can matter, and to celebrate/commemorate the Battle of Salamis as Aeschylus did in his inimitable way was to invent a grand tradition worthy of – suitably distanced and self-critical – perpetuation.

Notes

1 Sommerstein (2010), ch. 13, argues persuasively against its being autograph.
2 Hanink (2014).
3 The weight of scholarly opinion is firmly against its being actually by Aeschylus: Griffith (1977) and now Manousakis (2020).
4 The four plays by Aeschylus performed in spring 472 constitute one of the only five known tetralogies, though whether there was unity to the three

tragedies is a moot point: Flintoff (1992). The other tragedies beside *Persians*, which came second in order, were *Phineus* and *Glaucus*, the satyr-drama was a *Prometheus*. For the Great / City Dionysia, see Pickard-Cambridge (1988) and Cartledge (1997).
5 On the Achaemenid Persian Empire in general: Wiesehöfer (1978). For the Apadana stairway, see e.g. Curtis and Tallis (2005) (though 'Forgotten' will raise eyebrows in some quarters: by whom, pray?).
6 Medes: Momigliano (1975), ch. 6, 'Iranians and Greeks'.
7 On the Greek/barbarian opposition/polarity, see generally Skinner (2012). But the polarity could be and was 'deconstructed' in antiquity as in modern scholarship: both Skinner (ibid.) and Hall (1989) make use of that critical trope.
8 On the linguistics of communication in the *Iliad*, where are to be found the 'bar-bar-voiced Carians': Mackie (1996) and cf. Cartledge (2007). On Strabo's response to *Iliad* 2.867: Almagor (2000).
9 Scholarship on Herodotus, and translations of Herodotus, are legion. For ease and brevity of reference, I cite solely a recent, compendious (*c.* 2,500 entries), 3-volume *Encyclopaedia*: Baron (ed.) (2021). On the 'so-called human generation', see Herodotus 3.122, in reference to Polycrates tyrant of Samos in the 530s BCE, i.e. within three generations of Herodotus' own adult lifetime.
10 'above all explain' – and assign personal responsibility: see the famous Preface, which is notable not least for its ideal even balance between the 'famous deeds' of both Hellenes and non-Greeks alike.
11 On the 'Median' or 'Persian' War(s), as seen from a Hellenic perspective, see the lively accounts of Holland (2005), Garland (2017) and Shepherd (2020). There are other 'ancient voices' extant, but that of Herodotus is by far the most eloquent. For the relationship between him and *Persians*, see below.
12 'Controversial' because Salamis was not the finally decisive battle of the campaign; that was Plataea, a victory due chiefly to the senior partner in the anti-Persian coalition, the Spartans. Herodotus knew Sparta rather exceptionally well for a foreigner (3.55, 6.51–60), but he was more favourably impressed overall by the Athenians and their *nomoi* than by those of the Spartans.
13 On the development of ancient Greek life-writing: Momigliano (1993). It is sometimes simply assumed and asserted, e.g. by Romm (2016), not only that Aeschylus fought at Salamis but that he fought as a sailor. There is actually no positive evidence for either assumption.
14 Complexity of Athenian–Persian intercultural relations: Miller (1997). 'Medism' in general: Gillis (1979); terminology: Graf (1984). One extant *ostrakon* (Agora Inv. P9945) from the several Athenian *ostrakophoriai* of the 480s labels Aristeides 'brother of Datis': Robertson (1999).
15 Odeion: Miller (1997), ch. 6, at 218–42. It served among other functions as the site of the theatrical Proagon, but was constructed well after the staging of *Persians*: Pickard-Cambridge (1988). In the fifth century, play

performances were 'one-offs'; there were no repeats or revivals before the fourth century.
16 Interpretation of such images is sometimes far from straightforward, e.g. in the case of the famous/notorious 'Eurymedon' vase: Fisher (1998).
17 Cartledge (1997) argued that there was a tight, intimate, causal fit between the development of democracy at Athens and the development of drama, at first tragedy, later also comedy; none of the attempted rebuttals of that position has yet persuaded me.
18 'earth and water': Rung (2015).
19 Exactly what the Athenians thought they were doing, both in despatching ambassadors carrying the submission tokens and then in almost as quickly repudiating any such commitment, is unclear. At any rate, by the time the Milesian Aristagoras came begging for aid in 500/499, a majority of Athenians was clearly aggressively anti-Persian, a stance for which Herodotus (5.97.2) with the benefit of hindsight castigated them mercilessly.
20 Torching of Sardis 498: Greaves, Knight with Rutland (2020).
21 Date: Pickard-Cambridge (1988), 236–7 n. 6.
22 On the 'real' Xerxes and his varying receptions/image, see Stoneman (2015) and Bridges (2015). As for his 'character' as represented by Aeschylus in *Persians*, where he is not mentioned until line 144 and does not make his appearance on stage until after line 900, it is to be noted that he plays a particularly key and not unsympathetic role towards the end of the play in an antiphonal discourse with the Chorus of Persian seniors, an extended *kommos* or lament, the longest in extant Greek tragedy: Goldhill (1988), Hall (2010), 201, Hopman (2013) and Bridges (2015), ch. 1, 'Staging Xerxes: Aeschylus and Beyond', at 11–35 for *Persians*. Vlassopoulos (2012), 58 n. 25, cites Skinner (2012) for the view that Persians participated as much as Greeks in intercultural communication and reflected upon it as much – but did not preserve it in written form as Greeks did.
23 Note that the play does refer to the message of Sicinnus (a Hellenized non-Greek adjutant of Themistocles, later granted the citizenship of Thespiae in Boeotia), a reference which came 'as near as a tragedy could to mentioning a living individual': de Ste. Croix (1972), 185. On the 'Delian League'/ Athenian Empire, see for multiple aspects, Meiggs (1972), see also below, n. 31, de Ste. Croix (1972); and specifically on the attitude to it of Themistocles post-478 and on Aeschylus' politics then and later: de Ste. Croix (1972), 183–5.
24 On the 'politics' of Aeschylus in *Persians*, see Hall (1989), ch. 2, 'Inventing Persia': section 'Persians in the Theatre', subsection 'Politics', 93–8, see also ch. 3, 'The Barbarian Enters Myth', subsection 8, 'Politics', 154–9. Pelling (1997), 9–13, discusses Politics, including Ideology (later, 214, defined as 'a web of socially constituted normative axioms and thought patterns, especially when these affect questions of political or public interest'); cf. Pelling (1997), 13–19, on 'Ideology and National Stereotypes'.

25 Herodotus' attitude to and treatment of Xerxes were very different from those of Aeschylus: for the former, he was an oriental despot straight out of central casting: see Bridges (2015), 45–72, for Herodotus' Xerxes-narrative; and for a near-quotation of Aeschylus *Pers.* (728) by Herodotus (8.68γ), see Bowie (2007), 158.
26 'Orientalism' once had a fairly anodyne meaning, something like a profound scholarly interest and expertise of Westerners in oriental history and culture; but Palestinian Christian scholar Edward Saïd gave it the mainly bad name that it still carries: Saïd (1995), with Harrison (2011) and Skinner (2012) 45.
27 Hall (1989), 56–90, is the definitive account of why and how an Athenian audience or audiences would have seen things this way.
28 Roberts (1982).
29 On Herodotus 3.80–2, see Cartledge (2009).
30 The (ghost of) 'Darius' of Aeschylus' *Persians*, considerably hellenized, is a very different figure from that of the real, magniloquently autocratic Darius of, say, the Bisitun trilingual: Brosius (2000), document no. 44.
31 Meiggs (1963) is a beautifully succinct account of the Parthenon's 'political implications'; Meiggs is also the author of a satisfyingly comprehensive account of the 'Athenian empire', though Meiggs (1972) has, of course, been superseded in many particulars over the subsequent half-century.
32 See above n. 16.
33 See Hall (2007), as cited by Bridges (2015), 191 n. 2.
34 Stoneman (2015), App. 1, 'Xerxes in Opera and Drama', 219–22.

2

Athens and Persia, 472 BCE

Lloyd Llewellyn-Jones

Imagine, if you will, that you are among the first audience of Aeschylus' *Persians*. You are young and almost certainly a man, but that aside, you are now sitting on a long narrow wooden bench, one of many which have been inserted into a hollowed-out depression in the southern side of the Athenian Acropolis. This is the Theatre of Dionysus, although it is a much more rudimentary affair than the stone structure it was to develop into a hundred years later. It is early April, the weather is pleasantly warm, but not hot. You are settling into a day of watching a competition of tragic drama and you are hoping for a bit of stage spectacle, too, since Aeschylus, who is presenting his new trilogy, likes to dazzle his audiences with expensive props and costumes. Your expectations are doubly high because Pericles is the *chorêgos* and he likes to splash the cash. Besides, first up is a play about mad bad Xerxes and those weird half-men rag-heads he rules over. If anything spells 'spectacle' it is the Medes (or are they called 'Persians'? Whatever). You can't wait to see what they look like. Your father has told you all about his exploits at Salamis, when he fought hand-to-hand against them, looking them in their cold eyes (mascara-smeared) and enduring the sight of their crazy multicoloured leg-coverings and the animal-sound of their barbarian babble. But your dad forced the buggers back home, like your granddad did before, about twenty years ago, when you were just a kid, at the Battle of Marathon. And now you can see for yourself what these Medes or Persians or whatever are all about. There are prayers to the gods. Then music. The chorus dances in. They are wearing those legging things, looking *amazing*! This is crazy stuff! The crowd goes wild – clapping, whistling and there's happy chanting, too: 'Two World Wars! Two World Wars!' They finally settle down. The play begins.[1]

* * *

The Persians and their vast empire exerted a remarkable hold over the Athenian imagination. The Athenians – and all Greeks for that matter – were obsessed with their powerful eastern neighbours. Rightly so, for, after all, the

Persian superpower constituted a genuine threat to the hegemony of the numerous autonomous Greek *poleis*. Athenian art contains an endless catalogue of images of the Persians, showing them as pampered despots and defeated soldiers, and Athenian literature overflows with details about all kinds of diverse Persian exotica.[2] There are references to Persian-sounding (but fake) names, references to tribute, to law, truth-telling, hard drinking and gold. The Athenians speak of citrus fruit, camels, horses, peacocks, roosters, lion-hunting, gardens, and road systems measured in *parasangs*. They tell of great wealth, pride, hauteur, and a luxurious lifestyle exemplified by expensive clothes and textiles, fine food and drink, luxurious tableware, fans and fly-whisks, and ivory furniture. There are queens, concubines, harems and eunuchs, impalement, crucifixion and many hideous forms of drawn-out torture. This limitless directory of 'Persianisms' helped to mould Greek self-identity, although it said very little about the reality of Persian life. Athenian society during the Classical age was self-crafted to be a mirror-image to Persian civilization. The Athenians, it seems, were best aware of their 'Athenianness' when they imagined looking back at themselves through Persian eyes. In his *Histories* (5.105), for instance, Herodotus described King Darius' reaction to the burning of Sardis, a Persian-held city, during the Athenian abetted Ionian Revolt. Paying little mind to the Ionians themselves, the Persian king was focused, from the start, says Herodotus, on the Athenians:

> Darius asked who the Athenians were, and after receiving his answer he requested his bow. After taking it and loading an arrow, he shot it up towards heaven, and as it flew into the atmosphere, he exclaimed: 'O Zeus, may it be granted to me to take vengeance on the Athenians.' When he had said these things, he commanded one of his attendants to remind him three times whenever a meal was set before him, 'Master, remember the Athenians.'

Only a Greek – and a pro-Athenian one at that – could have composed such a scene. It is very unlikely that Darius ever gave *much* thought to the far-off Athenians; he had far more important things on his mind, like conquering Scythia and India. But the story informs us very clearly of the Athenians' sense of puffed-up pride and inflated self-importance. To visualize themselves as the Great King's nerve-wracking nemesis, gave the Athenians a sense of worth.[3]

Herodotus took this idea further. According to him, it was the memory of Athens' support of the Ionian Revolt that motivated the two Persian campaigns against Greece in 490 BCE (led by Darius) and 480 BCE (under Xerxes' command). The latter expedition is particularly notable because even though Xerxes had by this time succeeded his father as monarch, Herodotus continued to emphasize the depth to which Athens penetrated Darius' memory. It was the latter invasion which was the focus of Aeschylus' great tragic drama *Persians* of 472 BCE, which is the subject of this book. In the play, Xerxes is characterized as a monstrous tyrant who attempts to crush the freedoms enjoyed by Athens and the Greek city-states. The subsequent fortuitous repulsion of the overwhelming forces of the Achaemenid despots became something to celebrate in poetry, drama, art and in new narrative histories, such as that which was crafted some half a century afterwards Aeschylus by Herodotus.

This chapter asks a fundamental question: at the time of the first performance of Aeschylus' *Persians*, what did the Athenians know about Persia and its people? I have broken down this overarching question into a series of sub-enquiries, each of which focuses on a theme or element encountered in Aeschylus' tragedy. I raise the questions because of the potential the answers offer for understanding the overall position of the Persians in the early classical Athenian mindset. To answer them, I will focus on themes which arise from the play itself as well as on the literary and artistic evidence produced (largely but not exclusively) in Athens in the period before and directly after 472 BCE. Therefore, I exclude from this discussion references to the observations of later, predominantly fourth century BCE, writers such as Xenophon, Aristotle, Plato, Isocrates and others. These late classical authors tend to construct the Persians as decadent Orientals, a theme not so readily located in the earlier classical materials. Similarly, the iconographic evidence I briefly discuss here comes from artworks created before 472 BCE.[4]

The Athenians encountered the Persians in various ways: in warfare, through diplomacy, trade and economics, slavery and by scholarly observation.[5] Greeks were in service to Persian kings and satraps (provincial governors) as mercenaries, physicians, artists and craftsmen. Many Athenians could be encountered in Persia as refugees and political exiles. Persians were encountered in Athens, too, as royal diplomats and ambassadors, traders, war-captives and slaves. Opportunities for private interaction between Greeks and Persians were available in the periods before, during and after the Persian Wars and although language barriers and other difficulties in open communication might have prevented an easy and routine exchange of ideas, Aeschylus and his peers would have known something of Persian culture, even if at a very superficial level.[6]

Question 1: What did the Athenians know about the extent of the Persian Empire?

Judging from *Persians*, the Athenians rightly comprehended the scale of the Persian Empire, although Aeschylus' understanding of the geography of Persian territory, like that of many other Greeks of his age, is somewhat lopsided and tends to focus on the western part of the Persian realm.[7] This is unsurprising because the Athenians had predominantly encountered the Persians on the western seaboard of Asia Minor in the 540s BCE when they had occupied and colonized many Greek-speaking Ionian cities. Athens came into direct contact with the Persian Empire around 507/6 BCE when the *polis* appealed for help from Persia because its oligarchic neighbours (and Sparta) were proving to be antagonistic opponents towards Athens' nascent democracy. The Persian Great King Darius I ordered his half-brother, Artaphrenes, the satrap of western Asia Minor, to demand tribute of earth and water from the Athenian envoys who had arrived at the satrapal capital of Sardis, by way of sealing the alliance. Through these symbolic gifts, the monarch confirmed his domination over the lands that made up his empire (Xenophon, *Cyropaedia* 8.6.6 and 8.6.23). The gifting of earth and water (probably presented to the monarch in physical form – a silver jar of water, and a golden dish of soil, for instance) represented a country's unconditional surrender to Persia. The symbolic offering played a key role 'in initiating a relationship of ruler-subject and appears to have been a prime strategy used by the Persian king to attach himself to areas without resorting to military tactics' (see Herodotus 7.32; Strabo 15.3.22). The Athenian envoys duly presented the gifts to Darius' representative, much to the anger of the Athenians, whose wrath they encountered upon their return home. The Athenians were terrified that the gesture would be interpreted by Persia as an act of submission. But it was too late. The presentation of earth and water locked Athens in the nexus of Persian interests and the city remained entrenched in the imperial world view for well over a century.

In 499 BCE, supported by Athens, several cities in Ionia (as well as parts of Cyprus) rebelled against the Persian occupation. Ionian forces sacked Sardis, the great Persian stronghold, and set it aflame. The Persians quickly countered the attack, although it took them six years of intense fighting both on land and by sea to establish a sense of peace in the region. The final act of the uprising – a punitive attack on Athens – ended badly for the Persians at the Battle of Marathon in 490 BCE. Darius lost no territories during the whole protracted debacle, however – a testament to Persian staying power. Nonetheless, the Battle of Marathon became an advantageous propaganda opportunity for the Athenians. It provided them with material enough to launch legends that would sustain them for centuries to come. In truth, for Darius, the Ionian Revolt (as it has become known in Western eulogistic histories) was an inopportune and costly border skirmish on the peripheries of the Persian Empire. The revolt's major effect was on the plans Darius had drawn up for an extensive campaign of conquest in wealthy, sophisticated India. This had to be aborted in order to shift Persian military resources to the far west to put down the Greek insurgencies.

From the moment the Persians came into military contact with the Greeks in 499 BCE, it was certain that, one day, Greece would face invasion. Had Darius' ambition to integrate Greece into the empire not collapsed at Marathon, then the fate of the Athenians would have been the same as for other conquered peoples: deportation into Mesopotamia or further east. Athens would have been the centre of operations for the invasion of the Peloponnese, and, who knows, it might have become a satrapal capital, too. Darius' failure in Greece was behind Xerxes' ambition to conquer it, and his chief desire in the years after his accession was to incorporate mainland Greece into the Persian Empire.[8] There is no good evidence for why the Persians invaded Greece in 480 BCE. Herodotus insisted that the war was an act of retaliation against the Athenians, who had helped the insurgents in the Ionian Revolt, but there is no reason to take him at face value. A more likely explanation for the war was Xerxes' own territorial ambitions, which were very much in line with those of his father, Darius. Extension of power was, after all, the natural consequence of power, and like the Romans after them, the Persians, too, aspired to *imperium sine fine*, an empire without end.

Throughout his play, Aeschylus' attention is devoted to the Persian territories in Asia Minor and to the autonomous city-states in Greece. *Persians* demonstrates an acute awareness of the geographic separation between mainland Greece and the continent of 'Asia', a term which is used time and again by Aeschylus as a byword for the Persian Empire. Thus,

> sabre-wielding persians
> from every part of asia
> follow in the terrifying procession
> of the king
>
> these are the men
> the flower of persia
> who set out on campaign
>
> all asia
> reared them

all asia
sighs for them
in quenchless longing ...

When the Chorus of Persian elders refers to 'Asia', prophesying the break-up of Persian power, the reference is to the empire as a whole:

the peoples of
the land of asia
will not remain for long now
under persian rule
or pay the tribute
forced on them
by persian masters

Aeschylus' concentration is solely on the western seaboard of Asia Minor (which he even refers to as 'the continent'). Although references in *Persians* to Babylon, Bactria and Egypt suggests his broader knowledge of the scope of the Persian Empire, its vastness is quickly dismissed in favour of the polarized view of Ionian Asia. Aeschylus' knowledge of the Persian heartland is very limited, however. The action of *Persians* takes place in the imperial city of Susa in the south-western Iranian province of Elam.[9] It was a location well known to the Athenians and other Greeks as it was the destination of many Greek diplomatic embassies. Inscriptions dated to the reign of Darius I show that Greeks were also present in the city as workmen, charged with helping to construct the Great King's palace. Susa was the administrative heart of the Great Kings' realm and orders emanated from Susa to all provinces of the empire; it was a hotbed of officialdom.[10] All life converged at Susa for the purpose of imperial business. Yet Susa was not Persia's capital city per se. The concept of a single capital city was unknown among the Persians. The Persian kings built lavishly throughout the realm and their chief palatial sites, crafted from fine stone, mud-brick, glazed-brick and wood, were clustered in the ancestral regions of Iran at Susa in Elam and at Ecbatana in Media. Little remains of the once famed Achaemenid residence at Ecbatana near modern Hamadan, and much controversy surrounds even its archaeological location, but it must have once afforded quite a spectacle.[11] Aeschylus knew of it for sure and referred to the Persian war dead as 'the heroes of Ecbatana, the flower of Persia'. Puzzlingly, however, Aeschylus shows no knowledge whatsoever of the great places at Pasargade and Persepolis, the great Persian dynastic centres constructed by Cyrus the Great, Darius I and Xerxes, all of which lay at the heart of the empire. Today, the best known of all the ancient

Persian sites is Persepolis, whose magnificent haunting ruins rest at the foot of Kuh-e Rahmat ('Mountain of Mercy') some 500 kilometres east of Susa. Persepolis lies in a remote region in the mountains, making travel there difficult in the rainy season of the Persian winter. Its isolated location kept it a secret from the outside world and no Greek source speaks of it until the 'Alexander historians' in the first centuries CE.[12]

All in all, Aeschylus' understanding of the imperial territories is very limited. From his play one would not guess that the Persians ruled over lands which stretched out of Persia (modern-day Iran) to the west, towards the Mediterranean Sea and to India in the east. The empire extended south to the Gulf of Oman and far north, into southern Russia. The empire encompassed Ethiopia and Libya, northern Greece and Asia Minor, Afghanistan and the Punjab up to the Indus River.[13] There was no kingdom on earth to rival its size. At Naqsh-i Rustam in south-western Iran, on the façade of his rock-face tomb, Darius the Great had his artists sculpt a high-relief depicting him in the act of worshipping his divine protector, the god Ahuramazda. He stands on a throne-platform (a *takht* as it was known in Persian) which was raised high above the heads of representatives of the different peoples of the empire in a joyous act of reciprocal collaboration. It was a visual celebration of the diversity of Darius' empire.[14] An inscription carved into the rock in Old Persian cuneiform lettering invited the viewer to count the figures who represented the various geographical regions which made up the empire (each one clothed in 'national costume' to make the point clearer). To make sure that none were missed, the artist carefully labelled each of them:

> This is the Persian; this is the Mede; this the Elamite; this is the Parthian; this is the Areian; this is the Bactrian; this is the Sogdian; this is the Chorasmian; this is the Drangianian; this is the Arachosian; this is the Sattagydian; this is the Gandaran; this is the Indian; this is the drug-drinking Saca; this is the Pointed-Hat Saca; this is the Babylonian; this is the Assyrian; this is the Arab; this is the Egyptian; this is the Armenian; this is the Cappadocian; this is the Sardian; this is the Ionian; this is the Scythian from across the sea; this is the Thracian; this is the sun-hat-wearing Ionian; this is the Libyan; this is the Nubian. This is the man from Maka. This is the Carian.[15]

The royal rhetoric propounded on Darius' tomb emphasized the notion that all conquered nations were united in service to him, the Great King, a warrior-king whose 'spear has gone forth far', whose laws they obeyed and whose majesty they upheld. Darius the Great was thus lauded not only as the 'Great

King' and 'King of Kings', but also 'King of countries containing all kinds of men', 'King of many countries', as well as 'King in this great earth far and wide'. All subject-peoples were put under Darius' rule and he made it clear that he would tolerate no trouble or brook no resistance: 'What I said to them,' he stated with gravitas, 'that they did, as was my desire'. The strong visual brand employed by Darius to describe and depict his empire can be summed up in one Old Persian word *vispazanānām* – 'multicultural'.

Question 2: What did the Athenians know about Persian history?

During the Archaic period, in Greek-speaking territories, there had been an increasing interest amongst Greek scholars in writing treatises on the ethnography of Eastern societies and on the legendary genealogies of Greek gods and heroes, which were sometimes located in the Orient. Thus, for example, the Assyrian king known to the Greeks as Ninus, the so-called founder of the city of Nineveh, was thought to be the direct descendant of the Greek superhero Heracles (Herodotus 1.7). Rumours and stories about the Persians must have been in wide circulation, and no doubt tales were carried to the Greek cities in Ionia. But it was only after the Persian occupation of the Greek-speaking cities of Asia Minor in the 540s BCE that Persia itself became the focus of more intensely forensic study, with the Greeks trying to understand the nature of the (unwelcome) new Eastern superpower. A particular field of Greek history writing developed early in the fifth centuries BCE that we can classify as *Persica* or treatises written about the Persians and their empire.[16] Sadly, these have come down to us in short, broken fragments and in the citations of later authors. Nonetheless, they do bear witness to a desire amongst Greek intellectuals to understand the Persian foe. The first author of a *Persica* proper was Dionysus of Miletus who seems to have attempted an outline of Persian history from the end of the reign of Cambyses II (522 BCE) to the end of the reign of Darius the Great (486 BCE). He also authored a text called *Events After Darius* which comprised five books detailing the reign of Xerxes and the period of the Persian Wars from 480– 479 BCE. Also working within the same genre was Hellanicus of Lesbos who was born around 490 BCE and who is reputed to have lived to the age of 85. Throughout his long life he remained fascinated by ethnography and wrote several books on barbarian peoples. There are just 16 surviving fragments of his *Persica* in which he outlines the accession of Darius the Great, the invasion of Greece by Xerxes (to the Battle of Salamis), as well as details of Persian life and customs. As a contemporary of Herodotus, it is possible that Hellanicus'

Persica worked as a parallel (if more concise) redaction of the better known *Histories*. Finally, dating to *c*. 464 BCE was the two-book Persica of Charon of Lampascus. In another (unnamed) work, he told the birth-stories of Cyrus the Great, many decades before Herodotus did the same thing.

It would seem that when composing *Persians*, Aeschylus had some specialist works at hand. There were, no doubt, many more scholarly histories, in addition to oral tales, poems and long-lost songs for Aeschylus to draw on. Persian prisoners of war and Greek deserters might have added to the pot of 'knowledge'; anecdotes told by Athenians returning from Persia would have gone into the mix, too. Certainly, Aeschylus was sure enough in his knowledge of Persia's history to allow the ghost of King Darius to appear on stage to recite his royal lineage:

> Medos was the first to rule our people and our army. Next came his son, who kept up his good work and governed with sound judgement. Third, Cyrus took the throne, a man loved by the gods, and gave peace to all his people. He added to his empire the Lydians and Phrygians and he took all of Ionia by force. Yes, Cyrus was a gracious man, beloved by god. His son ruled next, the fourth king; and the fifth was Mardus, no credit to his country or to the ancestral throne. Brave Artaphernes and his trusted colleagues took him by surprise and killed him in the palace as was their duty. [The sixth king was Maraphis, the seventh Artapernes.] And then – by lot – I took the throne (I'd always wanted it), and I led my mighty army out on many a campaign – though I never brought catastrophe like this on Persia. But Xerxes, my son, a young man thinking young men's thoughts, does not remember my advice.

The Greeks associated Persians with the Medes and the conquest of Ionia was thus thought of as the sovereignty of the Medes. The Persian Wars, following the Ionian rebellion of 499 BCE, were considered as 'Medika' and the political cooperation with the opponent as 'Medism'. When Aeschylus presented the Persian kings on the Athenian stage, he portrays them as descendants of an eponymous Medos (later the prevailing belief was that they were descendants of Perseus or Perses). However, Aeschylus' knowledge of the Persian past is, at best, piecemeal – although, to give him credit, he was no doubt in step with other Greek attempts at creating a Persian historical narrative.[17] From what we now know of Persia's history from indigenous Iranian sources, Darius' articulation of his royal pedigree is littered with historiographic twists, not necessarily inaccurate but more misaligned.[18] For, as Edith Hall concedes, when it came to Persia's history, 'Aeschylus may have had only the foggiest of notions of what had taken place.'[19]

A strange omission from Aeschylus' play is the dynastic name of Persia's ruling house, the Achaemenids. They took their name from an eponymous founder, 'Achaemenes', an alleged ancestor of both Cyrus the Great and Darius the Great. 'Achaemenes' was also a Greek rendering of a Persian name: 'Haxāmanish', which in turn was derived from the Old Persian words *haxā-* 'friend' and *manah* 'thinking power'. Formed of a patronymic, the dynasty was known to the speakers of Old Persian as 'Haxāmanishiya' – 'Achaemenids'. The name is trumpeted again and again in the royal inscriptions of Darius the Great and Xerxes. The Old Persian texts proclaim the heroic and militaristic qualities of the Achaemenid monarchs and place their successes within the shadow of Ahuramazda, the great god of the royal dynasty. Yet curiously, no mention is made of the dynastic name in Aeschylus' play, a fact which suggests he simply did not know it.

The royal lineage which Darius recites in *Persians* is concerned with casting Xerxes as a feckless and disappointing royal heir. The whole point of the catalogue of kings is to emphasize Xerxes' inability to rule, overshadowed as he is by the noble warrior kings of the Persian past. Aeschylus is responsible for a powerful contribution to the dismal reputation of Xerxes. For the playwright, Darius is a 'blessèd king', quite without peer, a benevolent father, Susa-born and beloved of the gods. By way of stark contrast, Xerxes is weak, childish, a coward. The ghost of Darius denounces his son, who has lost his senses, and repeats the typically Greek accusation of *hybris* against Xerxes. He is responsible for unspeakable disaster, for the loss of a continent's worth of men, many of high nobility. In Aeschylus' play, the consequences of the defeat of Xerxes, are catastrophic for the empire of the Great King and Aeschylus attempts to show through the rag-bag figure of the humiliated Xerxes an empire that was in irreversible decline.

Question 3: What did the Athenians know about Persian queens?

The answer to this question is simple: the Athenians knew next to nothing about Persian queens, or any Persian women for that matter. In Persia, the high social rank of royal females, like that of the Great King himself, was stressed by their conspicuous invisibility (which is not to be confused with seclusion or a lack of agency).[20] It is clear from Iranian sources that the royal women of Achaemenid Persia did not live in the confinement of purdah, nor did they inhabit an Orientalist world of sultry sensuality, but they did form part of a strict hierarchical court structure which moved in close proximity to the monarch. As such they became touchstones in the Greek fantasy of

Persia. In Greek literature, Persian royal women are crafted as powerful and authoritative figures, but are very often rapacious, cruel and vindictive also.[21] For the Greeks, Persian degeneracy came to be embodied in the imaginary figure of the fearsome Persian queen who was 'psychopathically heartless, status-conscious, and obsessed with sartorial display'.[22]

The unnamed widow of Darius and mother of Xerxes who plays a central role in Aeschylus' *Persians* is traditionally identified as Atossa, a daughter of Cyrus the Great, sister and spouse of King Cambyses II, and sister-wife of King Bardiya. In the tragedy, she holds a position of great honour, although in the history of Herodotus, she appears less noble. She is encountered in connection with the story of the Crotonian physician Democedes, and it is said that Atossa incited Darius to prove his manliness by making war on Greece (3.134). Later, in connection with the advice of the Spartan king Demaratus on the Persian royal succession, it is said that her son Xerxes would have prevailed in the contest for the succession to the throne no matter what arguments were made from the order of birth of Darius' sons, because Atossa 'held all the power'. Yet, the queen is encountered but rarely in indigenous Persian sources and received only six scant mentions (in the Old Persian form of her name, Udusana) in the cuneiform texts dating to the reign of Darius found at Persepolis.[23] This suggests that whatever political power she had – if she had any at all – came to her only as the Queen Mother, after the accession of Xerxes, and not as the kingmaker, before his accession.[24]

Curiously enough though, the name Atossa was known among the Greeks in the generation between Aeschylus and Herodotus. According to Hellanicus of Lesbos, it was the name of a fabulously masculine Eastern woman:

> She was brought up by her father Aryaspes as a man, and inherited the kingdom. Hiding her female disposition, she wore the royal *tiara*, and also first wore leather trousers, invented the service of eunuchs, and communicated her decisions (lit. 'replies') through writing. She conquered many tribes, she was most warlike and manly in every deed.
> FGrH 4 F 178a [= 687a F 7]

It is not entirely clear if Hellanicus' Atossa is Persian (as opposed to, say, Assyrian). She may well be an amalgamation of Xerxes' (in)famous mother and the most famous Assyrian queen of all time, Semiramis, since both women have much in common in the Greek imagination. Whatever the situation, Hellanicus' Atossa is constructed as a figure from a Greek man's nightmare: she is raised as a male by her tyrant father and because of this she hides her true female nature behind clothes and protocol. She wears a kind of turban – the sort of soft headdress used by Persian kings – to disguise her sex and project her power and more than that, she wears *anaxarides*, the leather trousers commonly worn by horse-riding Persian men. Having blurred the boundaries of her gender, next Atossa goes about castrating men and boys, turning them into eunuchs, a curious third sex widely employed in the courts of the Near East, but an anathema to the Greek ideal of masculinity. Just as she uses eunuchs to control access to her person, so, too, Atossa communicates through the written word, rather than orally. She takes to the battlefield and celebrates numerous victories. Remote from her subjects, the clever, Amazon-like Atossa arouses awe and admiration, concealing from her people the great secret that she is in fact a woman.[25]

Did Aeschylus' Queen feed into the later Greek depiction of Atossa? It is possible. Whilst in the play she is calm, sensible and entirely sympathetic, her very presence on the stage, the fact that she is so vocal throughout the action, her arrival in a chariot and the obeisance performed to her by the Persian nobles, would have rankled with the Athenian audience. Here was a woman with too much to say and with way too much authority.

Question 4: What did the Athenians know about Persian religion?

It is Herodotus who provides us with evidence for Greek knowledge of the religious practices of the Persians. Believing that Herodotus made salient and accurate observations on the nature of the Achaemenid world, scholars once put all their trust in what the 'Father of History' had to say about Persian religion. 'The customs which I know the Persians to observe are the following: they have no images of the gods, no temples nor altars, and consider the use of them a sign of folly,' he stated dogmatically (1.131). Now that we can read and analyse the indigenous Persian texts for ourselves, we can categorically state that on each of his 'observations', Herodotus was simply wrong. The cuneiform Persepolis tablets contain evidence to show that in their worship, the Persians *did* use images, temples and altars. In his *Histories*, Herodotus was trying to depict Persia as a topsy-turvy world, the antithesis of Greece civilization. Because the Greeks routinely used temples, altars and images in their worship, to craft the Persians as the ultimate 'Other', Herodotus created for them a religious world which operated without the fundamentals of a 'civilized' organized religion.[26] But at last, the Persepolis texts are correcting Herodotus' very persuasive images of Persia's alien religion.

The religious rites and rituals of Aeschylus' on-stage Persians are essentially those of the Athenian audience. He makes no attempt to imagine a different 'oriental' sphere of worship. The gods worshipped by the theatrical Persians are those of the Greek pantheon and Aeschylus shows no knowledge of anything of the religious traditions of ancient Iran. On stage, Aeschylus depicts acts of libation and necromancy from a distinctly Greek perspective.

Aeschylus certainly understood that the Great King held, by virtue of his office, a mystical position and that he was, if less than a god, still more than a man. Therefore, Aeschylus calls the dead Darius *isotheos* 'equal to the gods', *theion* 'divine' and *akakos*, 'knowing no wrong', and while the Athenian playwright must not be taken literally on these points, he was capable, nonetheless, of thinking of Persian kings in this way. Indeed, some Greeks described the Great King as having a divine *daimon*, or spirit, and how Persian courtiers revered it and piled tables high with food offerings for the pleasure of the king's spirit. This Greek belief in the king's *daimon* is a reasonable interpretation of the genuine Persian belief in the *fravashi*, or 'soul', of the monarch. Moreover, Herodotus (1.131–2) says that the Persians were duty-bound to pray for the king and his sons during their private acts of worship, which, according to Kuhrt (2007: 473), demonstrates that the Greeks understood the Persian 'intertwining of god(s), king, and empire'.

Question 5: What did the Athenians know about Persian language and culture?

The sound world of Aeschylus' *Persians* has been well studied. Sadly, the musical accompaniment of the tragedy is long lost, but we can be certain that the performance of *Persians* was enhanced by 'the orientalising effect of the verbal ... elements'.[27] Meaningless 'Eastern' cries of lamentation filled the stage in an endless cacophony of strange Oriental cries: *otototoi, aiai, oi, popoi, totoi, pheu, oa, io, ioa, papai papai, ie* and so on. Sprinkled into the text, Aeschylus added some genuinely exotic words, too (*ballen*, for instance, was a Phrygian word for 'king'), and the frequent use of Greek Ionicisms in the play helped lend an added touch of the Orient to the proceedings.

Old Persian was an inflected language and so, like the Ionic Greek that Herodotus spoke, the suffix – that is the part at the end of a word – would change depending on its case. Herodotus (1.139) observed that, 'Persian names, which express the nature of some bodily or mental excellence, all end with the same letter – that which is called San by the Dorians, and Sigma by the Ionians. Anyone who examines will find that the Persian names, one and all without exception, end with this letter.' What he meant by that was the likelihood that the nominative form of Persian names which, in Old Persian can end in *-sh*, is close to but not the same as the *-s* denoted by the Dorian *San* or Ionian *Sigma*. This is just one example of the many observable mistakes in

Greek renderings of Persian names, and – more often than not – these names have passed through a number of mutations by the time they reach us. The personal names encountered in Aeschylus' text reflect their Greek rendition. The Greek 'Dareîos' (Latinized 'Darius') is a poor rendition of the genuine richly sounding Old Persian 'Dārayavaush'. Ancient Persian names were replete with meaning and acted as powerful statements, designed to reflect the nature and status of their bearers. Not only do they afford us knowledge of the sound values of spoken Persian, but the cultural world of Persia was reflected in personal names too, giving us a good insight into the Persian mindset. Dārayavaush, for instance, means 'Holding Firm the Good', a reflection of his kingly role for certain. Xerxes' true name was Xshayarashā, meaning 'Ruling over Heroes', while the four kings known to the Greeks and Romans as 'Artaxerxes' bore the Persian name Artaxshaça –'Whose Rule is Ordained by Truth'. Cyrus the Great was always Kūrush – 'Humiliator of the Enemy', an interesting moniker for a king whose reputation has been built on justice, tolerance and kindness.

The strange barbarian tongue of Aeschylus' on-stage Persians was interspersed with similarly alien actions – such as an action known to the Greeks as *proskynesis*.[28] The old men of the chorus threw themselves face down onto the earth in an act of abject humility before the Queen and Xerxes. For the Greeks, the gesture was a religious act and suitable only for performance before a god, so that for a Greek to do it before a man – let alone a woman – undermined the very concept of *eleutheria*, or 'freedom' (Xenophon, *Hellenica* 4.1.35). The fawning and kowtowing of the chorus of Persian councillors must have resonated with the Athenian audience as being typically, distastefully, Oriental. These eastern flavours were revisited later in the fifth century in some of Euripides' later plays such as *Iphigenia Among the Taurians* and *Orestes*, where a character like the Phrygian slave (clearly meant to be a Persian eunuch) is used as a device (typical of later Greek xenophobic tendencies) to barbarize and effeminize the Persians.[29]

It is very difficult to know how the Persians were physically portrayed on stage, but costume must have played a significant role in the presentation of the Oriental 'Other'. The earliest representation we have of a Persian in a visual medium comes from a black-figure vase dating to *c.* 520 BCE.[30] A seated male, perhaps a Great King or a satrap, wears a curious sleeveless tunic and a pair of patterned trousers. Something of this sort must have been worn as a visual 'code' when depicting Persians on stage, although by and large the painted image is not an accurate depiction of Persian dress. Of course, it is important to remember, as Margaret Miller emphasizes, that the hundred-or-so surviving images of Persians created by Greek artists over a century's worth of creativity, 'are not historical facts to be slotted into discussions of chronology or military history'. Rather, they express how the Persians were conceived of in the ever-shifting Greek mindset. She rightly notes that painters, 'drew on a variety of sources to inform their rendering of the Persians: autopsy, artistic traditions for depicting other Easterners (notably Scythians ...), and fantasy'.[31]

We know that the Persians wore garments common to all Iranian horsemen, chiefly consisting of sleeved tunics and tailored coats, and – most notably – long trousers.[32] Such was the standard dress of the nomads of the Iranian plateau. For the peoples to the west of Iran, encountering trouser-wearing Persians for the first time was an uncomfortably disconcerting experience; for the Greeks it was tinged with trauma. Herodotus noted (7.112) that the Athenians 'were the first of all Greeks to endure the sight of Persian clothing' – an extreme reaction, perhaps, but one which tells us much about Greek conceptions of their strange, powerful, but alien enemy. Throughout the fifth century, the Greek representation of Persians and other Orientals blurred the reality of dress with the costume of the stage, so that it is impossible to accurately tweak out the pure imaginary from the deliberately theatrical. Generally speaking, the Greeks expressed distaste for what might be perceived as 'modification of body shape' through clothing: this can be seen in their attitudes to 'barbarian' dress, and in particular the shaped garments of the Persians.

* * *

There can be little doubt that the Persia we encounter in Aeschylus' great tragedy of 472 BCE is by and large a locale of Oriental fabulousness. Aeschylus may well have met face to face with Persians as they clashed on the battlefield, but when it came to creating an on-stage Persian world, his Persians are based on little or no first-hand knowledge. The play may nod towards Persian history and to Oriental *realia* such as dress and equipment, language and gesture, but even these are, at best, rudimentary. *Persians* must be regarded as an important contributor to a long line of well-crafted, if deeply misunderstood and precarious clichés that permeate other Greek conceptions of the Achaemenid world.

The on-stage picture created for the audience of that first performance of *Persians* is of course an exotically fictionalized Persia of the imagination, a world in which all eyes are seduced into feasting upon the sights of the fabled hedonism of the royal court – the mandatory locale of all accounts of the Orient. But in no way should the play (even with its many distortions) be thought of as a caricature of the Persian world. Aeschylus does not lampoon the Persians, nor does he make any form of disdainful criticism of them in the style of, for instance, later fourth-century Attic oratory. No, in spite of his lack of knowledge, errors, misreadings and delusions, the Aeschylus' *Persians* offer an 'open sesame' to what they found to be a fantastical, puzzling and decidedly alien world.

Notes

1. For good introductions to the play, see especially Broadhead (1960), Hall (1996), Garvie (2009) and Rosenbloom (2006).
2. Tuplin (1996), 164. For a further discussion of the sheer variety of ways in which Greek culture encountered the Persians, see Miller (2006/7).
3. The theme propounded by Hall (1989) and Miller (2006).
4. On later Greek perceptions of the Persians see Llewellyn-Jones (2012).
5. On the Greek interaction with the Persian world, see Sancisi-Weerdenburg (2001). On the image of the Persian in Attic art, as well as on diplomacy between Greece and the empire, see most importantly in Miller (1997). See also Hirsch (1985). Further discussion of Persian–Greek interactions can be had in Vlassopoulos (2013) and Morgan (2016), also Harrison (2002).
6. As Miller (2006/7), 109, notes: 'it is unlikely that there was anyone in Athens who had not clapped eyes on a person or an artefact from the empire'.
7. On the scale of the Persian Empire, see Llewellyn-Jones (2017b).
8. For new interpretations on the cause and trajectory of the Persian invasion of Greece in 480/479 BCE, see Llewellyn-Jones (2022).
9. Harper, Aruz and Tallon (1992).
10. See Kuhrt (2007), 492–4.
11. Llewellyn-Jones (2013), 52.
12. Mousavi (2012).
13. Llewellyn-Jones (2013), 23–7.
14. Ibid., 224, fig. F17.
15. See further Kuhrt (2007), 483–4.
16. See Llewellyn-Jones and Robson (2009) for a full discussion of the genre of *Persica*. Of course, the Greek fascination with Persia was reflected in literary genres other than *Persica* proper: Persia is frequently alluded to in legal orations, histories, drama, poetry, novels and philosophy. See Stevenson (1997), 1–3.
17. Sampson (2015), 24–42.
18. For a narrative overview of Persian history, see Briant (2002), and Dandamaev (1989). See also Llewellyn-Jones (2022).
19. Hall (1962), 162.
20. Llewellyn-Jones (2013), 96–122.
21. Sancisi-Weerdenburg, (1983).
22. Hall (1996), 7.
23. Henkelman (2010).

24 Llewelyn-Jones (2013), 17.
25 See Gera (1997).
26 Llewellyn-Jones (2022).
27 Hall (1996), 20.
28 Llewellyn-Jones (2013), 71–2, 230.
29 On the feminization of the Persians, see Llewellyn-Jones (2017a).
30 Morgan (2016), 166, fig. 3.6.
31 Miller (2006/7), 109.
32 Llewellyn-Jones (2020).

3

Persians' First Audience

Robert Garland

Aeschylus' *Persians* was produced at the City Dionysia in 472 BCE, just eight years after the Greek naval victory in the straits of Salamis, to which the Athenians had made a major contribution. It is highly probable that a sizeable proportion of Aeschylus' audience – all male, I assume – would have fought in the battle. For them, pride in their stunning victory was no doubt tinged, as all victories are, with the memory of comrades they had lost. Others in the audience, either too old or too young to serve, evacuees from Attica primarily to the island of Salamis shortly before Xerxes invaded Attica, can never have forgotten the fact that, had the Persians prevailed and the Greek fleet been destroyed, they, along with the rest of the civilian population, would have been either butchered or enslaved immediately afterwards. They had thus had a ringside seat of the battle, which they had observed close up from the shores of Salamis. It is possible, too, that a few Greeks from other city-states were at the performance, though our earliest evidence for inviting foreigners to the City Dionysia dates to later in the century when the festival served in part as a celebration of Athens' empire. In sum, rarely has a historical play been performed before such an informed audience or one that was more invested in the treatment of its subject matter.

Persians is a puzzling work, to put it mildly. It has even been disputed whether it deserves to be classified as a tragedy at all. Its subject matter is the report of a catastrophic defeat of an invasion force whose objective was to burn Athens to the ground, annihilate its population and conquer the Greek mainland. Some scholars have charged the play with being little more than a triumphant dramatization of patriotic sentiment, tendentiously pointing to the fact that the future statesman Pericles was the *choregos*.[1] Others have offered a more nuanced reading by suggesting that it both evokes patriotic pride in victory and validates the resultant grief of the Persians.[2] If it had been Aeschylus' objective simply to encourage his audience to gloat at the sufferings of their enemies and to celebrate the superiority of Greek over barbarian culture, *Persians* would be of antiquarian interest at best. It might even be a candidate for cancellation from the canon. Aeschylus' objective, however, was not to encourage gloating.

A related but separate charge is that *Persians* has contributed to 'the dangerous myth of the Orient as decadent, effeminate, luxurious and materialistic'.[3] That claim, made over twenty-five years ago, has if anything become more pertinent in light of the attention that all forms of racism, wherever it has taken root, and however remotely in the past it is situated, now receives. In regard to *Persians*, it is a charge, because of its vagueness, that can neither be proven nor disproved.

The text which has come down to us may not be identical to the one that was performed in the Theatre of Dionysus in 472 BCE. It was not until the 330s BCE that the Athenian politician Lycurgus introduced a law requiring an 'official' version of all the plays of Aeschylus, Sophocles and Euripides to be preserved in the public treasury, a circumstance which obviously raises questions of authenticity that apply to every surviving Greek tragedy.[4] There is another issue to bear in mind. Later sources claim that a revival of *Persians* was staged in Aeschylus' lifetime in Syracuse 'at the urging of the tyrant Hieron'.[5] It is therefore possible that the version which Lycurgus canonized was a synthesis of the original performance and the Syracusan revival. Even if that is the case, however, I see no reason to suppose that there would have been an inclination to reduce its anti-Persian sentiment, a topic that is central to this discussion, since the Greeks did not concern themselves with such matters and there would have been no incentive to do so.[6] In other words, there is no reason to suppose that the original play was more 'racist' – to use an adjective that would have had no meaning to a Greek – than the version which has come down to us.

It is not my primary intention to interpret the play. Instead, I want to attempt to evoke the response of the audience to Aeschylus' language and to the events which he dramatizes. In other words, I am interested in the audience's *experience* of the play. Though interpretation and response are closely connected, they are hardly identical. It goes without saying that every member of the audience would have brought his unique perspective to the performance but in no other surviving tragedy did such an intimate relationship exist between subject and spectator. For that reason, I believe it is legitimate to seek to identify a *collective* response. The attempt to recover an audience's reaction to any pre-modern play is a partial exercise at best, given the fact that the visual impact which it made is irrecoverable. And the attempt is made yet more partial in the case of a Greek drama, since the accompanying music has not survived, and we have little knowledge of what dances the Chorus might have performed.

* * *

What knowledge of *Persians* did the audience members have prior to taking their seats on the day of its performance? It would make sense if everyone involved in the production of a Greek drama, tragedy and comedy alike, maintained a strict code of secrecy throughout the rehearsal period to ensure that any given play made the maximum impact, but there is no evidence to indicate that any such code was observed, added to which it would have been almost impossible to enforce in view of the numbers of people involved in its production. In particular, Pericles as *choregos* would have been hard-pressed to conceal the play's content from his circle of aristocratic friends. The majority of the audience, however, may well have been assuming they would witness a dramatized celebration of Athens' stunning victory over the hated invader, though they might have been somewhat puzzled by the play's title, which puts the spotlight on the vanquished rather than the victors. Even so, they could not have known that the play was going to concentrate on the Persian reaction to the news of the defeat at Salamis, though it is worth pointing out that Phrynichus' lost play *Phoenician Women*, which had been performed probably four years earlier and which provided the inspiration for Aeschylus' *Persians*, had previously focused on their grief. Some element of surprise would have been inevitable, however, if all they knew in advance was the play's title.

It is unclear, too, whether, even after they had settled in the theatre, the audience would have realized that the play they were about to witness was set at Susa, the seat of Achaemenid rule. The *skēnē*, the building which served as the actors' changing room, whose exterior was often decorated to resemble the façade of a palace or temple, might not have been introduced yet.[7] Its earliest attested usage is for the production of Aeschylus' *Oresteia* in 458 BCE.[8] Even if there was no *skēnē*, however, an indication of oriental pomp and splendour could easily have been suggested by hanging a decorated cloth or tapestry at both entrances to the orchestra and by placing a few simple props on stage suggestive of the extravagant wealth of the Persian court.

There may have been a mound of earth, or perhaps a representation thereof, indicating the tomb of King Darius, though whether the audience understood its significance before the play began is doubtful. (647–8, 684). Such an unusual feature might well have provoked curiosity without revealing anything about the subject matter of the play.

Whatever the audience saw or did not see or knew or did not know before the play began, the entry of the Persian elders wearing ornate and colourful clothing would have indicated that the action was taking place in the Persian court. Very likely the elders wore patterned costumes with long sleeves and headdresses, since this is how Persians are depicted on the famous name vase in Naples by the Darius Painter.[9] Their attire contributed significantly to the un-Greek flavour of the production, which, as we shall see, Aeschylus was keen to emphasize.

Their opening lines, too, suggest an exotic location, especially the repeated use of the adjective *polychrusos*, 'rich in gold', which they employ first to describe the palace at Susa, second the Persian army, third Sardis and fourth Babylon (3, 9, 45, 53). The adjective would have paid into the audience's stereotypical image of Persia as a fabulously wealthy country.[10] But it would also have reminded them of the dangers that excessive wealth poses, since excess in all its forms incurred the wrath of the gods, whether one happened to be a Greek or a Persian. Its prominence thus alerted the audience to the fact that Persia's wealth was a liability both to its people and to its king. Another adjective suggestive of the Persian lifestyle is *habros*, 'delicate', which appears three times in the course of the play in a variety of compounds, viz. *habrodiaitôn*, 'living delicately' (41), *habropentheis*, 'grieving delicately' (135) and *habrobatai*, 'stepping delicately' (1072).

A third defining feature of Persia is her military might, which, the Chorus state, is drawn from 'the whole of Asia' (12, cf. 61). They emphasize the army's size by enumerating the names of its commanders – 17 in total – some of which were probably falsified, and by listing the peoples and cities which the empire rules. Most of the names would have meant nothing to the audience but their recitation alone surely contributed to the atmosphere of strangeness and exoticism. References to the fact that the army is 'fearful to behold' further reinforce the idea of its overwhelming might (27, 48, cf. 116). The metaphor of the yoke, which occurs twice here and on several occasions later, reminded the audience, as if it needed reminding, that Greece's population came close to enslavement.[11]

The parodos does not, however, present an image of invincible strength. Far from it. In fact, the last word in the opening line – *oichomenon* – meaning 'gone', which the Chorus uses in reference to the army, conveys the idea of 'dead and gone'.[12] It is clear from the start that the Chorus are experiencing acute anxiety, first because the entire army has departed, leaving the empire undefended, and second because no report of the army's fortunes has been received (8–15). It was a state of mind with which an Athenian audience would easily have identified, given the fact that there was little if any contact with an expeditionary force once it had set out. After listing the forces at Xerxes' command, the Chorus undercut the impact of the preceding 80 lines by mention of the 'insidious deceit of god', which no man can resist (107). They speak of *Ate*, Delusion, which, seemingly benign, ultimately ensnares a man in its net (111–14). Though they refrain from identifying the victim of divine deceit and delusion, it would have been obvious to the audience that these words refer to Xerxes. In sum, the parodos creates an atmosphere of tension by suggesting that the Persian Empire, despite its wealth and vastly superior manpower, is by no means secure, while allusions to the sea hint at the possibility that the drama will focus on the naval disaster at Salamis (88, 90, 100).

Atossa's grand entrance, in a chariot that was no doubt accompanied by a large retinue, was surely spectacular.[13] The Chorus' observation that the light that radiated from her was equal to that which blazes from the eyes of the gods indicates that she was gorgeously apparelled (150-1). Prostrating themselves before her in a manner that would have been regarded with repugnance by the audience, the Chorus address the queen in exalted terms. They conclude by hailing her as 'mother of a god, unless some ancient divine spirit has wrecked the army' (158). Once again, they unwittingly hint at the disaster that is shortly to come to light.

After Atossa has described her inauspicious dream portending disaster, the Chorus counsel her to propitiate the gods and the dead. There follows a passage of stichomythic dialogue, in which she quizzes them about Athens (231-45):

'Where is the city said to be located?'
   'Far away in the region where Lord Helios sets.'
'Why did my son want to hunt down this city?'
   'Because all of Greece would then become subject to the king.'
'Is there a multitude of men in its army?'
   'It's large enough to have caused troubles for the Persians.'
'What else does the city have apart from men? Do they have much wealth in their homes?'
   'They have veins of silver, a treasure trove beneath the earth.'
'Do they fight with bows and arrows?'
   'No, they stand in close quarters armed with spears and shields.'
'Who is their ruler and commander-in-chief?'
   'Of no one are they called slaves or subjects.'
'How then can they withstand a hostile invasion?'
   'They were sufficiently powerful to defeat the large army that Darius sent to do battle.'

The Chorus has provided the audience with a brief description of how they, the Athenians, saw themselves. They had a sizeable army. They were not wealthy as individuals, but they possessed a common treasury which contained reserves of silver. They fought with spears (i.e. as hoplites), rather than with bows and arrows. Their governmental system was a democracy, not an autocracy. They had experience of defending their land against invaders. Very likely the audience would have risen to their feet and cheered ecstatically at this line, even as Greek audiences have done in modern times.[14]

As a result of what she learns, Atossa is reduced to a state of anxiety, not unlike the Chorus in the parodos. 'What you say is alarming for the parents of those who are going there,' she observes, perhaps in a solemn whisper (245).

The Messenger enters with news of the naval defeat. Before he delivers his account, however, he states that he was present at the events which he is about to describe. In so doing, he not only establishes his credentials as a reliable eyewitness but also puts himself on the same footing as those members of the audience who had either fought at Salamis or observed the battle from the shore (266–7). It is surely not accidental that in the parodos the Chorus repeatedly referred to eyes and sight (27, 48, 81, 102, 150). Atossa had been even more focused on eyes and sight (168, 179, 183, 188, 200, 205, 207, 210). I think it likely that Aeschylus is using this device to encourage his audience, to nudge them almost, to adopt the perspective of their adversaries. He will do so throughout the play.

The Messenger, too, encourages the audience to step outside their conventional frame of reference. Declaring that the flower of Persia has perished, he describes Attica's coastline to be chock-full of corpses (272–3). Many members of the audience would have witnessed this same sight, the retelling of which would have evoked extremely painful memories. Many Athenians, we may surmise, had been unable to retrieve their dead relatives for burial and been equally troubled by the thought of their bodies rotting at sea. Though the Greeks would have done everything they could to recover their dead, whereas the Persians had no opportunity to recover theirs, it's a fair assumption that their effort was only partially successful. The experience described by the Messenger was thus common to both sides. The Chorus' response – 'Alas, you speak of the bodies of our loved ones, buffeted by the sea, bobbing up and down constantly' – would thus have been as appropriate in the mouth of an Athenian messenger as it was in the mouth of a Persian (274–6).

After stating that the Greeks were heavily outnumbered – by 300 ships to 1,000 – the Messenger offers the suggestion that 'some divine power' assisted them in their victory (345), adding as a general principle his belief that 'gods preserve the city of the goddess Pallas' (347). A few lines later he attributes the victory to the craftiness of an unidentified Athenian (actually Themistocles, though he is never mentioned by name) and to the *phthonos* or resentment of the gods, both of which factors, he alleges, Xerxes had failed to take into account (361–2). He reports Xerxes' order that if the Greek fleet escaped from the straits of Salamis in the dead of night, which is what Themistocles falsely claimed to be their intention, he would behead all his officers (369–71). This is the sole allusion to the brutality that the Greeks believed was characteristic of Persian kings. Once again, the Messenger suggests that divine intervention contributed to their defeat by claiming that Xerxes 'did not know what was purposed by the gods' (373). It is striking that there is no suggestion that Xerxes was guilty of any moral flaw.[15] Nor is any blame attached to the Persian navy.

The audience's anticipation is increased by the Messenger's description of the night before the battle. The Persians, he states, were sitting at their oars in expectation that the Greek fleet would attempt to break through and make a dash for safety. Though some commentators have suggested that the lines 'The crews, well disciplined, obeying orders, prepared supper, and each oarsman looped his oar around the thole pin so that it fitted snuggly' refers to the Greeks (374–6), a Persian would hardly have had direct knowledge of what the enemy were doing before the battle and the lines might just as appropriately refer to the invaders. The ambiguity, however, may be deliberate, since the homely image of looping an oar around a thole pin would be familiar to every oarsman, irrespective of his ethnicity. Here again, Aeschylus is encouraging the audience to step outside their conventional frame of reference and envisage the mindset of the Persians by describing the tension on both sides before the commencement of hostilities.

The Messenger's description of the Athenian advance into battle is undeniably triumphalist in tone. As dawn broke, he declares, the Greeks gave voice to 'a cheer, a shout of triumph, which echoed forth from the cliffs of Salamis' (388–91). The sailors chanted a solemn paean to the accompaniment of a blast of a trumpet. The order to advance was given and a mighty shout went up, 'Forward, Greeks! Set free your fatherland! Set free your wives and children! Set free your fathers' gods and the spirits of your ancestors. The contest is at hand and it is all to fight for!' (401–5).

Very likely the audience once again erupted in cheers when they heard this chant, which might well approximate to that actually sung before the battle. But though the recollection of these stirring words might have evoked in the audience a sense of patriotic pride, a mere fifteen lines later the Messenger offers this chilling picture of what amounts to an atrocity:

> 'They (i.e. the Greeks) – like we were tuna or fish netted in a fishing net – kept on clubbing us with broken oars and bits of splintered wreckage.'
> 424–6[16]

How, we might ask, did the audience respond to such a brutal image, which a number had perhaps witnessed at first hand and which action some might even have perpetrated? Did it stir in any a sense of shame and remorse? What impact did it make coming so soon after the former patriotic call to arms? It is difficult not to conclude that the poet is inviting his audience to reflect upon the brutality of war, even though the cause itself was fully justified.

The Messenger concludes his account by condemning 'those Persians at the pinnacle of life ... the most brave-hearted ... the highest born ... the best ... and always first to earn the king's confidence ... who met the most dishonourable, most squalid death of all' (441–4). Damning though this judgement is, it applies solely to the Persian ruling class. The oarsmen, we are to assume, were betrayed by the cowardice and incompetence of their commanders. It is a strikingly bold statement to make in the presence of the queen.

He then describes an incident that took place subsequent to the main battle. The previous night the Persians had landed a force on a tiny island in the Saronic Gulf called Psyttalia, its mission being to rescue shipwrecked Persians and kill any Greeks who swam to its shores.[17] Following the victory, however, a contingent of Greeks landed on the island, surrounded the Persians, first threw stones at them, then shot arrows at them, and finally 'with one long endless roar rushed at them, cut them down, kept on hacking at their limbs and butchering those poor unfortunates, until every one of them was dead' (462–4). Though the slaughter was justified according to the norms of Greek warfare, the vividness of the Messenger's description is striking. It serves as another reminder of the brutal acts that combatants, irrespective of ethnicity, carry out in the heat of the moment.

The final section of the Messenger's report is devoted to the hardships that the army underwent on its journey back home. He concludes, 'Persia's capital will lament the loss of her country's youth, the best, the most beloved of men. Such horror did the god unleash against the Persians' (511–14). Divine intervention, which Xerxes' hubris had activated, is once again held responsible for the calamity.

Atossa departs without saying a word, though she may well have given vent to her feelings in a manner that roused the sympathy of the audience. In the following stasimon, the Chorus envision how the relatives of the Persian dead will react to the news of the defeat. They foresee the consequences for the empire. No longer will the Persian king receive tribute from his subjects and no longer will they prostrate themselves before him, since his royal power has been destroyed (585–90). They fantasize that democracy will replace autocracy, since henceforth commoners will openly express their opinions (590–4). Though some members of the audience might have cheered at the prospect of Persia's demise, the more thoughtful ones would have sadly shaken their heads: seven years after the Battle of Salamis, the Persian Empire had not visibly weakened and Xerxes was still on the throne.

Atossa returns, but on this occasion she is on foot and no longer dressed in sumptuous clothing. The audience understands that she has been humbled by the Messenger's report. She announces her intention to evoke the ghost of her dead husband Darius, whom she claims is a *daimôn* or divine spirit (628). The Chorus enthusiastically endorse her decision, describing Darius as 'blessed and godlike' (633–4).

The ghost's majestic appearance from behind its tomb was surely intended to create an electrifying impact upon the audience (681–2).[18] Precisely how this was achieved is a matter of speculation. Much probably depended on the stunned reaction of the Chorus, whose preceding choral song may have been accompanied by wild gyrations.[19] All that we know specifically of the ghost's apparel is that he was wearing saffron slippers and a feathered tiara (659–62).

After Atossa has erroneously, or at least exaggeratedly, declared that the entire expeditionary force has perished (721), the ghost cuts to the chase by inquiring how Xerxes succeeded in crossing the Bosporus. Learning that he constructed a bridge over the Hellespont, it condemns Xerxes for his folly in believing that he could 'gain control over all the gods, even over Poseidon' (749–50).[20] It then provides a brief account of the rise of the Persian Empire from Medos, the legendary predecessor of Cyrus, down to the present. It scrupulously makes no reference to the defeat which his army sustained at Marathon.

Aeschylus paints Darius in an entirely positive light in order to strike the sharpest contrast between him and his errant son. The ghost proudly states that, despite conducting many expeditions, it 'never inflicted so much evil upon my city' (780–1). When its advice is sought by the Chorus, it is simple: do not invade Greece again because the land itself is Greece's ally, since it does not have enough food to feed a large army (787–94).

The ghost goes on to predict the crushing defeat of the Persian army at Plataea, which it describes as 'the culmination of their' – or perhaps his (i.e. Xerxes') – 'suffering ... payback for hubris and sacrilegious thoughts' (807–8). After painting a lurid picture of 'the oozing mess of blood' that will be spilled on the battlefield, it produces a banal platitude:

> 'Let no-one drain great wealth by despising present fortune and lusting after more. Zeus punishes whoever entertains excessive arrogant ambitions. He is a stern chastiser.'
>
> 824–8

It instructs Atossa to provide Xerxes with new raiment and to speak to him gently. The reference to his attire underscores the calamity that has befallen his son (833–8). Though unaware that the Persians have been defeated at

Salamis, the ghost nonetheless knows that Xerxes has rent his garments. The audience might have thought it somewhat odd that the ghost fails to surmise the reason for the rending of the garments, but logic is not what is at stake here. Its parting words are, 'Despite your troubles, take pleasure every day from life, since, once you're dead, wealth brings no benefit' (840–2). Far from constituting an '"oriental" preoccupation with sensual self-gratification', this sentiment, too, is banal.[21]

The ghost scene, apart from its dramatic impact, enabled Aeschylus to extend the scope of Xerxes' tragedy beyond the defeat at Salamis. By revealing that a further, even greater, catastrophe is waiting in the wings, the ghost offers a broader perspective on life. You may think things are bad now, it warns, but there's worse to come. Human folly always comes a cropper in the end. Do not waste your precious resources by seeking to get more. Enjoy life to the full.[22]

We do not need to believe that the ghost of Darius is the mouthpiece of the poet to deduce that the audience would have identified with its comments, all the more so since Darius is portrayed as the exact antithesis of Xerxes.[23] In the final stasimon, the Chorus looks back nostalgically to the military successes achieved by Darius in contrast to the disasters wrought by Xerxes. They, too, diplomatically ignore any reference to Marathon.

Xerxes enters forlornly, in rags and with an empty quiver (cf. 1017, 1030) – evidently his mother did not have time to fetch him any replacement robes – and expresses the wish that he were dead. It is impossible to gauge what the audience's reaction would have been to his pathetic appearance. Would they have seen his discomfiture as tragic or as 'utterly ridiculous'?[24] Though I find it hard to believe that it was Aeschylus' intention to elicit ridicule before the commencement of the dirge with which the play ends, a section of the audience may well have taken pleasure in seeing him so reduced. Dionysus' character in *Frogs* claims to have taken pleasure in seeing the Chorus in a later production of *Persians* express sorrow on learning of the death of Darius.[25]

It has been suggested that the ritual lament or *kommos* in which the Chorus and Xerxes jointly engage is further evidence of Persian effeminacy. Lamentation, however, was a staple ingredient of Greek tragedy. Moreover, it is no mere 'add-on'. Rather, it brings closure to the drama. It is clear, too, that the Chorus and the feckless Xerxes, at whose door moments earlier the entire guilt for the tragedy was laid by the ghost, do not share a single grief. Xerxes is obsessed by his own wretchedness, whereas the Chorus lament the colossal waste of human life. 'Alas, I'm overwhelmed by my terrible suffering,' Xerxes declares in his opening line. 'Alas, O king, for our great army,' the Chorus echo a few lines later (910, 918). The distinction is telling. The Chorus inquire about the fate of the Persian aristocracy, instancing each of them by name, 27 in total, whom Xerxes in a telling phrase is forced to admit he 'left behind' (962, cf. 984).

The audience, unlike Xerxes, are aware that the misery of this moment will soon be dwarfed by the arrival of a second messenger reporting the defeat at Plataea, though this event lies outside the temporal frame of the play. As we saw, the Chorus were apprised of this further disaster by the ghost, but they do not share their foreknowledge with Xerxes. He thus remains to the end in a state of delusion regarding the scale of the tragedy he has engendered.

* * *

Persians conjures up a magical world of 'oriental' luxury and exoticism, but there is little in it that smacks of prejudice or jingoism.[26] The Chorus of Persian elders, though highly deferential to royalty, are by no means grovellers. It is hardly their fault that they are forced to kowtow to members of the royal family. They are aware of the dangers that beset the empire from the start and when the Messenger departs, they make a thinly veiled criticism of Xerxes by comparing him unfavourably to Darius (652–6).

Atossa is a loving mother but nothing about her, apart from her attire, is specifically Persian, though the dramatic contrast between her two entries might well have aroused some degree of pathos in the audience. It is true that she shows what we might regard as a heightened awareness of the fact that her son needs a new set of clothes since he tore his robes, but it is tendentious to claim that this indicates that Athenians thought Persian queens were 'psychopathically heartless, status-conscious and obsessed with sartorial display'.[27] We cannot rule out the possibility that it may merely be a device to facilitate her exit.

Xerxes alone is the object of criticism, both for his hubris, his selfishness and his barbarism. His barbarism, however, is merely a function of his sense of entitlement as a king. Despite his moral failings, moreover, we should not assume that the audience would have rejoiced in his discomfiture. We are all guilty of pride. His, however, had colossal consequences. Though *Persians* was inspired by a historical event, the audience was not simple-minded. They knew full well that the *dramatis personae* were independent of the characters they represented. Moreover, the criticism that is levelled at Xerxes is not a criticism of the Persian system of government as such. Darius is presented as an exemplary ruler. The Chorus berates the aristocracy for its incompetence and cowardliness, but it does not level any criticism at ordinary Persians, who are innocent victims of Xerxes' hubris. Finally, as the Messenger makes clear, it is the Greeks, not the Persians, who perpetrate war crimes.

In sum, it is undeniable that the Athenian audience which attended the first production of *Persians* would have found much to celebrate from a nationalistic point of view. However, it is worth pointing out that the role of the Athenian navy is presented as subsidiary to the intervention of the gods and to fate. I seriously doubt, therefore, whether *Persians* met with the wholehearted approval of those who had been expecting an uncomplicated endorsement of Athenian patriotism. Some might even have been put out by the fact that the poet was so even-handed in his treatment of an event that could have resulted in Athens' annihilation.

But while Aeschylus encourages his audience to visualize the Battle of Salamis from a Persian perspective, this does not mean that he intended them to adopt a Persian perspective. Far from it. When the play was produced, Persia was still a force to be reckoned with and would remain so until the Battle of the Eurymedon River brought peace of sorts some years later.

Persians nonetheless reminded Aeschylus' audience, as it does us, that suffering is the common lot of humanity, irrespective of ethnicity.[28] When in *Iliad* 24 Priam comes to the tent of Achilles to beg for the body of his son Hector, Priam grasps the hands of the man who has killed so many of his sons. Achilles remembers his own father and the two grieve jointly, their enmity forgotten, but only momentarily. *Persians*, notwithstanding its subject, is an authentic slice from the great banquet of Homer, as Aeschylus reportedly claimed all his dramas to be.[29]

Notes

1. Murray (1940), 115, 121.
2. Goldhill (1988) and Rehm (2002), 242–50.
3. Hall (1996), 6.
4. Garland (2004), 25–9.
5. Scholion on Ar. *Frogs* 1028; *Life of Aeschylus* 18.
6. *Pace* Librán Moreno (2005), 67–157, who, on the strength of Ar. *Frogs* 1026–7, argued that the original play was more patriotic than the one that has survived. For the Syracusan and Athenian revivals, as well as the possibility that two versions of the play existed, see Broadbent (1960), xlviii–lv, Podlecki (1991), 106–9, and Garvie (2009), liii–lvii.
7. The later tradition that the *skēnē* originated from the tent of Xerxes (or his commander-in-chief), which the Greeks acquired after Plataea, is generally rejected. As Couch (1944), 118, noted long ago, 'It is quite an assumption to believe that this tent was preserved in its entirety, brought to Athens, set up in the neighbourhood of the Precinct of Dionysus, and kept there for long enough period to influence the phraseology of the Greek theatre.'

8   Taplin (1977), 452–9. However, Librán Moreno (2002) argues that the *skēnē* was in use as early as 490.
9   Garvie (2009), xvi.
10 On the stereotype of Asian luxury, see Hall (1989), 80, 127–8 with Herodotus 5.49.7.
11 'Yoke' is used metaphorically at 50, 71, 139, 542, 594, 722, 736, and literally at 191, 196.
12 Podlecki (1991), 63.
13 We know the queen was riding in a chariot because when she makes a second entrance, she states that she is on foot (607–9).
14 Podlecki (1991), 76.
15 Garvie (2009), 188, sees no evidence to indicate that Aeschylus held Xerxes to be morally culpable for the defeat but merely guilty of a failure of judgement.
16 Ibid., 200, believes that we are to understand that the violence was perpetrated by Greek soldiers stationed on the shore but why would hoplites resort to 'broken oars and bits of splintered wreckage' rather than their swords? In addition, the image of fish being caught in a net more naturally evokes an action taking place at sea.
17 Herodotus 8.76; Pausanias 1.36.2.
18 The invocation alone would not have prepared them for his appearance. Agamemnon's ghost, more powerfully invoked in *Agamemnon*, makes no such appearance.
19 Podlecki (1991), 92.
20 Though folly is the chief offence that Darius levels against Xerxes (cf. also 725, 744), the charge carries with it the presumption that he has committed an offence against the gods. There seems little doubt in my view that his reference to hubris at l.821 represents a judgement on the actions of his son, viz. that he committed an offence against the gods, and that it would have been interpreted as such by Aeschylus' audience. Though Garvie (2009), xxii–xxxii, is right to argue that the function (his word) of the play was not to 'propound the moral that *hubris* is a bad thing' – they surely knew that – this does not discount the possibility, even the probability, that the play does indeed endorse that viewpoint.
21 Hall (1996), 165.
22 Some scholars, including Hall (1989), 89–90, and Ogden (2001), 129–32, have suggested that necromancy plays into the stereotype of Persian reliance on magic. I would argue on the contrary that Darius' ghost is a powerful, even essential, dramaturgical device. Though rare in extant tragedy, ghosts are hardly unknown, cf. Clytemnestra in *Eum.* and Polydorus in Eur. *Hec*. An Athenian audience would have found nothing odd about summoning the services of the dead.
23 Broadhead (1960), xxviii, writes, 'This imposing dignified and majestic figure … shows how far Aeschylus has risen above the level of a narrow

nationalism.' Winnington-Ingram (1983b), 218, is equally admiring. For the antithesis between Darius and Xerxes, see Podlecki (1991), 4–5.

24 So Blomfield (1830), *Praefatio*, xiv.

25 Darius does not, of course, die in *Persians*, which raises the question as to whether Dionysus is referring to a different version of the play. Alternatively, either he or Aristophanes might simply have got his facts wrong. Though the offhand remark offers a tantalizing glance into audience reaction, it is of dubious value, occurring as it does in a comic context.

26 As Gruen (2010), 20, writes, 'The play avoids any trumpeting any inherent superiority of Hellenes over Persians.'

27 Hall (1996), 7.

28 Garvie (2009), xxii, writes, 'If by the end of the play the audience had not, despite itself, come to sympathize or empathize with the Persians in their suffering, to identify with them as fellow human beings, *Persae* would be, I think, a failure.' The claim that *Persians* is a nationalistic play was already conclusively debunked by Broadhead (1960), xxix, who pointed out that Aeschylus delineated the Persians 'not with prejudice or malice, but with sympathetic imagination'. For the opposite viewpoint, see Hall (1996), 16–17. Though we should not assume that Aeschylus expected his audience to sympathize with the Persians, Gruen's claim (2010), 20, that the play 'eschews universalist preaching' is in my view equally tendentious. I see no reason to discount the possibility that the poet intended his play to be a commentary on the human condition.

29 Athen. *Deipn.* 8.39.

4

Imperial Stirrings in Aeschylus' *Persians*

Sophie Mills

This chapter will argue that the genre of tragedy compels Aeschylus to portray the sufferings of the Persians in such a way that his audience could feel deep compassion for them, but that *Persians* is also marked by a more aggressive Athenian triumphalism, already embryonic in Athens' self-image before the Persian Wars, and which came to its full fruition in the aftermath of the wars to shape Athens' relationship with the rest of Greece ever more strongly as the fifth century progressed.

Just eight years after the people of Athens evacuated their city, fought a navy many times larger than theirs and then returned to find their homes burned and sacked, some of them sat in the theatre with the ruined temples of the Acropolis in their view, watching a fictionalized representation of the pain of their former enemies reacting to unexpected and humiliating defeat at the Battle of Salamis. Aeschylus' *Persians* is unique among extant tragedies in dramatizing historical events that took place in the recent lifetimes of its audience. Aeschylus himself fought at Salamis. But in spite of this unusual connection between history and fiction, the tone of *Persians* is notoriously contested. How might his audience have reacted to what they saw? Did they – could they – feel genuine grief for the pain their victory had inflicted on those who had been their enemies for the past thirty years and more, as those enemies finally met fear, suffering and the shame of defeat? Did they see the play in bigger cosmic terms as a warning about the dangers of overreach when a vastly powerful person or nation wants even more power, and will do anything – even making sea into land and land into sea against the gods' provisions – to secure that power? This warning seems as relevant to Greeks, and perhaps especially the Athenians, as it is to foreigners.[1] Or did they enjoy the play primarily as a dramatic representation of the righteous triumph of Greeks over barbarians?[2] If so, was their enjoyment rooted in a high-minded patriotic celebration of sheer relief at the victories of the Greeks, or did the play stimulate feelings in them of active pleasure in seeing the humiliation of their enemies? For Aristophanes (*Frogs* 1026–7), a major theme of *Persians* was, quite simply, seeking victory over enemies, and while of course, he is trying to make his audience laugh and this is surely over-simplistic as an interpretation, there may be an element of truth in it. Did the audience see the play as a celebration of unified panhellenic action or did Aeschylus' words encourage his Athenian audience to believe that the Athenians, including many in the audience who first saw his play, saved Greece from the barbarians by their own efforts?[3]

None of these imagined interpretations of audience reaction to *Persians* necessarily excludes any other, since no audience reacts monolithically to any production. Indeed, even for those well disposed to seeing humiliated barbarians, the genre of tragedy by definition involves a degree of sympathy and an awareness of human vulnerability,[4] generated through the portrayal of suffering and the attempt to understand that suffering in a bigger cosmic framework, so a degree of sympathy for the Persians is more or less built into the play. Any dramatization of the Persian invasion – undoubtedly a topic full of dramatic potential – could only be written from the side of the losing Persians. Only a reckless tragedian would have dared to show the sack of Athens to Athenians,[5] and in any case, it is typical of tragedies in which Athens features that Athens saves others from tragedy but remains strictly outside tragic circumstances itself.[6] Thus tendencies innate in tragedy shape Aeschylus' portrayal of Xerxes and the Persians to allow sympathy for them, but other currents may also be flowing through the play. The Persians cannot lack any redeeming features, since the fall of completely unsympathetic characters would not be tragic, and yet the portrayal of their sufferings must also include some sort of contextualization of the reasons for their fall, to make it comprehensible and in some sense just.

All that said, within Aeschylus' play also lie multiple tropes about Athens that recur in later fifth- and fourth-century texts which discuss Athenian power and explain and justify the city's pre-eminent position in the Greek world.[7] I suggest that, even as audiences could pity the Persians in their misery, Aeschylus' text is also influenced by an ideology in which Athens is a, or even the, leading city in Greece already: when he wrote *Persians*, the Athenians were the acknowledged, and still admired, leaders of the Delian League.[8] As such, pity for the Persians must be balanced with a sense that the right side had won, thanks both to Greek efforts (especially those of Athens) and to the gods.

The Greek victory over the Persians was a remarkable surprise, given the relative power of either side. Such a surprise naturally requires explanation. An obvious explanation, from a Greek angle, was that the gods must have at the very least been favourable to Greek success, and at most actually enabled it: Aeschylus' Persians themselves make this claim (*Persians* 514, cf. 604), though with a rather different emotional tone from the claim in Greek mouths (e.g. Herodotus 8.109.3). And since the gods would clearly not reward anyone who did not deserve to be rewarded, then victory must have been deserved; and if deserved, it was proof of Greek moral and military excellence contrasting with their enemies' manifold failings.[9] Such a conceptualization of their defeat of the Persians was doubtless familiar to all the Greeks who fought and conquered them, but as Athens became more powerful, it turned a panhellenic conceptualization into a specifically Athenian version. Many later Athenian texts claim that the gods particularly support Athens because of the essential virtues of the Athenians and that the unique power of Athens and its success in peace and war were 'proof' of divine approval.[10] Athens used certain selected historical facts[11] to underline its unique status in Greece, above all, its supposedly lone stand against the Persians in 490 BCE and the city's supreme self-sacrifice in 480. Such actions could be used to prove the unique combination of virtue, wisdom and courage of Athens that outclassed that of other Greeks, found favour with the gods, and was both explanation of, and supported by, ever-increasing Athenian power. Aeschylus' play is marked by these Athenian tropes, sometimes implicitly and sometimes explicitly, usually in the mouths of the Persians themselves: that Athens' enemies endorse images of the idealized Athens gives those images an objective authority and truth.

Oppositions between Persians and Greeks shape *Persians*. Though the Persians are pitiable and certainly not one-dimensional villains, they are also given significantly negative characteristics. They are cruel (371), mere babblers (406), servile to their leaders (694–6, 700–3), fearful in spite of outnumbering the Greeks so greatly (391–3) and luxury-loving. Especially important in their characterization is their lack of understanding of why they are suffering. For Aeschylus' audience, the reason would have been clear, since the play unambivalently claims that hubris attracts divine punishment: Darius, wiser from beyond the grave, acknowledges this: 'When hubris flowers, it bears rich fruit – blind recklessness, a bumper harvest thick with tears' (821–2, cf. 827–31). It is hard to think that any Greek would doubt this claim, and the Persians are explicitly represented as behaving in typically hubristic ways. Both Aeschylus and Herodotus[12] moralize and mythologize the Persian Wars through narratives of events which illustrate a fundamental Greek law of human existence already expressed by Solon (13.9–22 West) which states that excessive prosperity brings a destructive hubris followed by divine punishment. Aeschylus gives multiple examples of the gods' hostility towards the Persians, and it is explicable as a punishment for their hubristic excess. Not only the hostility of the Olympians to Persia but that of the very land and sea themselves (389–91, 707–8, 792–4, cf. Herodotus 7.48–9) is emphasized throughout the play: gods and terrain even combine in malignity at Edonia as the Persians cross the frozen Strymon only to be drowned when the sun melts the ice, in a fitting revenge of water on those who had committed the crime of yoking the sea (495–512). Some Persians here are even accused of learning too late to worship the gods (497–9), and, with the exception of Darius, a ghost with greater powers of understanding than those he has left behind, the Persians do not really understand what the audience does understand through being primed with a specific theodicy in which the gods punish the Persians and help the Greeks. In a particularly striking use of dramatic irony at 215–25, the dreams and omens sent to the queen by the gods (176–214) are misinterpreted by her advisors, but every member of Aeschylus' audience would understand their real meaning. The Persians tend to ascribe disasters rather vaguely to 'some' god or spirit (*daimon*) (345, 354, 514, 573, 725) without further considering their responsibility for incurring divine hostility.

It is also a classic mark of hubris for a human being to aspire to divine status, as Darius explicitly states (820), but the queen is said to sleep with a god (643, 651, 654–5, 711) and to be a god's mother (157–8). Although Xerxes is generally called godlike rather than an actual god (80, 150–1, 634), by his bridge over the Hellespont, he attempts a divine act of linking lands separated by sea, yoking a holy entity as though it were a slave (65–71, 745–6, cf. Herodotus 7.36.1–5). His transgression of divine–human boundaries, combined with the excessive resources that he briefly controls, makes his punishment quite predictable, as his wiser father admits (739–52, 821–31). Human ignorance (454, cf. 361, 372–3) is inextricably bound up with divine malignity, and Aeschylus endorses the conventional Greek belief, already expressed by Homer, that the gods sometimes actively encourage humans to make destructive decisions (725.)

Every commentator notes Aeschylus' emphasis on the wealth and manpower of Persia. Their possession of 1,207 ships against a mere 300 Greeks (337–43) also represents an excess which is integral to hubris,[13] and a pride which according to cosmic law will bring about correspondingly catastrophic losses. The equation of the vastness of Persia's forces with the vastness of the disaster is replicated in Herodotus, for whom the sheer number of Persians is a similar obsession (e.g. Herodotus 7.56.1, 59.2–100.1). Similarly, Aeschylus' use of catalogues also points to Persian excess. Early catalogues of individuals and types of soldiers (21–60, 302–28) recall the magnificence of Herodotus' account of Xerxes surveying his army (7.60–100.1), a moment of impossible grandeur which, by virtue of its grandeur cannot be sustained, as Herodotus' Xerxes himself had realized even before this moment, when he observed his troops at Abydos and wept at the shortness of human life (7.44–6). Much later in the play, the spirit of the earlier catalogues is inverted as Xerxes is held to painful account when the chorus question him on the whereabouts of a catalogue of dead Persians (957–1001). The catalogues with their specific listing of multiple names also contrast with the anonymity of the 'Greeks' or 'Athenians': even Themistocles, arguably the architect of the Athenian victory, is reduced to 'a Greek man' (355). The anonymity of the Greeks here recalls the emphasis on democracy and equality between citizens that is emphasized in the annual speeches given to honour the war dead at Athens,[14] and also suggests a general restraint and modesty that aligns with the play's emphasis on Greek discipline and courage (e.g. 374–5, 394–405, 417), contrasting with the intense emotionalism with which Aeschylus characterizes the Persians (e.g. 537–83).

Thus, pitiable though they are, the Persians are also coloured by certain characteristics whose undesirability would have been clear to Aeschylus' audience. The portrayal of Greek virtues would have been equally clear. As one of the Greek cities, Athens naturally shares in those virtues, but as the fifth century went on and Athens gradually became increasingly dominant over so many of the Greek cities, the city developed a self-conception of what it meant to be Athenian in which qualities possessed by the Greeks became quintessentially Athenian characteristics instead, either by having originated in Athens, only being found at Athens, or by being possessed in somehow greater quantities at Athens, making Athens unique among the Greek city-states.[15] Athens' uniqueness is used for political ends to justify the city's pre-eminence in Greece as the fifth century wore on, while its pre-eminence is itself the 'proof' of its supposedly unique virtues: the same implied claim to divine favour that could explain the Greek victory over the Persians also explains Athens' greatness. Athens' supposedly unique stand at Marathon in 490 is both product and proof of a more overarching uniqueness. A further corollary of this ideology is the claim that since Athens is unique in its uniquely Greek virtues, Athens and Greece can be elided with each other.

All of these tendencies are evident in Aeschylus' *Persians*. Aeschylus speaks of 'Greeks' and emphasizes Greek unity in contrast to Herodotus' narratives of more fractured relations between participants in the Greek resistance, but he still privileges Athens and expresses Athenian self-assertion in the face of other Greek cities' claims to outstanding service in the Persian Wars. Like Herodotus, Aeschylus expresses what Athenian funeral speeches, some tragedies and other texts marked by their themes also emphasize, and what even Thucydides (1.73.4–74.2) offers, though with a rather different emphasis, that Athens is unique among the Greeks and their efforts saved Greece from the Persians. Several times in his histories,[16] Herodotus has his foreigners ask questions about the Greeks and Greek ways. One purpose of these is to reflect Greek-ness back to his Greek audience, to affirm their differences from, and usually superiority to, Persian customs and characteristics. Aeschylus produces a very similar effect by having his Persian queen ask the chorus questions about Athens at *Persians* 230–45. The exchange contains multiple contrasts between Athenians and Persians. All would have been unarguable truths to the audience, and they also have an ideological dimension beyond mere facts: Athenians fight with the more masculine weapons of shields and spears, rather than the bows which the Persians use (239–40). As king, Xerxes has absolute power over his subjects and no one to check him, but the Athenians need no autocrat to lead them (241–2, cf. 213–14, 762–4),[17] in spite of the queen's disbelief that they could withstand an invader without one (243). Edith Hall argues that a conceptual polarization between Greek and barbarian essentially began with the Persian Wars and then shifted into a contrast between Athenian democracy and barbarians' forms of ruling or tyranny:[18] *Persians* 230–44 clearly illustrates such a conceptual division between Persian and Athenian forms of politics.

Again, Persia is wealthy with gold belonging to individuals – at 237 the queen assumes that Athenian wealth would be in their houses – but Athens has a 'silver wellspring' since 'their very land's a treasure trove' (238):[19] through democratic agreement among the Athenians to use it for communal purposes, this silver was used to create the navy which defeated Persia (Herodotus 7.144.1–2) and ultimately brought Athens to pre-eminence among the Greeks. That Athens' enemies voluntarily endorse what Athenians know about themselves enhances the power and credibility of Athens' self-image of superiority and uniqueness that will increasingly shape the city's dealings with other Greeks later in the century. Similarly, the messenger's use of direct speech to recall the Greeks' exhortation to battle (402–5) stirringly recalls the triumphant resistance of that day, and the story is all the more powerful in the mouth of an enemy of Athens. At *Persians* 474, the queen herself calls Athens 'famous' ('starry' in David Stuttard's translation here), an epithet extremely familiar from fifth-century and later texts marked by Athens' supreme power in the Aegean,[20] even though earlier (230) she knew nothing about the city.

More importantly, when the Persian messenger claims that the gods save the city of the goddess Pallas (347), he elides Athens with the entire Greek army, and also endorses one of the great truths that would shape the Athenians' relationship with the rest of the Greek world long after the Persian Wars. The play often blurs the Greek resistance with the Athenian resistance, because Aeschylus has been influenced by Athenian conceptions of the Persian Wars. The Battle of Marathon is naturally not Aeschylus' focus, but the way that 490's triumph came to shape all the claims of the funeral speeches and other texts in which Athens is the 'first' or 'only' city in some noble attribute – for example, the false claim that they were the first to endure the sight of the Mede (Herodotus 6.112.3) – has also shaped Aeschylus' portrayal of 480's allied Greek triumph as the unique triumph of a specifically Athenian democracy, free speech, intelligence and order. These are precisely the claims that Athens would use throughout the fifth century to prove the rightness of its pre-eminence in Greece. Aeschylus is undoubtedly subtler in his portrayal of Athenian pre-eminence than some funeral speeches are. For example, when the queen recounts her dream of the two sisters who react differently to Xerxes' attempts to yoke them (181–99), the woman representing Greece is specifically described as wearing Dorian dress, linking her with Sparta rather than Athens. Later on, Darius will prophesy Persia's final defeat at the Battle of Plataea, a land battle in which Sparta's efforts were crucial in securing Greek victory, and which correspondingly tended to be less emphasized in later Athenian accounts of the Persian Wars. But overall, there is considerable emphasis on Ionian achievement throughout the play (178, 563, 950–1, 1011, 1025) and while Plataea is mentioned (816–17), the engagement at Psyttaleia (447–71), which was less significant in the bigger context of the war, is given a notable emphasis. Moreover, the only Greek state specifically named in the play is Athens (231, 285–6, 348, 474, 716, 824, 976) and the queen's questions to the chorus at 230–44 elicit the information that Xerxes' purpose in attacking Athens is to subject the whole of Greece to the king. To defeat Athens is to defeat Greece itself (234, cf. 824): Herodotus also gives pride of place to Athens in Persian hostility,[21] and similar claims are prominent in later ideologically inspired speeches on Athens. Herodotus already explicitly links Athens' service in the Persian Wars with the justice of its primacy among the Greeks (6.109.3) and the connection may also be found, if more subtly, in Aeschylus' play.

At 178, the queen refers to the 'land of the Ionians'. It is clear that at this early point in the play, she is referring to Greece (as Stuttard translates it here) rather than Ionia proper, but later references to the superior naval power of the 'Ionians' (950–1, 1025, cf. 563) would surely have recalled a specifically Athenian naval prowess at Salamis for Aeschylus' audience, especially since the historical Ionians had to fight on the Persians' side at Salamis. Thus, the elision of Greece and Athens is matched by a further elision between Athens and Ionia. The ambiguity between Athens and Ionia prefigures the claim made already by Solon, and which would be made especially forcefully later in the fifth century, that Athens was the mother city of the Ionians, whose position in Xerxes' forces in 480 Aeschylus is careful to obscure or absolve.[22] Athens' title as the mother city of the Ionians, many of whom were subsumed into its empire via their original membership in the Delian League, was a key plank in maintaining imperial power in the Aegean, and indeed, inscriptional evidence shows that later fifth-century Athens tried to make the mother-city colony relationship and obligations attendant thereon mandatory for all of its imperial possessions, even those of non-Ionian origin.[23] Euripides' tragedy *Ion* some 60 years later would make claims to Athenian primacy over the Ionians and also over non-Ionians (1571–93), but it is striking that already in 472, these claims are apparently lurking in embryonic form.[24] Later in the fifth century, Athens' Great Dionysia was an indisputably panhellenic festival, but it is possible that even in 472, there may have been a significant non-Athenian presence in the audience. If so, the play might have offered an early demonstration to other Greeks of an ideology of Athenian superiority that shaped the city's image of itself in the fifth century and recurs in texts long after the end of Athenian domination in Greece.[25]

The conclusion to Herodotus' *Histories* suggests that he considers that the Athenians were picking up as imperialists exactly where the Persians left off.[26] This prospective handover of power is also indicated within *Persians*. Aeschylus' Persians express fear that the end of their own imperial power is imminent: at 584–94 they prophesy that free speech, the hallmark of Athenian political excellence, is coming to a people no longer yoked under a king's power and that their subjects will soon pay them no more tribute. Athens' claim to overtake the Persians is also captured in the catalogue of places that Darius once easily conquered (864–902), especially the islands. By 472, these were part of the Delian League, led by Athens. Thus, within the middle of his play, Aeschylus shows that the seat of power is moving inexorably from Persia to Athens before our very eyes. The process was rather slower in real life, but by 472's play, an Athenian audience could suspect that the end of Persia's dominance was a foregone conclusion, thanks to the allied Greek army's victory. Audience members might also suspect, given that Athens was offered leadership of the Delian league by grateful and admiring allies, that the shift from Persian to Athenian primacy would be easy, undisputed and inevitable, as it appears in *Persians*. The fears placed in Persian mouths by Aeschylus indicate that, as early as 472, when Athens could not yet be completely sure that Persia had truly learned its lesson, some Athenians at least could express confidence in their city's powers as world liberators.

The roles of liberator and civilizer that were key to Athens' image of itself in the fifth century and its justification of its primacy among the Greek city-states actually existed long before the Persian Wars, and they were potent. Such roles are already evident in pre-Persian war Athenian narratives of the Theseus legend in the national (now lost) epic the *Theseid*, in the last decades of the sixth century: in the *Theseid*, Theseus, the quintessential Athenian civilizing hero, clears the road from Trozen to Athens of malefactors, punishing their cruelty to travellers by doing to them what they did to others and making the road safe for subsequent travellers. These localized stories are thematically close to the much older and more widely known story of Theseus killing the Minotaur in Crete: in its early incarnation, it was just a typical story of man conquering monster, but it came to acquire a distinctly political dimensional as a story in which an Athenian liberated the entire Aegean from a tyrannical Minos.[27]

Stories like the Theseus legends may also have worked as a template for Athenian military action in the Aegean prior to the Persian Wars, as Athens began to acquire the reputation for being an active, helpful city, like the active, helpful hero Theseus, as it accepted appeals from other cities for military aid.[28] This reputation was entirely congruent with narratives of Athens' service in the Persian Wars. In this way, mythology, pre-Persian War history and Persian War history can thus all be 'spun' to give a consistent and highly idealized version of Athenian action. Especially in fifth-century tragedy and funeral speeches, it is a central claim of Athenian self-publicity and public education that Athens is the city that liberates and civilizes because of its unique and divinely approved virtue.[29] This image of Athens continues to be promoted in public discourse long after the end of the Peloponnesian war which ended Athenian domination in the Aegean.

Aeschylus promotes beliefs about Athens that Athenians would have found uncontroversial by placing them in the mouths of their enemies, and he also uses the speech of their enemies to reassure his audience of their security for the future through the invocation of Darius' ghost. Darius was a successful conqueror in life and now, as a supernatural being, has special access to prophetic truth. The figure of Darius has knowledge of the past and present that Aeschylus' audience also has, and he also has knowledge of the future for the Persians – what will happen at Plataea – that is simultaneously the past for the Athenian audience. At 807–12, Darius gives explicitly theological explanations for his people's defeat: 'Yes, when they got to Greece they felt no compunction whatsoever about looting ancient wooden statues of the gods or torching temples. Altars have been smashed. Statues of divinities have been torn down from plinths and shattered. So. Since they acted so outrageously, they are suffering no less outrageously in turn.' Because the audience can align their knowledge with his predictions and know that what he says is true, when he talks about the future even beyond their experience up to 472 BCE, his predictions are given extra authority from the credibility of what he has said about what has happened between 480 and 472. Darius sternly warns the Persians never to engage with Greece again, because the land itself protects them and will bring only hunger and misery on future invaders (794, cf. Herodotus 7.49). By predicting the Battle of Plataea (816–22) – the future for those portrayed on the stage, the past whose outcome is already known for the spectators – framed in terms of hubris and impiety (820–22), his reassurance that Persia will not attack Greece again is made to sound highly credible (824). Moreover, just three lines later, he speaks of Zeus 'who punishes'. In later Athenian discourse, both in fifth-century tragedy and fourth-century funeral orations and other prose, a familiar image of Athens is that of preserver of Greek law and custom by punishing the wicked and rewarding the good,[30] as though they were agents of Zeus. Xerxes had planned to punish the Greeks for the humiliation inflicted on the Persians at Marathon (476) but had foolishly misunderstood divine intention.

Tragedies which explore Athens' relationships with other Greek cities, especially Euripides' *Suppliants* and *Children of Heracles*, embody the stories of Athenian courage and self-sacrifice on behalf of other Greeks which were repeatedly narrated in the funeral speeches in which Athenian ideology was most clearly represented:[31] Athens' historical service in the Persian Wars was also assimilated to those canonical deeds to tell an identical story that 'proved' the unique virtues of Athens which in their turn are both responsible for Athenian success and also justify Athens' pre-eminent power in Greece. In Euripides' *Suppliants*, for example, Athens restores the bodies of the dead who died in their failed attempt to sack Thebes, and it is repeatedly emphasized that the Athenians (unlike the Thebans who are blocking their burial) are following the laws of gods and men: above all, to the Theban herald who sneers at his efforts and accuses him of interfering, he responds that he only 'punishes' those who are wanton '*hubristai*', not those who are good, and that knowing the difference between the good and the wanton, and acting always on the side of good, is how his city has reached such great prosperity (*Suppliants* 574–7).[32] This was the image of Athens that, as I have argued elsewhere, became dominant in the fifth century and carried on into the fourth century and far beyond, long after Athens had lost the power that it first began to take for itself once it had assumed leadership of the Delian league with the full blessing of the other Greeks (Thucydides 1.96). Aeschylus' *Persians* is deeply marked by these early stirrings of imperial possibilities.

Notes

1 For interpretations emphasizing Aeschylus' sympathy for the Persians, promoting a message of a common human vulnerability for fictional Persians and contemporary Athenians alike, see, for example, Goldhill (1988), Dué (2006), 57–90, and Rosenbloom (2006).

2 For interpretations that consider *Persians* at least partly an expression of Greek superiority over non-Greeks, see the commentaries of Prickard (1879),

xxviii–xxix, and Sidgwick (1903), viii–xi. Harrison (2000), 135 n. 1, offers useful bibliography and a summary of scholars' arguments that have been offered for both interpretations.

3 Lattimore (1943), 90–3. One can get even more specific: Podlecki (1966), 15–23, argues that Aeschylus intended to glorify Themistocles and the Battle of Salamis over Cimon and the Battle of Marathon. See, however, Harrison (2000), 31–9, 98–100.
4 Pelling (1997), 13–17.
5 Even portraying the sack of Miletus brought Phrynichus a stiff financial penalty for reminding Athens of its 'own' troubles: Herodotus 6.21.2.
6 Mills (2017).
7 I do not have space here to discuss the validity of assimilating fourth-century post-imperial material with that of the fifth century, but see Strasburger (2009) and Mills (2020), 7–9, for an extensive argument.
8 Cf. Thucydides 1.95–96.1, Herodotus 9.106.4.
9 Lysias 2.43, Isocrates 4.88–90, 120, Plato *Menexenus* 240d.
10 The connection between Athenian virtue and Athenian success is frequently expressed in many different genres and time periods: see, for example, Sophocles *Oedipus at Colonus* 69–719, Eupolis fragment 330, Aristophanes fragment 581, Plato *Menexenus* 237c–238b, Isocrates 4.29–33, 12.124. In general, see Mills (2020), 11, 19, 21.
11 They were not always literally factual: it was well known that the Plataeans fought alongside the Athenians at Marathon, for example (Herodotus 6.111), in spite of claims that Athens was single-handedly successful in 490. Harrison (2000), 62, compares British views of the Second World War, in which they alone (omitting all the peoples of the British Empire) stood between freedom and Nazi tyranny.
12 Herodotus 7.8γ1–3, 24.1, 34–5, 8.109.3.
13 The 'few against many' trope is frequent in narratives which use Athens' performance in the Persian Wars to justify Athenian power: e.g. Lysias 2.24, Plato *Menexenus* 241b and Hyperides 6.19, 35.
14 The custom of the annual funeral speech at Athens is generally thought to date from around 470 BCE. One respected orator spoke over the dead of that year's military campaigns both to honour them and to remind his audience that they died for a glorious city. Because of this, these funeral speeches offer a highly concentrated collection of idealizing claims about Athens that appear more sporadically elsewhere in Athenian literature. Our only fifth-century specimen is that of Pericles (Thucydides 2.34–46): it is ostensibly somewhat different from the more homogeneous speeches of the fourth century and beyond, but contains many commonalities with these later speeches: Ziolkowski (1981), 133–6, 163, 173, and Mills (2020), 7–9.
15 Such claims in a wide range of fields can already be found in Herodotus: 1.60.3, 2.51.1, 4, 5.78, 6.109.6, 112.3, 7.139, 161, 8.11.2, 136.2–3. Herodotus 5.82.2 (cf. Sophocles *Oedipus at Colonus* 694–706) even claims that olives originally only grew in Attica. Even Thucydides, whose view of Athenian

power is different from mainstream Athenian ideology, refers to Athens' uniqueness: e.g. 1.70.7, 2.40.1–4, 41.2–3, etc. The claims continue to circulate in later texts: e.g. Isocrates 4.26–7, 41–2, 12.197, Demosthenes 60.17 and Plato *Menexenus* 238b. In general, see Mills (2020), 17–18.
16 Herodotus 1.153.1, 5.73.2, 5.105.2, 7.101–5, 8.26.
17 Compare the characterization of the Spartans at Herodotus 7.103–4, and also the portrayal of Athenian democracy in Euripides *Suppliants* 230–45.
18 Hall (1989), 16.
19 The earth in this play often has a divine dimension, so this is another implied sign of divine favour to the Greeks or rather, the Athenians.
20 Pindar fragment 76, Sopocles *Ajax* 961, Euripides *Children of Heracles* 38, *Hippolytus* 423, 760, 1459, *Trojan Women* 207, *Ion* 30, 262.
21 Herodotus 5.105.2, 7.5.2, 8β1–3, 11.2, 53.2, 138.1, 139.1, 9.3.1, Thucydides 6.33.6, Lysias 2.21, Demosthenes 18.202–3, Isocrates 4.94.
22 *Persians* 41–2. Hall (2007), 111, 162, 166.
23 Solon fragment 4a West, Herodotus 5.66.2, 7.94.1, 8.22.1, 44.2, Thucydides 1.95.1, 6.82.3–4, Pausanias 7.1.2–5: Meiggs (1972), 293–8. From the 440s, the allies were required to send a cow and panoply to the greater Panathenaea 'like colonists': Meiggs and Lewis (1969), 46:41–2, 69:56–8, 49:11–13, cf. 40:3–5. Those who refused were punished: Meiggs and Lewis (1969), 46:40–3.
24 Harrison (2000), 108–10.
25 Hall (2007), 11.
26 Moles (1996).
27 Mills (1997), 6–24. Plutarch *Life of Theseus* 15–19, offers many different accounts of the Theseus and the Minotaur story.
28 Already in the mid-sixth century, Croesus of Lydia appealed to Athens as well as Sparta for help against Cyrus. Sparta had long been the most powerful city in Greece, so that an appeal to Athens as well shows that the city's reputation as an effective ally was increasing beyond Greece: Herodotus 1.53.3. Some fifty years later, Athens accepted the Ionians' request for help in their revolt against the Persians (Herodotus 5.97.1), while Sparta turned them down (Herodotus 5.49.1–51.3).
29 These claims are especially strong in the portrayal of representatives of Athens in Euripides' *Suppliants* and *Children of Heracles* and Sophocles' *Oedipus at Colonus*: Mills (2020).
30 Gorgias fragment 6, 12–13, describes the Athenians as helpers of the undeserving unfortunate, and punishers of the undeservedly fortunate, and the topos is frequent in later sources which reflect idealized views of Athenian power: Lysias 2.19, 20, 56–7, Demosthenes 60.11, Isocrates 4.89, 120, and Plato *Menexenus* 240d.
31 The help given to Heracles' children and to Adrastus after his failed attempt to sack Thebes are two (the others being the defeat of the Amazons and of Eumolpus) of the four canonical deeds of Athens recounted in the funeral speeches and other texts recalling their themes: as early as Herodotus

(9.27.2–4) they are used to assert the generosity and courage of Athens through which the city deserves leadership of the Greeks, but they are especially prominent in later rhetoric (e.g. Lysias 2.3–16, Demosthenes 60.8, Plato *Menexenus* 239b–c) and also art, for example on the temple of Athena Nike of the 420s: cf. Hanink (forthcoming).

32 Compare also Demophon's exchange with Eurystheus' equally obnoxious herald in Euripides' *Children of Heracles*. See also Lysias 2.7–11, 16, 20, Demosthenes 60.8, 11, Plato *Menexenus* 239b, 240d, Isocrates 12.170, 174, Hyperides 6.5.

5

Homeric Echoes on the Battlefield of *Persians*

Laura Swift

In Homer's *Iliad*, Achilles is given fabulous armour crafted by the blacksmith god Hephaestus, including a shield decorated with images which represent the entirety of human existence (*Iliad* 18.483–608). The first thing Hephaestus chooses to put on the shield, after the earth, sea, and stars, are two cities: one in a state of peace (409–508), the other in a state of war (509–40). These cities, and their prominent position on the shield, encapsulate something important about the Greek conception of war: it was an inescapable part of the human condition. To be sure, peace was regarded as a preferable state. Homer's city of peace is filled with music, wedding festivities and dancing, while disagreements are resolved through a judicial system. But the presence of the city of war indicates that armed conflict is part of the life of a human community. Indeed, the description of the city of war is almost twice as long as that of the city of peace, and includes a detailed battle narrative. Though the city of war is filled with bloodshed and destruction, and the gods who participate on the battlefield are grim ones – Strife (Eris), Turmoil (Kudoimos) and Death (Kēr) – the lengthy description also suggests the value that war held to poets, since it enabled great deeds worthy of commemoration: the 'glorious deeds of men' that Achilles delights his heart by singing of during his absence from the battlefield (*Iliad* 9.189).

The *Iliad* is a poem of war, and it is not surprising that conflict is central to its conception of human experience. It is also the text above all others to which later Greeks ascribed cultural authority, and which no poet dealing with a martial topic could ignore. An ancient anecdote claims that Aeschylus described his plays as 'slices taken from the great banquets of Homer' (Athenaeus 8.347d), and whatever the truth of this, it reflects the debt that his plays owed to Homeric epic.[1] It is thus unsurprising that in a play which deals with the greatest conflict of the audience's lifetime, we should find frequent evocations of Homer, and specifically of his account of the Trojan War. Many of those who attended the original performance of *Persians* in 472 BC would have fought in the Battle of Salamis only eight years previously, as well as having spent their lives from adolescence onwards training for and then participating in military activities. However, Aeschylus and his audience had regular experience of *contemporary* warfare, which both in practice and in ideology was very unlike that of the Homeric poems. This chapter will investigate the depiction of war in *Persians*, with a particular interest in how Aeschylus echoes and adapts Homeric precedent to suit his audience's beliefs regarding contemporary conflict. It will argue that *Persians* makes rich use of Homeric allusion in order to aggrandize the conflict between Greeks and Persians, and to cast it in a heroic light. In particular, it will examine Aeschylus' descriptions of the Persian army, both in its initial glory and in its destruction at Salamis, and discuss how these passages evoke Iliadic battle scenes. It will also discuss the presentation of Xerxes as a quasi-epic figure. As we shall see, however, the Homeric references are not put in simply to add grandeur, but are used in a way which underscores the play's political leanings, and which celebrates not only the victory over the Persians, but the Athenian movement from archaic aristocracy towards democracy.

War in life and thought

Accounts of Greek history stress the pervasive role that war played, and the figure is often given that during the fifth and most of the fourth century, Athens was in a state of war for an average of two out of every three years.[2] In recent years, however, scholars have pushed back against the assumption that the Greeks considered war to be their default state. Thus, for example, Simon Hornblower argues that our understanding of fifth-century BC history has been skewed by the historian Thucydides' focus on war, and his suppression of other mechanisms by which Athens achieved success, such as diplomacy, or cultural 'soft power'.[3] Similarly, Hans van Wees has stressed the role played by alternative strategies to armed conflict, arguing against the often-stated idea that Greek cities were in a near-permanent state of war.[4] Nonetheless, war was a normal part of Greek life, especially when we compare it to the modern Western mindset which tends to regard it either as something enacted by professional soldiers, or as a cataclysmic event that defines a generation. As such, it was an important mechanism for a Greek city to increase its wealth and status, and it played a crucial role in masculine identity.

Political rights and military obligations were intertwined in Greek cities, following the generally accepted belief that those in the leisured classes had the duty to contribute to their community through politics and war, the two best ways for a man to spend his free time.[5] In early fifth-century Athens, all men above a certain level of wealth (an annual harvest of 200 *medimnoi* of barley) were legally bound to serve as hoplites, and liable to be fined if they failed to arm themselves or ensure they were adequately trained.[6] It was this same wealth-bracket who were at this time eligible for political office: thus the soldier's life was one of prestige and aspiration.[7] For a man of this class, participating in military service was a basic responsibility of adulthood, and in the absence of a professional army he would expect to act as a soldier whenever required. In practice, Athens could not field an adequate army from the leisured elite alone, and many poorer citizens such as working farmers and craftsmen would also have served on the battlefield, especially in times of crisis. Thus, being a warrior was a core part of manhood and civic duty, and as such was valued highly. Though literary sources present war as a male sphere, we find hints that in real life women would have played a role in supporting military efforts, from stories that they hurled down roof tiles on the enemy (Thucydides 2.4) to references to their deployment as cooks for military garrisons (Thucydides 2.78).[8] The stakes could be high, since in the most extreme scenario, defeat in war could mean the destruction of an entire community, with the inhabitants killed, enslaved or driven off their land. The experience of the Persian invasion, where the Athenians had been forced from their city and seen their temples destroyed, would have therefore acted as a reminder that the safety of the whole community depended on military endeavour. In Athenian collective memory, the sack of the acropolis came to represent the arrogance and impiety of the Persians, as well as their capacity for brutality, and was influential in shaping perceptions of Persians (and Easterners in general).[9] For the audience of *Persians* in spring 472, these would have been recent memories, and the destruction would still be evident in the cityscape around them. The Athenians left the temples of the acropolis in ruins until the building programme of Pericles some thirty years later, and from the Theatre of Dionysus, located on the slope of the acropolis, these ruins would be a powerful reminder of how close their community had come to destruction.

For these reasons, warfare played an important role in Greek cultural and artistic life. Greek art is filled with images of fighting, whether at the grand scale of temple friezes or the more intimate images on painted pottery for drinking parties. Popular mythological images such as Amazonomachies and Gigantomachies use martial imagery to express core values such as the triumph of order over chaos. Similarly, war was a popular subject for poetry, from epic tales of Troy to narrative poems celebrating recent victories (or combinations of both, such as Simonides' elegiac poem on the Battle of Plataea, which uses the Trojan myth to honour the warriors of his own day) through to light-hearted drinking songs. The association between war and renown is highlighted in the *Iliad*, where Achilles sings of the 'glorious deeds of men' (9.189), and Helen weaves images of the exploits of Greeks and Trojans into her tapestry (3.125–8), and where Hector consoles himself in the moment of his doom by the thought of how he will be remembered (22.304–5): great deeds in battle give the poets a topic for their song, while the poems commemorate the warriors and ensure their valour is not forgotten. The lionization of heroic valour thus fits with this agenda, and partly explains the abiding appeal of the Homeric poems as a model for Greek masculinity, despite their very different social contexts. Greek culture valorized competition, both at an individual and a community level, and success in war meant that a city accrued honour, which reflected on the personal honour of its inhabitants.

The importance ascribed to war helps explain the cultural value of the *Iliad*, and of epic ideology, despite its obvious differences from fifth-century Athens. Heroic epic focuses on the figure of the hero, his personal prowess and his individual pursuit of honour. Although individual duels were not a feature of hoplite warfare, brave conduct on the battlefield won honour for an individual and his family. The war dead were individually commemorated on casualty lists and the state supported and honoured their orphaned children. Nevertheless, fifth-century Greeks were well aware that the ethos of heroic warfare, with its pursuit of individual glory, was not compatible with the qualities required of a hoplite, whose duty was to hold the line firm as part of a collective effort, and so subsume his personal ambition to the greater good. This tension between individual prowess and community well-being is part of a broader pattern in the way that fifth-century writers use the figure of the epic hero, who is to be admired, but has no place in contemporary society. This is particularly clear in Athenian tragedy, which regularly depicts the problems caused by the individualistic behaviour of heroes.[10] Thus, when *Persians* presents contemporary soldiers in language that evokes the heroic age, the comparison should not be taken as uncritically positive. Rather, the play indicates ways in which the contemporary conflict and its underpinning ideology is unlike that of Homer.

In the context of a play which depicts the triumph of Greeks over Asians, the *Iliad* offers a model for how to present the suffering of war as well as its glory. The scale of the Persians' defeat magnifies the Greek triumph, but the play also confronts the loss of young life on both sides, and the grief felt by the innocent wives and parents of the war dead. The use of epic resonances, which casts the conflict in heroic terms, allows *Persians* to aggrandize the Greek achievement while also encouraging audience members to feel empathy with their defeated enemy.

The 'catalogues of Persians'

Homeric allusions enter the play from early on, as the opening choral parodos takes the form of an epic style 'catalogue of ships', as in Book 2 of the *Iliad*, where the poet describes the marshalling of the Greek and Trojan army, and spends several hundred lines listing the various contingents and their leaders, and identifying where they came from (*Iliad* 2.493–759, 816–77). Although the *Iliad* is set in the final year of the Trojan War, this evokes for the audience the beginning of the conflict, as though the Greeks were only now arriving at Troy. Thus, it gives the sense that the poem encompasses the war's full scope, while also reminding us of the scale and grandeur of the army. Similarly, the Chorus of *Persians* lists the contingents of their army to suggest the original departure of their forces, and to indicate the scale of the endeavour. As in the Homeric catalogue, the passage is full of names, both of Persian leaders and the places they came from. This clustering of foreign names also establishes the alienness of the Persians, and differentiates them from the 'us' of the audience. For example, the first Persians identified are given as a consecutive list of four names (Amistres, Artaphernes, Megabates and Ataspes, 21–2), and this confluence of foreign names creates a sense of foreign speech.[11] Unlike the precise numbers given in the Homeric catalogue, the Persian army is presented as innumerable: the chorus introduces the army with the hyperbolic claim that 'all Asia has left us on campaign'. The detailing of the contingents also creates a sense of incomprehensible scale as opposed to any sense of numeration: we are told that the oarsmen from the marshes are 'so many . . . that you could not count them' (40). Similarly, the chariots of Sardis are 'countless' (45–7), and the Babylonian contingent is 'from many lands' (53).[12] This magnifies the achievement of the Greeks, who face a challenge greater than the heroes of old, while also foreshadowing the disaster faced by the Persians. By implication, when such an army is destroyed, the effect on those left behind will be vast, and the grief will be as innumerable as the army's might was. Even at this point of the play, the Chorus anticipate how 'all Asia / sighs for them / in quenchless longing' (61–2) and the mention of 'wives and parents' reminds us of the multigenerational impact the loss will have. Similarly, the Chorus imagine the 'crowds / of weeping women' (122–3) who lament the loss of all the men of the city of Susa. Unlike the crowds of mourners for Hector at the end of the *Iliad*, this mass mourning is not for a single hero, but rather reflects the vast scale of bereavement caused by the disaster.[13]

Another difference from the Homeric catalogue comes in the way in which the Persian commanders are introduced, where the Chorus make it clear that, though they are lords in their own right, they are subservient to Xerxes: ('all kings / yet subjects / of the great king', 24). This tight control by a single ruler reflects the political difference Aeschylus wishes to stress between Greeks and Persians, unlike the much looser set of alliances within the Iliadic armies, where, for example, we are told Agamemnon is pre-eminent among the Greeks not because he has superior rank, but because 'he was the greatest of men and brought by far the largest army' (*Iliad* 2.579–80). Yet the *Iliad* is hardly a proto-democracy, and its social system presupposes a hierarchical relationship between leaders and led. The common epithet 'shepherd of the people' indicates how this relationship operates: the kings wield authority over those they lead but also have a duty to care for them. This apparently benign Iliadic phrase is used in *Persians* so as to take on new connotations. The Queen, seeking to better understand the Athenians, asks 'who herds them into place?' (241) a phrase which evokes the idea of king as shepherd. In response, however, the Chorus reply, 'They're slaves of no man' (242). Thus, the Homeric relationship of ruler to subject is reconfigured, through fifth-century Athenian eyes, as really being one of master to slave. The Chorus' words hint that Athenians have moved on from this system, and that the world of heroes is an outdated model through which to understand the soldiers of Salamis.

In contrast to the *Iliad*, where the leaders and troops of both sides are named and celebrated, *Persians* avoids naming a single Greek. This is particularly striking in the Messenger's description of the battle, where epic language evokes the great Homeric battle scenes, and in particular the *aristeias* of the heroes: scenes which describe their greatest achievements on the battlefield. The Messenger begins by listing the names of the Persian dead, and here the clustering of names is reminiscent of a Homeric *aristeia*, which frequently includes lists of men the hero has killed in his battle frenzy. Such Homeric scenes often include gruesome details of how the warriors die, or a tiny snapshot into their life before the war. In *Persians*, similarly, the list of names is broken up by such details, for example Dadaces, who 'dived like a dancer from his ship' (304–5), a death modelled on two Homeric passages where falling men are compared to divers (*Il.* 12.385–6, 16.745–50). Similarly, Matallus of Chrysa died 'drenching his long tumbling beard, staining it blood red' (314–16). The description hints at Matallus' pride in his beard while alive, and implicitly compares the horror of his death to a harmless peaceful process (dying hair: cf. Garvie 2009: 167). Both are techniques reminiscent of Homer.

Echoes of the Trojan War continue through the Messenger's account of the Battle of Salamis. For example, the Messenger attributes the Greek victory to 'some divine agency that tipped the scales' (345–6), an allusion to how the Homeric Zeus uses a set of scales to weigh the fates of the two armies (*Iliad* 8.69–74).[14] Further into the battle narrative, we are told of how the sea was 'a dense mass of shipwrecks and the bodies of the dead' and 'choked with corpses' (420–1), a close verbal parallel to how Achilles in his battle frenzy chokes the River Scamander with the corpses of the Trojans (Aeschylus twice uses the same verb, πλήθω, plêthô, that the river uses to complain about how Achilles has sullied his waters, *Iliad* 21.218). The Messenger then uses a vivid simile to describe the carnage wreaked by the Greeks: 'like we were tuna or fish netted in a fishing net – they kept on clubbing us with broken oars and bits of splintered wreckage' (424–6). Edith Hall relates this simile to the Homeric simile which compares Patroclus to a fisherman dragging his catch from the sea (Hall 1996: 140, *Iliad* 16.406–8). Yet in the context of a bloodbath in water, it is also reminiscent of Homer's simile comparing Achilles to a dolphin chasing down and devouring a shoal of terrified fish (*Iliad* 21.22–6).

However, these echoes of Homeric *aristeias* also highlight the major difference with Aeschylus' account. The function of an *aristeia* is to celebrate the achievements of a particular hero. Conversely, the Messenger identifies no Greeks by name, even when it would seem natural to do so, as with the anonymous Athenian who approached Xerxes to give him misinformation about the Greek plans (355), or the man who exhorts the Greeks to show courage in battle (401–5). The lack of individuation forms a striking contrast to the detail with which Persians are identified. Thus, the *aristeia* celebrates not individual heroism or courage, but the collective efforts of those who followed their orders to 'set free your fatherland' (404). This lack of naming is thus an anti-epic feature, highlighting the ways in which this war was won by a different type of ideology.[15]

Xerxes as an epic hero

In contrast to the absence of individuals on the Greek side, Xerxes is predominant among the Persians, and he is depicted as personally culpable for the defeat of his army. Aeschylus' descriptions of him are filled with epic allusions, encouraging the audience to imagine him through a Homeric lens. Although the Chorus mention Xerxes from the opening of the play, he first comes into focus at line 74, where he is described as setting his army in motion:

> as the lord of teeming Asia
> > unbridled
> > drives his herd
> > > his superhuman herd
> > > to conquer the whole world
>
> > > > > > > > 74–6

The adjective used to describe Xerxes, *thourios* (translated by Stuttard as 'unbridled') is an alternative form of a Homeric epithet (*thouros*) meaning 'violent' or 'raging', which when used of individuals is only applied to the war god Ares, the least sympathetic of the Iliadic gods. More specifically, it is used of Ares in the passages in the *Iliad* where he is undermined and made to look foolish: in *Iliad* 5, he is called *thouros* when reminded by Athena that Zeus has asked them not to take part in battle (5.30); it is then used three times around Ares' wounding by Diomedes, under Athena's guidance (5.454, 830. 904). Later in the *Iliad* it is used on two occasions when Ares is humiliated: when Athena prevents him from recklessly disobeying Zeus and joining in battle (15.127), and when he is defeated by Athena in the battle of the gods (21.406). While the chorus may intend this as a compliment (cf. Garvie 2009: 74), to an alert audience member the adjective is associated with folly and blind rage which leads to a comeuppance. In this moment, Xerxes, too, is in a position of quasi-divine power (driving his superhuman army), but like Ares, he is a being the audience have little liking for, and they know that he, too, will face a humiliating setback, and one in which Athena is also involved.

Xerxes' Homeric references are then heightened in what follows. He is described as 'a godlike man' (*isotheos*, a common Homeric epithet),[16] and then the glance from his eyes is said to resemble that of a snake: 'He casts from his eyes the dark glance of a lethal snake.'[17] As several commentators have noted, this comparison is modelled on the Homeric simile which describes Hector when he ignores his parents' pleas to return inside Troy and instead waits to face Achilles.[18] He is compared to a poisonous snake coiling around his hole who 'stares terribly' (*Iliad* 22.92–5). Hector here is about to face his doom, and has just rejected the advice that would save his life and the city of Troy. Again, the epic language is used to foreshadow Xerxes' failure, and to create irony between the Chorus' initial confidence and the audience's awareness of what will happen to his expedition. When the Chorus go on to express their fears in the stanzas that follow, they observe how easily a mortal can be deceived by *atē* (folly). Anthropomorphizing her into a goddess, they say that she 'lures mankind deep / inside her snare / and no-one can escape / unbroken' (97–100). This evokes the Homeric Agememnon, whose poor leadership, and particularly his error in dishonouring Achilles, causes great damage to his own army. When Achilles finally rejoins the army, Agamemnon in his apology admits that he was blinded by *Atē*, and describes how she 'has entrapped others before me', using the same imagery of traps and snares as we find in the *Persians* passage (*Iliad* 19.94). The allusion suggests that Xerxes, like Agamemnon, has made mistakes out of pride and a desire for glory, which will cause damage to his people.

Xerxes' heroic demeanour before the battle stands in contrast to his conduct during it. The Messenger makes it clear that the king is a distanced observer, who watches the battle unfold from afar rather than leading his troops in person (465–7). While this is no doubt realistic (Herodotus recounts that Xerxes watched the battle from Mount Aigaleos, 8.90.4), it sits oddly with the Homeric language used of him earlier. Epic warriors must lead their troops from the front, and their social status depends on their courage in battle (cf. *Iliad* 12.310–21). This military prowess justifies their authority over the common people, as well as the wealth they obtain. Conversely, Xerxes' leadership offers none of these reciprocal benefits, and his relationship to his troops is merely that of a tyrant, as emphasized by his pre-battle speech, where he threatens his admirals with beheading if they let the Greeks escape (369–71). Xerxes' response to the destruction of his army is also unlike the resolute behaviour shown by epic heroes on the battlefield in moments of defeat: 'And he ripped his robes and wailed – a high-pitched wail – and he issued the command to his land army to turn and flee immediately with no concern for order' (468–70).[19] Xerxes' poor leadership qualities, foreshadowed in the early part of the play, are here exemplified, and the speech which follows this passage describes how most of the troops who had survived the battle died on their return from Greece (480–511). Thus, the epic language highlights the irony of Xerxes' failure to live up to the standards of Homeric heroes, as well as hinting at how this undermines his authority as commander.

When we see Xerxes at the end of the play, he has completed his journey from epic warrior to crushed and forlorn figure. Nevertheless, epic resonances are used to underscore his suffering and thus the magnitude of his own tragedy, as well as the tragedy facing Persia.[20] Early in his initial lament, he cries, 'I can scarcely stand' (913). The Greek literally refers to his limbs being loosened (λέλυται ... γυίων ῥώμη), a phrase which in Homer is commonly used of a warrior's death. Thus, Xerxes' humiliation and grief is imagined as a symbolic death (as in *Iliad* 18.22–31 where Achilles' grief for Patroclus is presented as a form of death), yet Xerxes immediately goes on to wish he really had died along with his army. Thus, the phrase also reminds us that he did not achieve the glory of a brave death on the battlefield, and instead must live to suffer the consequences of his actions. What prompts this quasi-death is the sight of the elderly Chorus. The shame one should feel before one's elders is also an echo of the *Iliad*, first of the passage where Priam tries to use this trope to persuade Hector to come inside the city (*Iliad* 22.59–76), and later where he hopes his age will shame Achilles into giving back Hector's corpse (*Iliad* 22.419).[21] When the Chorus ask about the whereabouts of their dead youth, however, Xerxes must admit that he has left them all 'battered / on the shores / of Salamis and / on the jagged / rocks' (964–6). Whereas

Achilles' respect for Priam allows the *Iliad* to end on a note of temporary reconciliation, and with Hector's corpse being restored to his family, no honourable burial is possible for these young Persians, and the play can end only in grief. The *Iliad* ends with lamentations for Hector by the women in his life, and throughout the play we have been given references to the lamentation that the Persian wives and mothers will carry out for the fallen men (e.g. 63–4, 115–25, 134–7, 542–4). Within the play, however, it is Xerxes himself who takes on the feminine role of mourner, taking part in the same kind of antiphonal grieving as the women of Troy do in the final part of the *Iliad* (24.721–76).[22]

In its depiction of war, then, *Persians* makes rich use of the *Iliad* both as a model for Xerxes and for the army he commands. Yet, if Xerxes is presented as a Homeric hero, he lacks an antagonist, for as we have seen, the *aristeia* which leads to the Greek victory belongs not to a single hero, but to the collective resolve of the unnamed mass of warriors. The allusions to Homer are therefore connected to the play's broader political agenda, which presents the victory as the triumph of Greek freedom over Persian despotism. This is foreshadowed by the Queen's dream, in which Greece refuses to submit to Xerxes' yoke and instead smashes his chariot. Xerxes' attempt to annexe Greece is presented as a personal decision, motivated by greed (which the Greeks believed to be a common vice of tyrants),[23] as is noted by the ghost of Darius (824–8):[24]

> 'Let every one of you be satisfied with what they have already. Do not drain great wealth by lusting after more. Zeus punishes whoever entertains excessive, arrogant ambitions.'

Thus, the Persian defeat is represented as the natural end-point of autocratic rule, and affirms the superiority of the Athenian political system.[25] Xerxes' flaws highlight the dangers of a system which gives too much power to a single individual. Yet the sympathy the audience may feel for the individual Persians who have died is heightened by the lack of control these men had over their fate. The Homeric resonances make this message more broadly applicable, reminding the audience that this is not simply a question of barbarian 'slavishness', but rather the natural consequences of a political arrangement that they have now outgrown.

* * *

Throughout *Persians*, then, Aeschylus makes rich use of language influenced by Homeric epic, to cast the conflict in terms reminiscent of the Trojan War.

These epic intertexts are not used simply to add colouring, but are used strategically, to encourage the audience to compare Xerxes to what they know of Homeric heroes, and to contrast the broader ethos of the Homeric poems with that of the Persian and Greek armies. Homeric language is used to highlight the ways in which Xerxes is a flawed leader, inviting comparisons with the doomed Hector and the foolish Agamemnon, as well as increasing his feminization at the end of the play, where he is transformed from Hector to an Andromache or Hecuba. Nevertheless, these Homeric echoes make it easier for the audience to engage with his suffering and to feel empathy towards him, and so increase the emotional power of the play. Similarly, the initial description of the Persian army mirrors the Iliadic catalogue of ships, yet subtle differences foreshadow the doom that the expedition will face. In defeat, the deaths of the Persians echo Iliadic battle narratives, and this, too, increases the pathos of their loss of life.

Moreover, the epic resonances applied to the Persians draw our attention to the lack of any epic figures among the Greeks. Xerxes is given no Achilles to face, and the *aristeia* which describes the mowing down of the Persian commanders lacks a proponent. This lack of heroization draws our attention to the collective achievement of the Greeks, whose courage and glory comes not from individual deeds, but from their resolve in the face of danger and their willingness to play their part in a broader battle strategy. Homeric style individualism, it is implied, has no place in this new order, and is presented as a precursor to folly. In the context of a newly confident Athenian democracy, this message of community strength is a powerful one.

Notes

1. On Aechylean tragedy's debt to Homer, see Sommerstein (2012), 241–53. For a brief discussion of epic diction in *Persians*, see Hall (1996), 24.
2. E.g. Sage (1996), xi.
3. Hornblower (2007), 25.
4. Van Wees (2004).
5. See ibid. (2007), 273–7.
6. See Aristotle *Politics* 1297a29–35, b2–13.
7. This system was changed in the 450s BC, with the introduction of pay for military service and public office, which acted as a formal acknowledgement that poorer citizens should contribute equally to the workings of the *polis*.
8. For women's role in classical Greek warfare, see Wintjes (2012), 21–5.
9. For a description of the Persian destruction, and how this was memorialized by the Athenians, see Kousser (2009).
10. For detailed discussion, see Allan and Kelly (2013), 95–8.

11 Cf. Hall (1996), 109.
12 On the Persian obsession with numerical superiority, see Harrison (2000), ch. 7, and Rosenbloom (2006), 40. For Persian pride in numbers as instrumental in their defeat, see Papadimitropoulos (2008), 454–5.
13 On the mass scale of mourning and its role in highlighting Xerxes' ignominy, see McClure (2006), 85–6.
14 The image is repeated at *Iliad* 22.209–13, for the fates of individuals (Achilles and Hector).
15 Ebbott (2000).
16 Cf. Garvie (2009), 76, who notes that Darius will later be called 'godlike', while Xerxes loses this status.
17 On this line, I follow the translation of Hall (1996) rather than Stuttard, as Stuttard translates as 'dragon' rather than 'snake'. The Greek can mean either, but I find the latter more likely here.
18 See Smethurst (1989), 263, and Hall (1996), 114.
19 See Garvie (2009), 214, on Xerxes' humiliation and feminization here.
20 The extent to which Xerxes embodies an 'everyman' figure with whom the audience can relate is disputed: nevertheless, the play would not be effective if the audience can feel no empathy towards him. For discussion, see Pelling (1997), 16–17, and Griffith (2007), 101–2.
21 Cf. Hall (1996), 170.
22 On the feminization of the Persian males throughout the play, see Hall (1989), 81–6, and ibid. (1993). On the ritualistic nature of the antiphonal lament here, see Seaford (2012), 216.
23 The relationship between acquisitiveness and *atē* is a traditional warning, as exemplified by the Athenian poet Solon (fragment 13.7–13 W): see Rosenbloom (2006). On the role of wealth in the Persians' downfall, see also Thalmann (1980), 275–8, and Winnington-Ingram (1983a), 1–2.
24 For a recent discussion of the role of this scene, see Seaford (2012), 210–14, and Martin (2020), 67–76.
25 The classic account of the political polarization of Greeks and Persians is Hall (1989), 57–8. Hopman (2013), 66–7, notes that after Xerxes' defeat, the Chorus' questioning of and antagonism towards him appears to break down the political certainties of Greece vs Persia.

6

Individual and Collective in *Persians*

Michael Carroll

One of the most influential of the arguments put forward by Aristotle in the *Poetics* concerns the desirability of a unified plot. A tragedy ought to be structured around a single action, Aristotle maintained, which is to say that it should contain a coherent sequence of events with a clear beginning, middle, and end.[1] How does *Persians* – composed close to a century before Aristotle was born and our earliest surviving tragedy – measure up to this principle? The verdict of the famous German scholar Wilamowitz, writing towards the end of the nineteenth century, was that it falls significantly short. Wilamowitz was satisfied that each of the three main sections of the play forms an adequate unit in itself: the foreboding of the early scenes culminates in the devastating news of the Persian defeat delivered by the Messenger and the song of lamentation that follows (the first *stasimon*), while the scene with the ghost of Darius and the concluding dirge sung by Xerxes and the Chorus both function as effective set pieces in their own right. Wilamowitz's main objection was to what he saw as the looseness of the connections between these three sections, and he took this as evidence that Aeschylus had not yet mastered the technique of shaping his material into a cohesive whole.[2]

There is more than one way of defending *Persians* against this and similar criticisms, but an important starting point is to recognize that the play does not have a single focus throughout: it dramatizes the tragedy both of Xerxes the individual and of Persia as a whole.[3] The first of the three sections identified by Wilamowitz is primarily concerned with the fate of the army that has set off for Greece, but the presence of Atossa means that we cannot forget about the consequences of the defeat for Xerxes in particular; he is the central figure in the dream that has so disturbed the Queen, and it is to Atossa rather than to the Chorus that the Messenger reveals that Xerxes is still alive (299). In the second section, the tragedy of Xerxes comes to the fore, as Darius and Atossa consider the factors that induced their son to embark on the expedition. We continue to be reminded of the broader impact of Xerxes' faulty decision-making, however, especially when Darius looks ahead to the defeat that the Persian forces left behind in Greece will soon suffer at Plataea.

In the closing scene, finally, both aspects of the plot reach a shared climax, with Xerxes forced to acknowledge – under sustained pressure from the Chorus – the scale of the losses suffered under his leadership as well as the ignominy of his own return from Greece.[4]

How closely are these two strands integrated in the course of the drama? Garvie has put forward a detailed interpretation of *Persians* along the lines sketched out in the previous paragraph, and his view is that, until the final scene, the tragedies of Persia and Xerxes are always presented alternately rather than being 'interwoven'.[5] This principle of alternation can be observed even within individual passages. At the end of the ghost scene, for example, the Chorus refer to the sufferings of Persia as a whole (843–4), while Atossa dwells on the shameful rags (torn by his own hands) that Xerxes has worn since the defeat at Salamis (845–51).[6] Such juxtapositions, on both a small and a large scale, are certainly integral to the structure of *Persians*, but they are not the whole story. As we shall soon see, in the first choral song of the play (the *parodos*) Aeschylus uses the full richness of his poetic resources to illuminate the nature of the relations binding Xerxes, his subordinate commanders, and the rest of the army together within a single hierarchical structure, and to hint at the consequences of defeat both for that complex whole and for the empire of which it forms part. When in later scenes the focus moves from one aspect of the disaster to another, therefore, the spectators continue to be able to grasp the connections between them in light of the patterns established in the *parodos*. After examining the style and structure of that opening ode in some detail, we shall turn to a number of passages later in the play where Aeschylus' use of language serves to remind the audience of the interdependence of the tragedies of Persia and Xerxes.

The opening section of the *parodos* (lines 1–64) is in a metre known as the 'marching anapaest' and was probably chanted (rather than sung) by the chorus members as they filed into the performance space and took up their positions for the singing and dancing to follow.[7] The Chorus begin by identifying themselves as members of the Persian royal council, left in charge by Xerxes since his departure to Greece. They explain that they are anxious about 'the return of the King and of his army supplied with plentiful gold' (8–9), a choice of words that immediately identifies the two main strands of the impending double tragedy.[8] The most striking feature of this opening section comes into view some lines later when, after referring to the great size of the Persian forces, the Elders proceed to list some of the names of the leaders from various parts of the empire who set off under Xerxes' command. The historical accuracy of this extended catalogue is questionable – some of the names here and in the two later catalogues may well have been Aeschylus' own invention[9] – but as a dramatic device it is a masterstroke. In the first place, the catalogue (comprising seventeen names in total) offers a vivid sense of the vastness and ethnic diversity of the army, with each new name indicating the participation not only of the leader in question but of a whole contingent of soldiers under his command.[10] At the same time, even this very partial roll call is a reminder that every member of the expedition, including the common soldiers, was an individual with his own personal history and place of origin,[11] while the accumulation of foreign-sounding names is central to the distinctly exotic atmosphere of these opening lines.[12]

A further effect of the catalogue, however – and one that has received comparatively little attention from scholars – is to stress the importance of these leaders in their own right. The description that follows the first four names sets the tone in a number of respects. Amistres, Artaphrenes, Megabates and Astaspes, the Chorus tell us, are 'marshals (*tagoi*) of the Persians, kings subject to the Great King', and 'overseers (*ephoroi*) of a huge army' (23–5). The designation of these men as kings suggests that they hold the position of satrap (provincial governor), but that is not to say that their authority remotely approaches that of Xerxes. Even those immediately below the Persian king in rank were apparently referred to as his slaves,[13] and the gulf in status is highlighted later in the play when the Messenger reports that before the Battle of Salamis, Xerxes threatened to have all of his admirals beheaded if the Greek ships escaped (369–71). The emphasis here at the start of the catalogue, however, is on the honour and high standing of these four leaders, and others are subsequently identified as rulers of cities (36, 38) and as kings (44). The Greek words translated above as 'marshals' and 'overseers' indicate why their authority is crucial to the success of the expedition: *tagoi* is related to a verb (*tassein*) that in a military context refers to the arranging or stationing of troops, while *ephoroi*, like 'overseers' in English, conveys the idea of directing through observation. And as the Chorus' reference to the size of the army in line 25 reminds us, the larger the number of troops, the more vital such a supervisory function becomes. The commanders also prove their value by the example they set to their men, moreover, and the Chorus go on to describe the qualities of bravery and fearsomeness possessed by the first four individuals (26–8).

Fewer leaders are named towards the end of the catalogue, as the Chorus' attention turns to the size of the contingents that have joined the expedition from parts of the empire outside the Persian and Medean heartland, and this enables a gradual transition back to the double motif of the magnitude of the Persian forces and the supreme authority of Xerxes (56–8). The final few lines of the anapaestic section then return to the anxious mood of the opening, as the Chorus describe the longing felt by 'the entire land of Asia' (61) for the safe return of those who set off for Greece. What all of this means is that by the start of the lyric section the audience have already been encouraged to think of the Persian army as a hierarchy consisting of three divisions – the mass of common soldiers at the bottom, Xerxes at the pinnacle and his commanders in the middle – while the empire as a whole has been presented as temporarily divided into the army on the one hand and those who have been left behind on the other.

The rest of the *parodos* offers a deeper insight into the relations between these various parts and wholes, and it does so by exploiting an important formal feature of tragic choral lyric: strophic structure.[14] The vast majority of choral odes in surviving tragedy contain one or more pairs of stanzas referred to as the strophe and antistrophe, with the antistrophe repeating the – often very complex – metrical pattern of the strophe. In tragedy, each new strophe has its own metrical structure (shared only with the corresponding antistrophe), and in fact across the whole tragic corpus no strophe is metrically identical to any other.[15] The metrical symmetry of strophe and antistrophe was presumably also reflected in the dancing of the chorus members, and Wiles go so far as to argue that the choreography in both stanzas would always have been identical: 'the antistrophe effects a transformation of the strophe, so that the same visual image receives two meanings'.[16] We may object to the generality of Wiles' hypothesis in the absence of firmer evidence, but there is no reason to doubt that continuity of movement and gesture was an important option available to the dramatist. In what follows, particular attention will be paid to the layers of meaning that emerge from correspondences between strophe and antistrophe on the level of imagery, correspondences that are very likely to have been reinforced, in some way or another, by the dancing of the Chorus.

The Elders begin by describing how the army succeeded in crossing the Hellespont, the strait separating Asia from Europe (65–72):

> It has already passed, the city-sacking,
> kingly army, over to the neighbouring land on the other side of the channel,
> after crossing the strait of Helle, Athamas' daughter, on a flax-bound floating bridge,
> a many-bolted road cast as a yoke on the neck of the sea.

Repeated 'p' sounds in the opening line of the Greek text draw a link between the action of traversing the Hellespont (*peperaken*, 'has crossed') and the army's destructive power (*perseptolis*, 'city-sacking'), with the latter word recalling in punning fashion the name of the Persians themselves (*Persai*).[17] The implication is that it is in the very nature of the Persians – or their destiny, if we prefer – both to range widely through space and to crush their enemies. The focus then turns to the remarkable construction that, by transforming the Hellespont into the neck of a beast of burden weighed down by a yoke, enabled the Persian forces to cross from one continent to another. The yoke metaphor helps to convey the sturdiness of the 'roadway' that has tamed the Hellespont, but the Chorus' choice of language also points to the fact that that, unlike the single cross-beams used in an agricultural setting, this was a yoke of many parts held together by flaxen ropes and bolts.

In the antistrophe the army is again on the move, but now its own structure is at issue (73–80):

> The fervent leader of many-peopled Asia
> is driving his divine flock over the whole earth
> by two courses, trusting for the leadership of those on land and at sea in firm,
> unyielding commanders – descended from a gold-begotten race, a man
> the equal of the gods.

The flock metaphor of the second line reflects the gulf in status between Xerxes and the rest of the Persian forces,[18] but the starkness of the divide is softened somewhat by the reappearance in the following clause of Xerxes' subordinate commanders. While there is no doubt that these individuals form part of the 'divine flock' along with the common soldiers, the catalogue in the anapaestic section has already underlined their prestige and Xerxes' reliance on them is now made explicit. But more is conveyed about these commanders than is apparent if we concentrate on the surface meaning of the Elders' words, and this is where the principle of strophic structure becomes crucial. In both stanzas a complex whole is used as the means to achieve a particular purpose: the bridge of many parts enables the Persian forces to pass from Asia to Europe, while driving his army from place to place allows Xerxes to move across the whole world. The result – reinforced by the formal symmetry between the two stanzas – is an implicit analogy between bridge and army: in the same way that the bolts and ropes hold the bridge together, it is only thanks to the leadership of the commanders that the army has the cohesion to be able to do the King's bidding. The Greek words I have translated as 'firm' and 'unyielding' (*ochuroisi* and *stuphelois*, respectively) can, like those English words, be used in a physical as well as a psychological sense, and both are relevant in this context. Xerxes relies on these men not just because of their doggedness as individuals but for their structural role in bolstering the (metaphorical) stability of the army.

At the start of the second strophe, a much more extreme form of unity is attributed to the Persian forces. The Chorus describe Xerxes as having the glare of a deadly snake and possessing 'many hands and many ships', a monstrous image that recalls the fearsome 'hundred handers' of Hesiod's *Theogony*.[19] In the antistrophe this mythical prodigy has transformed into a surging body of water (87–92):

> No one has the mettle to stand up
> to a great stream of men
> and with firm barriers keep back
> the invincible wave of the sea:
> there is no way to oppose the Persian
> army and its stout-hearted people.

If the idea of the army as a single colossal organism captures its unity of purpose and action, the focus now turns to the effect of this unity on those who refuse to yield to Xerxes' might.[20] The Persian army has such strength in numbers, the Chorus suggest, that its power resembles that of a torrent or breaking wave. We have already been reminded, however, that – unlike an undifferentiated mass of water – the army's unity is underpinned by a particular complex structure. The strength of barriers designed to hold out the sea, too, depends on the effectiveness of their design, and in fact the word I have translated here again as 'firm' (*ochurois*) is one of the two adjectives used to describe Xerxes' commanders in the first antistrophe.[21] The Chorus will later hear of the crushing defeat suffered by the Persians in the sea battle at Salamis, and scholars have been sensitive to the ironic resonances of this boastful comparison of the army to the 'invincible' sea.[22] More significant for our purposes, though, is the manner in which this stanza exposes the potential fragility of the kind of complex unity exemplified by the Persian army, and the image of shattered sea barriers will indeed prove prophetic of the fate that awaits the army.

The third strophic pair returns to the subject matter of the opening two stanzas, but this time in reverse order (a structural pattern known as 'ring composition').[23] In the strophe, the Chorus declare that destiny has allotted to the Persians the task of fighting wars and razing cities, while the antistrophe focuses on the maritime prowess that has made possible the empire's continued expansion. The antistrophe begins by acclaiming the general achievement of learning to cross the open sea before alluding to the traversal of the Hellespont in particular: the Persians have put their trust 'in cables fashioned from fine strands and in army-conveying devices' (113–14).[24] The language of trust recalls the reference in the first antistrophe to Xerxes' trust in his commanders, but in this case all who crossed the strait were required to put their trust in the bridge's stability, and the achievement of those who constructed it is underlined by the reference to the delicacy of the cables holding the design together. The Hellespont was crossed successfully, but the reappearance of the theme of trust and the acknowledgement of the flimsiness of the cables are further reminders that the robustness of any complex structure cannot be taken for granted.

Though there is much that we do not know about the choreography of tragic choral odes, one thing we can say for certain is that the choral ensemble performing in the theatre was itself a whole formed of multiple parts. In the period when *Persians* was written there are likely to have been twelve chorus members,[25] and it is not much of a stretch to imagine the Persian elders positioned side by side as they sang and danced the opening strophic pair, embodying first the bridge over the Hellespont and then a line of soldiers. And if the analogy between bridge and army were indeed given such perceptible, dynamic expression, we can only begin to conceive how powerful the effect would have been of seeing the Chorus enact, in the second antistrophe, the smashing of just the kind of composite whole they had represented in the opening two stanzas and proceed to evoke again in the third strophic pair.

The Chorus themselves may be oblivious to these patterns of darker significance, but something prompts a sudden change of tone in the following stanza (which has no metrical double and is therefore described as an 'epode'). What mortal man, the Chorus mournfully ask, can escape the deception sent by a god bent on his destruction? The shift to the level of the individual reflects the fact that, despite Xerxes' reliance on the army and his commanders for the success of the expedition, the decision to proceed in the first place was his alone. The atmosphere of gloom lingers in the following strophic pair, but the Chorus' perspective broadens, as it had done towards the end of the anapaests, to include all of those left behind in Asia. They first describe their own minds as 'dressed in black and torn with fear' (114–15), while the corresponding picture in the antistrophe is of women lamenting and rending their clothes if news of the kind of devastating defeat dreaded by the Elders were to be delivered.[26] In this way, just as happened towards the end of the anapaestic section, we are reminded that the army itself forms part of a larger whole and that there is a 'massed crowd of women' (122–3), not to mention parents and children, waiting at home for each troop of Xerxes' men.

The final strophic pair juxtaposes a picture of the army on its way to Greece with one of Persian women mourning their husbands' absence (126–39):

> For the entire host, both horse-drivers and plain-treaders,
> has left, like a swarm of bees, with the leader of the army,

crossing over the sea-spanning promontory yoked together
so as to be shared by both lands.

Beds are filled with tears through longing for the men who have left.
Persian women, softly grieving, each with the longing of love for her husband,
the fervent spear-bearing bedfellow she has sent away,
leaving herself yoked alone.

To an even greater extent than the earlier description of the army as a flock, the bee simile conveys both the scale of the Persian forces and the stark contrast between the mass of soldiers and their solitary leader. The Chorus' attention then turns once again to the construction that allowed the army to cross to Europe, but this time it is the bridge's astonishing capacity to unite two continents rather than its own structure that is at issue. The description is expressed in terms that verges on the paradoxical: 'where logic insists that there are two promontories, the Asiatic and the European, [Aeschylus] uses the singular ... to emphasize that Xerxes has turned them into one'.[27] The language of yoking recalls not only the description of the bridge in the first strophe but also the first yoke metaphor of the play: towards the end of the anapaestic the Chorus had referred to the eagerness of those who live near the mountain Tmolus in Lydia to 'cast the yoke of slavery around Greece' (50). The Chorus' hope, of course, is that, just as Europe has been physically bound to Asia, the cities of Greece will be incorporated into the Persian Empire. But in order for this outcome to be achieved, a significant proportion of the population of the empire – the 'flower' of its men, as the Chorus earlier put it (59) – has had to cross the borders of Asia, and the consequences for those left behind are explored in the antistrophe. This time the parallelism of strophe and antistrophe highlights a crucial disanalogy between the situations described in each stanza as well as their similarities. Whereas the bridging of the Hellespont has united land masses on either side of a natural boundary, we are now presented with a separation whose anomalousness is brought out by the oxymoron 'yoked alone' (literally 'single-yoked'). The military expansion required to bring Greece under Xerxes' rule has brought about a temporary severance of the yoke joining husband and wife, and the Chorus evoke to powerful effect the emotional strain caused by this undoing of the bond of marital intimacy. Both states of affairs run contrary to the natural order of things, but in opposite ways.[28]

Scholars have long been alive to the thematic importance of the chain of yoke metaphors in *Persians*.[29] We shall shortly turn to two passages where the disastrous outcome of the expedition is imagined in terms of a shattered or loosened yoke, and in the ghost scene the motif is also associated with the reasons for the disaster. When Atossa tells Darius that Xerxes 'yoked' the Hellespont, his initial reaction is one of incredulity, and to Atossa's suggestion that a god must have 'touched' their son's mind when he did so, Darius responds that only a very powerful divinity could have had such an effect (722-5). Some lines later Atossa again uses the language of yoking in reference to the bridge (735), and in his next speech Darius adds a startling twist to the motif when he declares that Xerxes fettered the Hellespont as if it were a slave (745-8), an act whose foolishness and impiety Darius sees as representative of the expedition as a whole. If in the *parodos* the emphasis was on the astonishing human achievement represented by the bridging of the Hellespont, from Darius' perspective Xerxes' disrespect for natural boundaries and the gods who have established them is symptomatic of the mindset that has led to disaster: in joining the two continents, Darius gloomily observes, Xerxes thought he could gain mastery over Poseidon, the god of the sea (749-50).[30] Already in the *parodos* the yoke metaphors had established a link between the progress of the expedition (the bridge), its objective (the subjection of Greece), and the potential consequences for the empire as a whole should the expedition fail (the wives grieving for their absent husbands), and the recurrence of the motif later in the play helps to reinforce and deepen those connections.

What I hope has emerged from our examination of the *parodos*, however, is that the yoke metaphors there do not simply anticipate various aspects of the disaster and its interpretation by Darius in a way that adds to the thematic coherence of the drama (all of which is certainly true). They also – in tandem with other aspects of the ode's language – cast light on the *nature* of the vulnerabilities in both army and empire that will be exposed by the expedition to Greece. The effectiveness of a yoke depends on the firmness with which it binds the animals to one another and to the plough or vehicle they are intended to pull. The bridge over the Hellespont needed to be stable enough to allow the whole Persian army to cross over to Europe, but the first strophe reminds us that only a construction of very many parts could meet the challenge, and in the third antistrophe, as we have seen, the Chorus refer to the trust which those who crossed the Hellespont were accordingly required to place in the design of the bridge. The main source of Persian military might, as the anapaestic section of the *parodos* makes clear, is the sheer number of soldiers at Xerxes' disposal,[31] and the danger in this case is that the multiplicity of parts will come at the expense of organization and tactical coherence. The hope of all those favourable to the Persian cause is that Xerxes and his army will display the cohesion of a single monstrous organism, but the catalogue of leaders in the anapaestic section and the implicit analogy between their function and that of the ropes and bolts in the bridge underline how essential those subordinate commanders are to the success of the mission.

The description of the wives left behind as 'yoked alone', on the other hand, not only foreshadows the permanent separation from their wives of the soldiers who are to lose their lives in Greece but also, in broader terms, points to the existence of countless individual bonds between those who have set off with Xerxes and the rest of the empire's population. The huge scale of the expedition carries with it the risk that very many of those bonds will be severed, and the repercussions of such an outcome would not be confined to the emotional devastation of the bereaved. The first hint that the failure of the invasion would also have severe political consequences is found in the dream that Atossa relates to the Chorus (181-99).[32] The Queen describes how she saw Xerxes yoke two women – one representing Greece, the other the areas under Persian rule – to his chariot, before the Greek woman put up resistance and 'shattered the yoke through the middle' (196). There follows a significant detail: the breaking of the yoke caused Xerxes to fall from the chariot (197). In other words, the failure to control the Greek woman after she has been yoked to the Persian forces leaves Xerxes worse off than before he made the attempt, with the shattered yoke forcing him from his position of authority in the chariot and exposing him to the pity of his father Darius (197-9).

The messenger scene is full of the language of striking and smashing, imagery that helps to link the brutal physicality of battle to the far-reaching political ramifications of the Persian defeat. The messenger begins by lamenting the 'single blow' that has destroyed the great prosperity of Persia (251-2), before some lines later identifying the 'ramming of ships' (279) as responsible for the destruction of the Persian forces. As his long account of the battle at Salamis later reveals, the Greeks succeeded precisely by immobilizing the Persian ships and preventing them from fighting as a collective. If the size of the two fleets were all that mattered, the messenger insists, Xerxes' forces would have been victorious (337-8). Instead, the Greeks managed to force the Persian ships into a narrow space that left them unable to come to one another's assistance and exposed them to accidental blows from Persian rams as well as from the Greek ships surrounding them (413-18).[33] Amid the wreckage and mayhem, every ship that was in a position to row away from the fighting made a disorderly escape, while helpless individual Persians were battered or speared to death (422-6). It is not just the maritime setting, therefore, but the manner in which the cohesion of Persian's superior numbers is shattered and the catastrophic loss of life that results which is foreshadowed by the image of the breaking wave in the *parodos*.

Particularly significant in the light of our earlier discussion, however, is the catalogue of dead leaders in the first of the long speeches delivered by the messenger (302–30). If the roll call of commanders in the *parodos* was reminiscent of an epic catalogue of warriors,[34] this speech may rather have reminded an Athenian audience of their own custom of inscribed (and perhaps also publicly recited) casualty lists.[35] Alongside their names, a scattering of details about the nineteen men listed by the messenger adds to the poignancy of his speech:[36] we learn in some cases about their homeland, the circumstances of their death, or the current fate of their corpse, and there are even more personal touches, such as the mention of the bushiness of Matallus' beard (316), or the skill with which Amphistreus' wielded his spear (320–1), or the good looks of Tarybis (323–4). The loss of these men has not only deprived the army of their own individual qualities, however, but of vital leadership, and this is brought to the fore by the repeated references to the number of men under a particular commander's charge: Artembares was commander of ten thousand cavalrymen (302), Dadaces was in charge of a thousand (304), and so on. And it is not just the running of the army that will inevitably be impaired by this devastation of the officer class. The opening of the *parodos* has already made it clear that these commanders were in many cases also governors of large portions of the empire, and, just like the army, the empire is a hierarchical structure whose operation depends on those who mediate between Xerxes and his subjects. In the final strophic pair of the first stasimon, the Elders spell out the consequences of the destruction of so many of Xerxes' subordinate commanders (584–97):

> Not for much longer will the people throughout
> the land of Asia be under Persian rule,
> nor will they continue to pay tribute
> by lordly compulsion,
> nor will they show awed reverence by prostrating
> themselves on the ground, because the king's
> power is utterly undone.
>
> Nor any longer will mortals keep
> their tongues in check: the people have been
> released from the limits on free speech,
> since the yoke of power has been unfastened.
> The sea-washed island of Ajax
> with its bloodied soil
> holds what was Persia.

Critics have been puzzled by the fact that, apart from the Chorus' prediction here, there is little evidence to suggest that the Persian defeat led the Empire to unravel.[37] Garvie accordingly stresses their dramatic purpose: '[Aeschylus] must present total tragedy for both Persia and Xerxes', and Xerxes' tragedy 'consists in the destruction of his empire and loss of his subjects' confidence'.[38] But if that makes the anxieties voiced by the Chorus seem rather *ad hoc*, it should be clear from our discussion so far that they in fact follow directly from the logic of the *parodos*. The stress there was on the importance of the commanders in binding the army together, while now their structural role in the empire as a whole is in question. It is only thanks to their power that tribute was gathered and the yoke of force remained bound, and now that they are gone there is nothing to underpin Xerxes' authority. The basis of Persian power is now in the soil of Salamis precisely because, as we heard in the ode's second strophe, that is where those seized by necessity were 'smashed' (571), and there is a strong sense as the ode comes to a close that the shattering of the fleet was only the physical manifestation of the shattering of Xerxes' power.

In conclusion, let us turn back to Garvie's claim that until the final scene the two aspects of the double tragedy are always presented alternately. What I hope has emerged is that the design of the *parodos* ensures that from the very start the nature of the hierarchy with Xerxes at its head is brought into focus, as the Chorus act out the capabilities and vulnerabilities of complex wholes through their singing and dancing. This means that, as attention later shifts between the immense loss of life in Greece and Xerxes' own dishonour, we are able to make sense of both in terms of the disintegration of a previously robust totality. Especially important in keeping the two strands interwoven are the catalogues of names in the opening anapaests, in the messenger speech, and in the exchange between Xerxes and the Chorus with which the play ends. One effect of these three roll calls is to underline the extent to which Xerxes' military and political authority depends on the steadfastness of his commanders, and this is a key point of contrast with the political system in Athens; as the Chorus tell Atossa in the scene following the *parodos*, the Athenians are reputed to be 'no man's slaves or subjects' (242). On the other hand, the bravery and martial prowess attributed to many of the commanders are qualities that an Athenian audience too would have valued highly. If the personal details in the messenger's speech encourage us to think of the dead leaders as individual casualties as well as symbols of the scale of the Persian defeat, in the final scene we are offered a vivid insight into the grief and anger felt by the aristocratic Elders at the loss of so many men of fighting age from the ruling class. In a striking contrast to the deference they showed to the ghost of Darius, the Chorus repeatedly ask the Xerxes where he left the commanders whose names they have listed,[39] and in the face of this questioning the King himself is moved to express yearning for his 'brave companions' (987–9). Those vassal kings were the source both of his power and prestige and of Persia's, but they were also individuals deserving of lamentation as such, and in this regard their names stand for the many thousands of men under their command whose deaths have left families across the empire permanently severed.

Notes

1. Arist. *Poet.* 1450b22–34. On the concept of unity in the *Poetics*, see Halliwell (1986), 96–108.
2. Wilamowitz-Moellendorff (1897), 383, 389.
3. For an overview of such criticisms and arguments in favour of understanding *Persians* as a 'double tragedy', see Garvie (2009), xxxii–xxxvi (this position is further developed throughout Garvie's commentary). Schenker (1994) similarly argues that *Persians* is marked by an interaction of national and personal perspectives (represented by the Chorus and Queen, respectively). For a selection of other possible responses to the objections of Wilamowitz and like-minded critics, see Hall (1996), 17–19.
4. Cf. Schenker (1994), 284: '[I]n the interaction between Xerxes and the Chorus, that tension [between national and personal perspectives] is finally released as the king and his people become united in mourning for the Persian losses.'
5. Garvie (2009), xxxiv.
6. Ibid., 321–2.
7. For more on how these lines may have been delivered in performance, see Hall (1996), 106, with further references.
8. Garvie (2009), 52.
9. See ibid., xiv–xv, with further references.
10. See e.g. Saïd (2007), 72, Rosenbloom (2006), 40–1, and Sommerstein (2010), 51.
11. Garvie (2009), xv.
12. See e.g. Rosenmeyer (1982), 114, Hall (1996), 109, and Garvie (2009), xiv–xv.
13. Garvie (2009), 138, with further references.
14. For an introductory discussion of strophic structure (among other aspects of the language of tragic lyric), see Battezzato (2005), 149–53.
15. West (1987), 50–2.
16. Wiles (1997), 96–113, quotation on p. 104.
17. Garvie (2009), 71–2.
18. The idea of the leader as a shepherd has strongly Homeric associations; on the significance of those associations in this context, see e.g. Saïd (2007), 76–7, and Garvie (2009), 74–5.

19 See e.g. Rosenmeyer (1982), 139, and Saïd (2007), 77–8.
20 Saïd (2007), 79, notes that these and similar images in the *parodos* are 'designed to reveal the essence of an absolutism which concentrates all powers in the hands of a single man', and that the ode as a whole 'suggests the transformation of many into one'.
21 From this perspective, the repetition is far from 'casual' (as suggested by Garvie 2009: 80).
22 See e.g. Rosenbloom (2006), 44, and Garvie (2009), 79.
23 I follow the majority of scholars in accepting that lines 93–100 (the epode) should be transposed to come after the third strophic pair. For arguments in favour of the transposition, first suggested by Müller, see Garvie (2009), 47–9. Hall (1996), 115–16, is one recent editor who follows the order of lines in the manuscripts.
24 For this way of understanding the train of thought in the stanza, see Garvie (2009), 81–3.
25 For a recent review of the evidence, see Sansone (2016, Sansone argues against the standard view that this number later increased to fifteen).
26 On the striking impersonation of the voice of these women on the part of the Elders here, see Hopman (2013), 64–5.
27 Garvie (2009), 90–1.
28 Petrounias (1976), 9–10.
29 For a concise overview of the imagery of *Persians*, see Anderson (1972, the yoke metaphors are discussed on pp. 167–8). For a comprehensive treatment of the imagery of yoking in the play, see Petrounias (1976), 7–15.
30 For a sensitive discussion of these lines, see Garvie (2009), 295–6.
31 See e.g. Harrison (2000), 66–7, and Saïd (2007), 71–3.
32 The significance of the action of yoking in this context is explored well by Rosenbloom (2006), 54–6.
33 Cf. Harrison (2000), 69–70, and Saïd (2007), 85, 'Number, in such conditions, far from constituting an advantage and a help, is merely an obstacle and a factor in destruction.'
34 See e.g. Michelini (1982), 15, 17, and Rosenmeyer (1982), 109, 114–16.
35 Ebbott (2000).
36 Garvie (2009), 161–2.
37 See e.g. Harrison (2000), 28, 74–5 (with further references).
38 Garvie (2009), 234.
39 Hopman (2013), 66, notes that this 'abrupt questioning ... is reminiscent of the practice of frank speech that defines Athenian democracy'.

7

Land, Sea and Freedom: The Force of Nature in Aeschylus' *Persians*

Rush Rehm

When discussing geography and the environment, we try to separate the man-made from the natural. The Greeks of Aeschylus' day did the same; however, the close relationship between their anthropomorphic gods and the natural world tended to blur the boundaries. Although the immortals did not create the earth or the surrounding cosmos, the Greeks associated the gods with what they saw as numinous aspects of the phenomenal world. Because of this interrelationship, nature often appeared to take on a purposefulness that responded to human behaviour.

Zeus (to whom we will return later) provides a case in point. The god had almost a hundred cult titles, linked to a range of elements, locations and events – rain, darkness, lightning, thunder, moisture, dust, fair winds, harvest, friendship, guests, hospitality, suppliants, deliverance, victory in battle, the marketplace, the household hearth, the city council, oak forests, tall mountains, among others. As many of today's school children know, the Greeks also imagined the peak of Mount Olympus inhabited by Zeus and his extended immortal family, who looked down over the human domain from on high, with varying degrees of interest or apathy. Anyone who has caught sight of the peaks can understand why the ancient gods chose Olympus as their home, in and above the clouds.

Approaching Mount Olympus from our scientific perspective, we eliminate the gods and differentiate the sedimentary rocks forged at the bottom of the primordial sea from the much later alluvial deposits produced by melting glaciers. We distinguish both of these geological phases from the recent surface scars made by human activity: rock quarries, timber-cutting, agricultural-terracing, olive plantations, viniculture, goat-grazing, refuge huts for hikers and so on. For all the effects of human use and misuse, however, Mount Olympus still stands an impressive 2,917 metres above sea level, much as it did in Aeschylus' day.[1]

In spite of the manifold changes since the premiere of Aeschylus' *Persians* in 472 BCE in Athens, natural features like Mount Olympus remain; the island of Salamis still rises in the Saronic Gulf; the River Strymon still flows in western Thrace; the plain of Plataea still lies between Mt Kithairon and Thebes. These continuities of land and sea lend credence to what Lawrence Durrell has called 'the spirit of place', which – *mutatis mutandis* – affects humans across different times and cultures. Its persistence helps account for the identification of certain places and natural phenomena with divine forces, a way of thinking that informs Aeschylus' *Persians*. As we shall see, the physical environment – the sea, land, rivers, climate and their associated deities and daemons – proves crucial to the defeat of the Persian expedition. In the words of the ghost of Darius, 'the Greek earth herself fights with her people' (*Persians* 792).

Representing the physical world in the ancient Greek theatre

Performed in large outdoor theatres during broad daylight, Greek tragedy took in the elements and what the audience saw and heard around them. At the City Dionysia, the main theatre festival in Athens, the production schedule involved four different plays by three tragedians – one tetralogy a day – staged consecutively over three days, followed by five comedies by five different playwrights on the fourth day, as well as another day dedicated to the performance of 20 dithyrambic choruses.[2] This meant that any scene-setting for the plays depended primarily on verbal description rather than complicated stage scenery. Consider, for example, Aeschylus' *Oresteia* tetralogy: *Agamemnon* takes place before the house (palace) of Atreus; *Choephori* begins at the tomb of Agamemnon, then shifts to the palace; *Eumenides* begins at Apollo's temple at Delphi, then moves to the temple of Athena on the Athenian acropolis, and then to the Areopagus for the trial of Orestes; finally, the (lost) satyr play *Proteus* takes place before Proteus' palace in Egypt or perhaps on the beach nearby. Aeschylus accomplished the shifts of setting within and between the plays almost exclusively by the language of characters and Chorus, and so did the other playwrights who competed at the City Dionysia.

As for Aeschylus' *Persians*, scholars have long debated where exactly the play takes place, given ambiguities in the text and staging problem, particularly involving the 'ghost-raising' of Darius.[3] Whatever one decides, we should not forget that the scenic space of *Persians* simply provides the backdrop for the far more important evocation of the *distant space* of Greece – its geography, terrain, sea, shoreline, rivers and plains. Each arrival onstage – the Chorus, the queen, the Messenger, Darius' ghost, Xerxes – brings new information that encourages the audience to create (in their mind's eye) the far-away world of Hellas, and the Persian defeat that takes place there. Although foreign to the Persian characters, Aeschylus' audience knew most of this world well: Athens, the Saronic Gulf, Salamis, Psyttaleia, the Plain of Plataea, the Spercheios River in central Greece, the Asopos River in Thessaly, the Strymon River in Thrace, and – further afield – the Hellespont, that narrow body of water separating Europe from Asia. These locations represent the important settings for the narrated 'action' of the play, where the disasters that destroy the Persian forces in Greece take place.

A fatal yoking

Xerxes' military invasion depends on moving a massive land army onto foreign soil, accomplished by a floating bridge of ships across the Hellespont. This feat generates admiration and praise early in the play (66–80, 87–90, 109–13, 126–31), only to prove the first step in the ignominious defeat of the Persian forces. The ghost of Darius delivers just such a judgement on his son Xerxes' overreaching:

> He planned to stop the flowing water of the Hellespont, divine stream
> of the Bosporus,[4] putting chains on it, as if it were a slave;
> he altered the nature of its passage with hammered fetters
> and created a great pathway for a great army.
> Wrong-headed, ill counselled, he thought that he, a mere mortal,
> could lord it over all the gods, even Poseidon.
>
> *Persians* (745–50)

Darius calls the Hellespont's 'flowing waters' (*rheonta*, 745) a 'divine stream' (*rhoon theou*, 746), literally 'the flowing of the god', evoking the presence of Poseidon in the channel that divides Europe from Asia. By 'yoking the neck of the sea' (70) and 'yoking the two lands together' (736),[5] Xerxes insults the god by treating his domain like a slave. Poseidon does not react immediately to this outrage; the gods in Aeschylus frequently take their time.[6] As the story unfolds, however, the audience comes to recognize the impact of Poseidon in the defeat of the Persian fleet at Salamis (353–434).

Yoking provides a network of imagery that runs through the play, interweaving four different meanings: to harness animals to a plough, cart or chariot; to join things together not normally united (Asia and Europe); to indicate the subjugation of people placed under 'the yoke' of slavery; and to describe the 'conjugal' union of husband and wife. The idea of animal-yoking arises implicitly in the Chorus's reference to the war chariots that make up part of the Persian military (29, 46–8, 84, 106). A regal manifestation appears onstage when the queen arrives on a horse-drawn cart (150).[7] She recounts her dream of the sisters Persia and Greece yoked to a chariot driven by her son, until the Greek sibling rebels, ripping off the harness straps and smashing the yoke (181–99). Her act of resistance causes Xerxes to fall from the chariot and rip his clothes in shame, foreshadowing his arrival at the end of the play in tatters (908, described at 1017).

The Chorus develop the idea of yoking as subjugation, announcing that the Persian forces wished 'to throw the yoke of slavery [*zugon doulion*] over Greece' (50). When they learn of Xerxes' defeat, the elders predict that the Asian peoples will reject Persian rule (584–94), now that 'the yoke of force [*zugos alkas*] has been removed' (594). The only occurrence of yoking in *Persians* with a positive valence involves the 'yoke' of marriage that joins together a man and woman.[8] The Chorus use the image for the heartbroken wives of Persia when their husbands depart for Greece:

Marriage beds overflow with tears, longing for their men;
Persian women, softly grieving, each with deep longing
for the bedmate she sent off with his war-raging spear
is abandoned, yoked alone [*monzux*] in her marriage.

Pers. 134–7

The grief felt by Persian women would have resonated with Aeschylus' Athenian audience, who conceived of marriage as a yoke assumed by the wedded couple for the purpose of 'ploughing legitimate offspring'. The image of marriage as a shared yoke brings together agricultural productivity and human fertility, a prospect that Xerxes undermines by 'emptying' Persia of its men (119, 718, 730, 761).[9]

The Chorus lament the Persian casualties in terms of blighted natural growth: 'The flowering of men [*anthos* ... *andrôn*] / from Persian soil, / nourished by the whole land of Asia, / is dead and gone [*oichetai*] ...' (59–62). In the same vein, the Chorus tell the queen that 'the flower of Persia [*Persôn d'anthos*] [has] fallen, dead and gone [*oichetai*]' (252).[10] Rising from the underworld, the ghost of Darius asks if 'the thunderbolt of plague' (715) has hit the land. When he learns of his son's invasion of Greece, Darius returns to the image of growth gone bad: '*Hubris* flowered forth [*exanthous*'], producing a crop of ruin, / and from it reaped a harvest of endless tears' (821–2). When Xerxes finally arrives on stage, the Chorus echo his father's language: 'The earth [*gâ*] laments its native [*eggaian*, 'of the earth'] / youth, killed by Xerxes, who crammed / Hades with Persians ... / ... The flower of the land [*chôras anthos*] / ... / ... has perished completely' (922–7).

In *Persians*, Aeschylus frequently invokes the earth (*gê, gaia*) as the place where humans dwell, its divine power manifest in the life that it brings forth, and the dead that it takes back. The Chorus urge the queen to make 'drink offerings / to the Earth [*Gêi*]' (219–20), which will enable her dead husband Darius to rise from the underworld and reveal what lies ahead. Moved by their request, the queen vows to return from the palace with gifts she will dedicate 'to the Earth [*Gêi*] and to the dead' (523).

In the ghost-raising scene (607–80), the Chorus fall to the ground and pound the earth with their fists (indicated at 683). The queen then makes a series of ritual offerings that honour the productive capacity of the soil, to which the gifts are, in a sense, returned:

> From a pure cow, delicious white milk;[11] and from the flower-
> working bee, the essence of bright-shining honey,
> along with a libation of water from a virgin spring;
> this too, the unmixed liquid from its wild-growing mother,
> the juice that comes fresh from her time-honoured vine;
> and in the foliage of those pale trees that live
> as if forever, the fragrant oil of the olive;
> and woven floral garlands, children of the all-bearing earth.
>
> *Pers.* 611–18

Unlike Xerxes' perverse harvest of dead soldiers, the queen's offerings bring someone *back* from the dead, albeit for a short spell. The elaborate ritual lends even greater weight to Darius' condemnation of his son for turning the earth's generative forces upside down, sowing and reaping only death.

With this interrelated imagery – unyoked couples, a land emptied of the flower of its youth, the earth filled with corpses, a harvest of ruin – Aeschylus suggests the scale of the Persian disaster. All of those alive in Persia, both young and old, will be haunted by this devastation, as if the fertile earth generated nothing but death. Prophesying Xerxes' defeat at the Battle of Plataea, Darius' ghost laments 'the heap of Persian dead that will grow to a third sowing of generations' (818). The Chorus bring this image home when addressing the man who brought on the annihilation: 'The gods have scythed away the Persians' (929).

The land and seas of Greece

Few (if any) Greek tragedies include as many references to the land and its features as *Persians*. Words for country, earth, ground, dry land, soil, plain, cliff, headland, gulf, island, reef, rock, crag, coastline and the like occur throughout the play.[12] Like a litany, we hear of 'the land' [*aian*] of Greece (2), of Persia (59, 250, 646, 1070, 1074), of Zeus (meaning Greece, 270–1), of the Dorians (486), of the Edonians (495); the 'ground' or 'soil' or 'hard surface' (*chthôn*) of Asia (61, 929), of Athens (231, 238), of Psyttaleia (310), of Boeotia (482), and of the Phocians (485); the 'earth' (*gê*) of Persia (173, 511, 922, 929), the Ionians (178, meaning 'the Greeks'), Greece (186–7, 792, 809), Asia (249, 270, 584, 881),[13] Magnesia (492), of Plataea (817); the 'land' or 'territory' (*chôra*) of the Persians (7, 856, 929), of the Hellespont (on the European side, 69), of Greece (271), of the Macedonians (492–3); the 'physical area' (*topos*) of Salamis (273, 447) and Greece (790); the 'plain' (*pedon*) of the Spercheios River (487), of the Malian Gulf (488), of Thrace (566), where Darius' grave lies (683), and the land watered by the Asopos River (805).

The Persians meet their doom on the 'island' (*nêsos*) of Salamis (307, 309, 368, 390, 596–7) and Psyttaleia (447, 451, 458). On the 'rugged coast' (*aktai*) of these islands (273, 303, 421, 449, 570, 954, 964, 966), the Persian soldiers wash up from their ships or are cut down by the Greeks. The Greek war song echoes off the 'island rocks' (*nêsiôtidos petras*, 390) of Salamis, while Xerxes watches the disaster from the mainland, sitting on a 'high mound, overlooking the sea' (466–7).

The role played by the land and waters of Greece in the victory over the Persians centres on three locations and events: (1) the naval battle off the islands of Salamis and Psyttaleia in the Saronic Gulf; (2) the land battle at Plataea in Boeotia; and (3) the Persian retreat through northern Greece. The Athenian triumph at Salamis begins with an event not directly referred to in the play, but essential to its narrative: Themistocles' interpretation of the 'wooden wall' that the Delphic oracle claimed would defend Athens from the Persians.[14] Themistocles, the Athenian political and military leader, understood that the prophecy did not suggest building a palisade to enclose the city, but rather a fleet of ships to engage the Persian armada.

We know from Herodotus that the oracle also stated the following: 'Holy Salamis, thou shall destroy the offspring of women, / When men scatter the seed, or when they gather the harvest.'[15] Many at the time interpreted this prediction to mean that the Greeks would suffer defeat if they engaged the Persian fleet near Salamis. However, Themistocles pointed out that were this the case, the Delphic priestess would have called Salamis 'Luckless' rather than 'Holy'. By its choice of adjective, the oracle implied that the 'offspring of women' referred to the Persians, not the Greeks, and boded well for the Athenian fleet. Assuming that Aeschylus knew the wording of the oracle, its language of sowing and harvest – properly interpreted 'of the Persians' – may have influenced his description of Xerxes' defeat. In any case, the Chorus confirm the devastating truth of Themistocles' reading of the oracle: 'In its blood-soaked soil, / the sea-washed isle of Ajax [Salamis] / holds the power of Persia' (595-7).

Aeschylus also refers to a lying Greek messenger who convinces Xerxes that the Athenian navy will try to flee under cover of darkness.[16] Xerxes commands his fleet to sail up and down all night, 'to guard the exits and the surging straits' (367), on the lookout for any Greek ships attempting to escape. At daybreak the well-rested Greek navy have the advantage over the exhausted Persians, as the Messenger reports:

> When the day drawn by her white horses
> spread brilliant light over all the earth,
> at that moment there rang out a loud, joyful song
> from the Greeks, and its echo resounded
> at the same time from the island's cliffs.
> Fear seized us, all of us from the east,
> because we had been tricked: far from taking flight,
> the Greeks were raising a holy hymn to battle,
> eager to fight, emboldened with secure confidence.
> Then the call of their trumpet set the whole place on fire.
> For at this clear command, they pulled on their oars, all
> together, striking the deep water till they made it thunder,
> and, suddenly, they were there, all of them, in plain sight.
>
> 386–98

The Persians find themselves facing a full-on assault from those they feared would flee in the night. Familiar with the islands and narrows, operating from lighter and more navigable warships, and fresh from a restful night, the Greeks triumph over the invaders. We will return to the thematic importance of day and night, when we look at the role played by elemental forces in helping the Greeks.

The Persian defeat at Salamis offers a negative image of Xerxes' 'success' in yoking the Hellespont. Describing the boat-bridge that spanned the water, the Chorus emphasize the conjunction of earth and sea, allowing both the Persian navy and army easy access to Greece:

> The bold ruler of Asia, so full of men,
> drives his divine flock across the entire world
> on both elements, confident in commanders
> stern and strong who lead the ground forces
> and those at sea ...
>
> 74–80

The ghost of Darius pursues the question of a naval, as opposed to a land, invasion, only to learn that both took place, with disastrous results:

> **Ghost**   My poor son – did he take up this fool's mission by land or by sea?[17]
>
> **Queen**   Both – it was a double front made up of two forces.
>
> **Ghost**   How did so large an army manage to cross the water?
>
> **Queen**   By clever means Xerxes yoked the strait of Helle, making a pathway.
>
> **Ghost**   And he succeeded, actually closing up the mighty Bosporus? [meaning the Hellespont]
>
> **Queen**   Yes, he did .... / ... /
> But the naval force was savaged, which doomed the troops on land.
>
> 719–23, 728

The totality of the Persian defeat – on both land and sea – reflects the size of Xerxes' forces, swollen in number as a direct consequence of his yoking the channel between Asia and Europe. The Greeks 'destroyed the whole [*pās*] army' (716), 'emptied the entire [*pāsan*] expanse of the continent' (718), 'killed the entire [*pās*] host' (729), the word *pās* ('all', 'every', 'total') repeated here, and throughout the play.[18]

Xerxes harnessed the water separating Asia from Europe, only to watch his fleet find itself trapped in the straits between the mainland of Attica (near Eleusis) and the island of Salamis: 'The massive number of our ships [*plêthos*] got caught / in the narrows, with no way to help one another; / our bronze-sharp rams kept striking our own vessels, / smashing each other's oars' (413–16). The Messenger characterizes the disaster as a literal overturning: 'The hulls / of our ships turned keel-up, and the sea was no longer visible, / teeming [*plêthousa*] with wrecked ships and human carnage. / The shoreline and reefs filled up [*eplêthuon*] with corpses' (418–21). The Greeks kill the Persians who swim from their ships, 'clubbing them like tuna or some other / catch' (424–5). With their ships topsy-turvy, the sea's surface coated with blood and wreckage, and the shoreline covered with dead bodies, the Messenger concludes: 'So massive [*plêthos*] was our suffering ... / ... / Never before has so vast a number [*plêthos*] / of human beings died in a single day' (429–32).[19]

In her reaction to the news from Salamis, the Queen's choice of metaphor sounds a bitterly ironic note: 'What a sea of troubles overwhelms us' (433).

The Messenger adds a greater irony, describing how the naval defeat leads to the massacre of Persians on the small island of Psyttaleia, near Salamis. Xerxes stationed a group of his men there before the sea battle, in order to kill any Greeks who might try to swim ashore for safety, and to rescue any Persians who might make their way there. Given the crushing defeat of their navy, the Persian soldiers – now surrounded and trapped – struggle to defend themselves and the enemy island they occupy. The Greeks slaughter them all (447–64).[20]

This unexpected land engagement anticipates the second major defeat of the Persians, the famous pitched battle outside the town of Plataea on the Boeotian plain. Mentioned only in passing by the Messenger (482–3), the Battle of Plataea enters the play more fully from the underworld, via the ghost of Darius. He begins his account with the sacrilege perpetrated by Xerxes' soldiers when they reach Athens, plundering the statues of the gods, destroying altars, burning temples and 'uprooting' (*prorrhiza*) their foundations (807–12).[21] Because of this outrage, 'the fountain of Persian suffering / has not stopped flowing, but pours out more and more. / So great is the blood that thickens on the earth / of Plataea, shed by Dorian spears' (814–17). Darius offers no further information on the battle other than crediting (correctly) the Greek victory to the Dorians, meaning the army of Sparta. Developing the image of 'uprooting' that he used for the desecration of Greek sacred sites, Darius links the blood of the Persian dead to the 'crop of ruin' and 'harvest of many tears' that Xerxes has brought on his own people (821–2, a passage quoted above).

The final stage in the Persian debacle brings natural forces and the environment directly into play, working against the invaders as they retreat homeward (480–514). After Plataea, the Messenger reports that 'in the land of the Boeotians, / we kept dying, some suffering from thirst / for a spring's fresh water, others from hunger' (482–4).[22] The survivors, 'panting and out of breath' (484), seem to find relief when they reach the Malian Gulf and the Spercheios River, 'which waters the plain and offers plentiful drink' (487). The river appears to benefit both the Greek farmers and the foreigners in retreat, but the respite proves all too brief for the Persians: 'Then the soil of Achaea received us, and the cities of Thessaly, / where we were desperately short of food, and a great many perished / from thirst and hunger [*limôi*] – not just from one, but from both' (488–91). The fate of his countrymen leads Darius to conclude that Persia's future does 'not lie in invading the land of Greece, / not even with a greater force, / for the Greek earth herself fights by their side / ... / killing by starvation [*limôi*] a multitude that is too vast' (790–4). The very size and ambition of the Persian expedition exhausts the resources of the land they sought to conquer, and from which they desperately try to flee.

Elemental and celestial allies

Deprived of food and water, the remaining Persians reach the natural barrier of the Strymon River in Thrace: 'That night [*nukti*] the god / brought on an unseasonable cold snap, and completely [*pān*] froze over / the flowing stream of the holy Strymon' (495–7). Buoyed by their unexpected good fortune, the Persians pray in thanksgiving to the earth and the heavens before making their way across: 'Those who started before the [Sun] god scattered / his rays [*aktinas*] made it safely to the other side. / But the burning [*phlegôn*] glow of the rising sun [*hêliou*] / heated the ice with its flames, melting it mid-river' (502–5). The Messenger reveals the horrific aftermath: 'The men fell on top of one another / and he was lucky – believe me – who lost his life the soonest' (506–7).

Night and day play an essential role in turning the Strymon River crossing into a disaster for the Persians. In his earlier account of the Battle of Salamis, the Messenger also emphasizes the importance of dawn, daylight, and darkness. Xerxes ordered an all-night watch to begin 'when the fiery rays of the sun [*phlegôn aktisin hêlios*] ceased to burn / the earth, and darkness seized the sky' (364–5). The Persian ships took up their position as 'the light of the sun [*pheggos hêliou*] disappeared / and night [*nux*] came on' (377–8). The Persians kept watch 'all through the night [*pannuchoi*]' (383), but 'as night [*nux*] wore on' (384), no Greek ship tried to escape. 'When day with her white horses / spread her brilliant light [*eupheggês*] over all the earth' (386–7), the Greek fleet came into view, fresh and in good order, and they overwhelmed the Persians. The cries of the dying sailors only faded when 'the dark face of night [*nuktos*] blotted them out' (428).[23]

At the Battle of Salamis, a multitude of Persian sailors drown in the sea, their corpses battered against the rocky coastline. After the defeat at Plataea, the Persian soldiers fall prey to thirst and starvation. For those who survive, what looks like a god-sent passage over a frozen river proves to be a death trap. Once again Persians drown, but this time in the icy waters of the Strymon. Allied with the land and waters of Greece, the night, the dawn, and the bright sun seem to fight on the side of the Greeks, both here and at Salamis. In the face of these natural phenomena, the Persian's confidence at the outset of their expedition seems the height of arrogance: 'No one can withstand / this great flood of [our] men / or form a barrier to ward off / its surge, irresistible as the sea. / The Persian host is / invincible' (87–92).

Back to the earth – Persian and Athenian

The arrival of Xerxes (908) – alone, on foot, in rags, and carrying an empty quiver – provides a powerful image of the once 'great flood' of the Persian army reduced to a pitiful drop. Unlike the Chorus's welcome for the Queen (152), and their obeisance to the ghost of Darius rising from the dead (694–6),[24] the elders do not prostrate themselves before their defeated emperor. By failing to perform *proskynesis*, they fulfil their earlier prediction that 'those in the lands of Asia no more will / . . . / fall face down on the earth / in worshipful awe' (584, 588–9).[25] To be sure, 'the 'land of Asia is on its knees' (930), but from abject defeat, not from humble subservience to imperial power.

Xerxes laments 'how cruelly a destructive god [*daimôn*] has trod / on the Persian race' (911–12). As the play ends, he bids the Chorus depart with him for the palace: 'Grieve, as you tread lightly.' The Chorus respond, 'Ah, ah! The Persian earth [*aia*] is hard to tread on' (1071–2). Puzzled by these lines, Sommerstein wonders if the Chorus are 'perhaps walking barefoot, having cast off their shoes as a further gesture of mourning.'[26] Another explanation seems possible: the ground is hard to tread upon because 'the earth [*gâ*] laments its native-born [*eggaian*] youth, / . . . the underworld is filled with Persians . . .' (922–3). It is hard to walk over the bones of countless countrymen whom, as noted above, 'the destructive god [*daimôn*] has scythed away' (921).

At the original performance at the City Dionysia in 472 BC, the ground to which the Chorus refer – the beaten earth of the theatre *orchêstra* in Athens – represented an area near the Persian capital, Susa. But Aeschylus' audience also saw reminders of the Persian sack of their city seven years earlier, the rubble built into the city's walls. The Saronic Gulf appeared in the distance, where many of spectators would have rowed in the Athenian fleet. Behind the theatre rose the Acropolis, where the Persians had torched and 'uprooted' the temples (807–12, quoted above). As the Persians onstage mourned their defeat and their dead, the audience surely remembered their own losses, the family and friends who fell defending the city. The fact that Athenian male citizens made up the Chorus of Persian elders, and that Aeschylus himself probably played the role of Xerxes, encouraged this split vision.[27] The play views the Greek victory as a triumph for them, and an unmitigated disaster for the Persians. However, the loss of life on both sides is cause for lamentation and ritual mourning, making the earth (both Persian and Athenian) 'hard to tread'.

'Natural' justice

By refusing to present the deaths of the enemy as risible or comic, our oldest surviving tragedy continues to demand our attention.[28] In spite of his might and resources, Xerxes learns the limits – indeed, the ultimate folly – of imperial ambition. His invasion generates resistance of a special sort, arising from the land and waters of Greece and the elemental forces working with them. History offers many examples of nature appearing to choose sides in a war of aggression. During the First War of Scottish Independence, Wallace and Moray defeated the English at the Battle of Stirling Bridge in 1297, taking advantage of the river and its marshy lowlands. The devastating Russian winter wreaked havoc on the Swedish assault of Russia in 1707, Napoleon's expedition in 1812, and Hitler's invasion of the Soviet Union in 1941. The jungles of Vietnam helped the Vietnamese resistance defeat a succession of Japanese, French and American invaders until the last quarter of the twentieth century.

It should come as no surprise that national mythologies tend to focus on such 'home-pitch advantage', and Aeschylus' *Persians* is no exception. The miraculous freezing and thawing of the Strymon River, for example, defies scientific explanation. In Broadhead's view, the event springs from 'the poet's imagination ... which betrays his theological bias'.[29] Be that as it may, Aeschylus' 'theology' reflects the wider Greek sense that elemental forces participate in a form of cosmic justice, sharing equally in the alternating pattern that informs the natural world. Night follows day, day follows night, and so they must. The changing seasons come in sequence, agreeing to divide the year and not impinge on another's 'rule'.[30] The cyclical workings of nature give rise to what we might call 'natural' justice. Trying to extend one's rule or power beyond those limits creates a fundamental imbalance that must eventually right itself. As for Xerxes, 'the violator of natural boundaries has in the end found retribution in Nature herself'.[31]

Winnington-Ingram argues that Zeus in *Persians* serves as the guarantor of this ordered pattern: Aeschylus 'interprets the campaign not in terms of Athena saving her city [Athens], but of Zeus maintaining a moral order in the world'.[32] The Persians would like to blame what befalls them on a malignant *daimôn* (911–12, 921, quoted above), akin to our idea of 'accursed luck'.[33] However, Aeschylus paints this *daimôn* not as the random effects of fate or fortune, but as a moral direction working through the natural world, responding to human excess and outrage. As Dodds points out in *The Greeks and the Irrational*, 'what to the partial vision of the living [Xerxes, Chorus, queen] appears as the act of a fiend, is perceived by the wider insight of the dead [Darius' Ghost] to be an aspect of cosmic justice'.[34]

Xerxes treats the natural world as his slave, yoking it to his ambition, and the forces of nature take their revenge. Zeus punishes those who 'despise the good fortune they possess and, / lusting for more, let their great prosperity go to waste' (825–6). This warning proved increasingly applicable to the imperial ambitions of fifth-century Athens, as Winnington-Ingram observes:

Yet the subsequent course of fifth-century history may well make us doubt whether the lesson of *Zeus kolastês* ['punisher of pride', line 827] was really grasped by the Athenians. Aeschylus might indeed have felt it a deplorable thing, if the patriotic emotions which the play aroused did more to determine Athenian policy and actions than the warning against acts of hubris which he had employed the resources of his art to make effective.[35]

The history of foreign wars across the globe has made *Persians* sadly relevant across the centuries. Given the play's focus on the natural world, we also can read the play as a dire warning against our ongoing assault on the environment, our systematic disregard for the continuation of life on the planet. Rising sea levels, global warming, the climate crisis and the mass extinction of animals and plants represent nature's response to the excesses of the modern world. To be sure, these issues have no direct bearing on *Persians*; Aeschylus would have thought it incredible that humans could perpetrate so great a disaster. *Mutatis mutandis*, we have come to resemble the Persians, incredulous to our ever-mounting losses, forced to face the truth that inconceivable and overwhelming disasters are already upon us.

Notes

1 Movement of the continental plates causes the mountain to rise between 1 and 4 millimetres a year. Until recently, this 'growth' kept pace with the rise in sea level, but the increasing effects of human-generated global warming will cause Mount Olympus to 'shrink'. See Price (2015), 20, and MedECC (2016), 5.
2 On various interpretations of the performance schedule at the City Dionysia, see Csapo and Slater (1995), 105–8; Pickard-Cambridge, Lewis and Gould (1968), 63–7.
3 The play seems to take place in the vicinity of the imperial palaces, either at Persepolis or Susa; see Garvie (2009), xlvi–liii, and Seaford (2012), 206–10. When focusing on the tomb of Darius (619–842), the specific setting becomes significant. However, the tomb later 'disappears'; no one mentions it following Darius' return to the underworld.
4 The Bosporus ('cow-ford', named after Io, who crossed here from Greece to Asia, described in Aeschylus' *Prometheus Bound*) actually lies 150 miles north-east of the Hellespont; tragedians often confuse this narrow channel with the Hellespont (Sommerstein 2008: note to line 723).
5 Aeschylus suggests that Xerxes stopped the sea in its natural flow, as if filling in the channel to create a land causeway. We know from Herodotus (7.34–6)

that the Persians used a bridge of boats to 'yoke' the continents (Sommerstein 2008: vol. 1, note on line 747).
6 See, for example, Aeschylus' *Agamemnon* 362–72.
7 In the 472 BC performance, the yoked team probably remained in the *orchêstra* until the queen exited at line 531. When she returns to the stage at 598, she emphasizes that she now comes on foot (607–9).
8 The metaphor of yoking for marriage occurs frequently in tragedy: both man and woman yoked together (A. *Pers.* 139, Eur. *Med.* 24); a spouse as 'yokemate' (*suzugos*, A. *Cho.* 599, Eur. *Alc.* 314); Iphis wishes he had remained 'unyoked in marriage' (Eur. *Supp.* 791); 'unyoked' used for unwedded girls (Eur. *Hipp.* 1425, *Ba.* 694) and for unwedded men (Eur. *Med.* 673, *IA* 805). One of Hera's cult titles as goddess of marriage was *Zygia*, 'Yoker'.
9 As well as in the 'yoked alone' passage, the Chorus bring up the painful separation of wedded couples (61–4, 287–9 and 541–5). The image with its link to fertility does not always evoke equality; in Sophocles' *Antigone*, Creon insists that his son Haimon 'has other furrows' [than Antigone] to plough (569).
10 The verb *oichomai* ('depart') occurs in the first line of *Persians*, then five more times over the course of the play, meaning 'departed in the sense of never coming back, dead and gone'.
11 Sommerstein (2008: vol. 1, note on line 611) thinks that this phrase means milk from a cow that has never worn a yoke; if so, the offering avoids the negative associations of yoking elsewhere in the play. All the Queen's offerings derive from a grammatically feminine source in ancient Greek: cow, bee, a virgin spring, a mother vine, the olive tree and mother earth (Hall 1996: on 611).
12 Also, roughly thirty different locations – cities, islands, countries, regions, continents, rivers – are mentioned *by name* in the play, some of them (Persia, Asia, Greece, Athens, Salamis) multiple times. For example, the Chorus refer to the 'sea-girt islands' (880) in the Greek Aegean, naming Lesbos, Samos and Chios off the coast of Asia Minor (884–5); the Cycladic islands of Paros, Naxos, Mykonos, Tinos and Andros (885–6); and the islands of Lemnos, Ikaria, Rhodes and Cyprus (891–4).
13 The numerous references to the earth (*gê*) of Persia emphasizes that Xerxes' harvest of death has perverted the fertility associated with the land.
14 Herodotus 7.139–44.
15 Herodotus 7.141.
16 Although unnamed in the play, Aeschylus refers to the slave Sikinnus, whom Themistocles sent to deliver this false report to trick the Persians (Herodotus 8.75–6). For Aeschylus' implicit praise of Themistocles in the play, and the relationship between Themistocles and Pericles (who provided the *leitourgia* [sponsorship] for the production of *Persians* in 472 BC), see Podlecki (1966), 8–26 and 125–9.
17 Darius' question points back to his earlier gnomic statement, 'There are many evils that befall mortals, both on the sea / and on dry land' (707–8), and more

directly to the Chorus's claim of 'the ever-lamented twin failure' (677) that has fallen upon Persia.
18 *pās, pān* in various forms (found in English compounds like 'pandemic') occurs over seventy times in the play.
19 The Messenger earlier reports that 'the shores of Salamis, and the whole neighboring area, / are full [*plêthousi*] of the wretchedly slain corpses [of Persians]' (272–3). The word *plêthos* ('immense number', as in the English 'plethora') occurs in different combinations some fifteen times in the play. As Garvie (2009; on 401–6) notes, 'the *plêthos* of the Persian forces, which earlier had seemed to ... guarantee a victory (235–6, 333–6), has now turned out to be a fatal disadvantage ...'.
20 The summary line reads 'they [Greeks] utterly destroyed the life of every [*hapantôn*, from *pās*] man' (464). The island is 'the haunt of Pan' (449), the demigod's name suggesting that 'all' [*pān*] the gods delighted in his energy (*Homeric Hymn to Pan*, 44–7).
21 In their prayer before Salamis, the Greeks call on one another to fight for their country, their families and for 'the temples of the gods of our fathers, / and tombs of our ancestors' (405–6), the holy sites that the Persians sacked. Herodotus (8.50–53 and 109, 9.65) and Thucydides (1.89) describe how the Athenians chose to abandon their city and trust in their fleet; the Persians burnt the acropolis and other sacred places in Athens twice, both before and after the Battle of Salamis.
22 For the textual difficulties of this passage, see Garvie (2009), on 482–5.
23 Compare the relief that the Queen expresses on hearing that her son Xerxes still lives: 'like bright day shining out after a pitch-dark night [*nuktos*]' (301). After the news of the drowned men in the river, however, the Queen recalls her 'clear dream vision of the [previous] night [*nuktos*]' (518) that predicted horrific disaster.
24 This action seems to be indicated by the Chorus' awe before Darius, afraid to speak to him face to face. See Sommerstein (2008: vol. 1, stage direction, line 693).
25 The Messenger reports that the desperate Persian forces prostrate themselves (*proskynôn*, 499) to the earth and sky before they begin crossing the frozen Strymon. Seaford (2012: 214–20) presents a strong case for the return to the political *status quo ante bellum* for the Persians at the end of the play; the Chorus' behaviour here suggests otherwise. Xerxes never speaks a single iambic trimeter line in the play; he only shares a ritual lament sung with the Chorus, rare for a Greek male character but not for female tragic characters. The 'feminization' reduces his symbolic potency (Hall 1999: 96–7, 100, 116–17).
26 Sommerstein (2008: vol. 1, note 151 on line 1072).
27 McCall (1986).
28 Hall (1989) makes a strong case for the racist 'orientalizing' of *Persians*; cf. Rehm (2002), 239–51.
29 Broadhead (1960), on 495–7.

30 Hesiod, *Theogony*, ll. 116–33; see Miller (2018), 207–23.
31 Wilson (1986), 57.
32 Winnington-Ingram (1983b), 3. Note that the Chorus call Greece 'the land [*aian*] / of Zeus' (270–1), a reference to Hellen, the eponymous ancestor of the Hellenes, ostensibly the son of Zeus.
33 The word *daimôn* occurs 19 times in the play, 12 times referring to the 'force' that has led Xerxes' astray.
34 Dodds (1951), 39.
35 Winnington-Ingram (1983b), 15.

8

The Persians Love their Children, too: Common Humanity in *Persians*

Alan H. Sommerstein

It would be idle to deny that one of the effects that *Persians* was designed to produce in its Athenian audience of 472 BC was an enhanced sense of pride in the victory gained at Salamis, by a fleet that was preponderantly Athenian, over an enemy who according to the script of the play outnumbered them more than three to one (*Persians* 338–43) and had the human and material resources of a whole continent behind them (12, 56–62, 73, 268–71, 548–9) – or that when it was restaged at Syracuse,[1] it was likely to evoke admiration of Athens' achievement alongside regret at not having been able to take part in it and proud recollection of the victory won almost simultaneously by a Syracusan-led army at Himera.[2] It would be equally idle to deny that Aeschylus' audiences believed that their political system was superior to that of the Persians and believed also that the average Greek had a greater share than the average Persian of the qualities that make a man a formidable warrior. But *Persians* is not about a Greek victory; it is about a Persian defeat. Every word of its script is spoken or sung by a Persian, or, to be more precise, by a performer impersonating a Persian. None of the characters, not even King Xerxes, is demonized or presented as a villain; on the contrary, we are encouraged to empathize and sympathize with them. In this chapter I shall be exploring several aspects of the play that provide evidence supporting this claim.

What, as the play presents things, is the principal cause of the Persians' defeat?

Their defeat is not due to any inferiority in fighting qualities. They lose the Battle of Salamis because they were successfully deceived. An unnamed Athenian (actually Themistocles, or someone sent by him) told Xerxes that the Greek fleet was going to attempt to break out and escape by night from their location off the north coast of Salamis Island (355–60). Xerxes, seeing an opportunity to destroy the enemy fleet, ordered his own navy to guard the straits through which the escaping Greeks would have to sail (361–73). The admirals duly manned their ships, patrolled the straits all night – and absolutely nothing happened (374–85) until the morning, when the Greeks did indeed sail out through the straits, not to escape but to fight (386–405). Thus, when battle was joined the Greeks were fresh, their enemies tired; moreover, the Persian fleet, taken by surprise (391–2), had suffered a severe psychological blow, and a tactical one, too, as, caught in the narrows, they were unable to manoeuvre and sustained as much damage from each other as they did from the Greeks (413–20).

Further back, though, the Persians had been the all too willing victims of a greater deception, or rather delusion. They had never expected to have to fight a naval battle at all. Up to the point at which the Messenger arrives with news of the disaster of Salamis, what notions do the Queen[3] and the Elders have of the war-making capabilities of the Greeks? In the first 229 lines of the play, all we hear about them is that they are 'renowned for spear-fighting' (85, cf. 147–9). Then the Queen asks the Elders some questions about Athens (230–45), and they tell her that Athens has an army that 'has already done the Medes a great deal of harm' (236, 244), an army that relies (they say again) on spear and shield rather than on archery (240), and also that she is not without financial resources thanks to the silver mines at Laurium (238). That is all. The Elders clearly expect that the Persian army may have to fight a tough land battle – but not a word has been said[4] to suggest that the Greeks have any ships at all to oppose Xerxes' powerful navy (cf. 19, 39–40, 54, 77). And even when the Messenger enters, and announces that a catastrophe has occurred, there is at first no indication that the catastrophe has been a nautical one. On the contrary, when the Messenger says (255) that the whole invading force has been destroyed, he calls it a *stratos*, a term which more often denotes an army than a fleet; and the Elders have evidently understood him in that sense when they sing (269) that 'those many weapons, all mingled together' were sent to Greece in vain. Only from the Messenger's next reply (278–9)[5] do they learn that the defeat was at sea, and even within that reply the revelation is delayed: the Messenger begins,

Yes, our archery was of no avail; the whole host perished, destroyed by . . .

. . . and the Elders are surely expecting his next words will be 'the Greek spear' or the like (cf. 85–6, 147–9, 239–40); but no, it is the naval host that has been destroyed, and it has been destroyed by 'the ramming of ships'. And the loss of the fleet, as we shall learn later (468–70, 724), also spelled the doom of the land army. The Persians' error is understandable, since most of the

Athenian fleet was of very recent construction, but it was still what a modern analyst would call a massive intelligence failure.

At a deeper level still, Xerxes' and Persia's downfall is presented as being due to a more fundamental deception or delusion, caused by a god or gods. Already in the *parodos* (93–100) the Elders are apprehensive on this score:

> But what mortal man can escape
> the guileful deception of a god? . . .
> For Ruin begins by fawning on a man in a friendly way
> and leads him astray into her net,
> from which it is impossible for a mortal to escape and flee.

Ruin (or Delusion, *Ate*) 'fawns' on a man (or family, or nation) by causing him/them to enjoy great success, as Persia had done in the generations preceding Xerxes' accession to the throne (cf. 102–7), the kind of success that too easily leads men to believe themselves invincible (cf. 86–92).

The idea reappears several times thereafter. The Queen is 'very fearful . . . that great wealth may make the dust rise from the ground by tripping up the prosperity that Darius, not without the aid of some god, had built up' (162–4). Xerxes gave the order for the fleet to mount a night patrol 'not understanding the deceit of the Greek or the jealousy of the gods' (357–8). When the Queen has heard the whole terrible tale of Salamis, she exclaims, 'O cruel divinity, how I see you have beguiled the minds of the Persians! My son has found his vengeance on famous Athens [for the defeat at Marathon] to be a bitter one' (472–4).

No explanation or motivation is suggested for this divine deception, except for the single word *phthonos* 'jealousy' (358). But that word may be enough to guide us to an understanding. It was a widespread belief that the gods are jealous of human success and delight in bringing low those whom fortune has favoured – especially perhaps if they lay claim, or others lay claim on their behalf, to a status equal or nearly equal to that of the gods. Such a claim is repeatedly made by the Elders in *Persians* on behalf of Darius and Xerxes[6] (80, 157, 634, 641–3, 651, 655, 856), and phrases like 'a god of the Persians' (157, 643, cf. 655, 721) imply that the Persian public in general took the same view, which might well be thought to make the whole nation liable to divine retribution.

In the second half of the play, however, the theme of divine deception recedes, and there is an increasing emphasis on the personal responsibility of Xerxes. This idea is first articulated by the Elders (550–3):

> Xerxes took them – *popoi!*
> Xerxes lost them – *totoi!*

Xerxes handled everything unwisely,
he and his sea-boats –

and is later analysed more fully by the ghost of Darius (739–86). According to Darius, Xerxes has brought about the early fulfilment of prophecies of doom which Darius had imagined would come true only in the distant future. In the past Persia has had good kings (like Cyrus, 768–72), bad kings (like the usurper Mardus, 774–5) and indifferent kings, and between them they acquired a great empire. At the end of his life, Darius – like Augustus half a millennium later[7] – apparently advised his successor not to seek to extend this empire further. Xerxes took no notice. He was 'a young man thinking young man's thoughts' (782),[8] and he was pressured and taunted by his contemporaries who called him a 'stay-at-home warrior ... doing nothing to increase the riches he had inherited' (753–8). Meanwhile, not only the ignorant masses, but (as we have seen) some of the wisest men in his kingdom, were assuring him that he was the equal of the gods. How many young men in his position would have successfully resisted this unholy alliance of flatterers and taunters? Xerxes, at any rate, did not. Not only did he invade Greece; he also, in the course of doing so, performed two actions that constituted gross insults to powerful gods. He marched his army across the Hellespont by means of a bridge of boats, 'putting fetters on a divine stream' (745–6) and angering Poseidon;[9] and once in Greece, that army angered all the gods of the land by destroying their temples and altars (809–12). Do we have here, after all, evidence of a distinctively Persian villainy?

Yes and no. Yes, the destruction of sacred sites and buildings is a crime by any ancient standards, and contrasts with the behaviour of Darius' general Datis ten years earlier, when he refrained from attacking the sacred island of Delos (Herodotus 6.97);[10] and yes, the bridging of the Hellespont can be seen as an attempt to turn sea into land contrary to the ordinances of nature,[11] and the bridge cables as chains or fetters put on the water as if to enslave it.[12]

But we can hardly ascribe these hybristic acts to some kind of Persian national character when they are denounced in vehement terms by a Persian king. Rather we should see them as the natural consequences of the situation in which he is placed. Young men tend to be highly competitive, and often have more energy than judgement, and absolute power attained at an early age is and was particularly likely to corrupt: even in democratic Athens, where no individual had very much formal power and no public office had a longer tenure than twelve months, no one aged under thirty was allowed to hold any office at all. Xerxes has done great harm to Persia, but in a well-organized political system he would never have had the opportunity to do so. As it is, the Elders condemn him to his face (923; so later 1016), and he fully accepts responsibility for the catastrophe (913–17, 931–3). But even now, we are still told that his blunder was caused by 'a powerful divinity that ... put him out of his right mind' (725) and made him forget his father's warnings (783); similarly, once Xerxes arrives, both he and the Elders ascribe the disaster now to him, now (Xerxes at 911–12, 942–3; the Elders at 921, 1005–7) to a god or gods.

There is no contradiction here, any more than in many other passages of early Greek poetry in general, and of Aeschylean tragedy in particular, where an event such as the death of Achilles (*Iliad* 19.416–17, 22.359–60) or the murder of Agamemnon (*Agamemnon* 1485–1507) is said to have been caused both by divine and by human will.[13]

There, but for the fall of the lot, go we?

When the Persian queen-mother first comes on stage, she explains that she has come to seek the advice of the Elders after having had a terrifying dream that seemed to portend ruin for Xerxes and Persia, a dream which she narrates in detail (181–99). First, she saw two women, whose contrasting clothing (182–3) made it evident that one represented Greece and the other either Persia (182) or the 'barbarian' world generally (187).[14] The two women quarrelled (188–9), and thereupon Xerxes appeared, attempting to 'restrain and calm' them (189–90) and then yoking them to his chariot (190–2) as if they were horses.

> One of them ... towered up proudly and kept her jaw submissively in harness, but the other began to struggle, tore the harness from the chariot with her hands, dragged it violently along without bit or bridle, and smashed the yoke in half. My son fell out. His father Darius appeared, standing beside him and showing pity; but when Xerxes saw him, he tore the robes that clothed his body.
>
> 192–9

The Queen does not tell us which of the two women submitted to the yoke of servitude and which resisted; we, the Greek audience, know that already – Greeks demand and cherish freedom, whereas barbarians are natural slaves.

But is it as simple as that? I have thus far almost completely ignored what the Queen says about the two women when she first mentions them, particularly in lines 184–7. They are both tall, both 'of flawless beauty' (184–5) – and crucially, they are *sisters* 'of the same stock' (185–6). Presumably this is a reference to the myth, already alluded to in 79–80[15] and mentioned three times by Herodotus,[16] according to which the Persians, or at least their royal house, were ultimately of Greek ancestry, being descended from Perses, son of the great Greek hero Perseus; but be that as it may, the statement is not germane to the Queen's reason for narrating her dream, namely that it made her fear for the fate of Xerxes and Persia. Since it does not serve any purpose of the Queen's, it probably serves some purpose of the poet's. Its effect is to make us see the Graeco-Persian conflict as a conflict between kinsfolk, and therefore one to be avoided if possible. Nothing that we have heard, or will hear, suggests that Xerxes viewed his war in that light.

> But Aeschylus now has more to say about the sisters:
> One, *by the fall of the lot,* was a native and inhabitant of the land of
>   Greece, the other of the land of the barbarians.
>
> 186–7

We will shortly be told that the 'barbarian' was a willing slave while her Greek sister was ready to fight for freedom. We, the Athenian audience, know that most of us did fight at Salamis. But while we are entitled to pride ourselves collectively on our courage, we should not think that our courage is a special endowment granted by the gods to Greeks alone. Being courageous or cowardly is part of one's personal character, which can be modified, for better or worse, by training, experience and associations. Being Greek or 'barbarian' is a matter of chance, depending on where, and to what parents, one happened to be born. If that lottery had turned out differently, any of us might have found ourselves fighting on the other side – as of course many Greeks did, both at Salamis and at Plataea.

The wives and the mothers

'Few out of many returned home'. Thus, Thucydides (7.87.6) concludes his narrative of the disastrous Sicilian Expedition of 415–413 BC, echoing *Persians* 800, his own words (1.110.1) on the Athenian expedition to Egypt forty years before, and the traditions of the Trojan war.[17] In *Persians*, out of an expedition which emptied all the cities in Asia of their young manhood (12–13, 718, etc.) we see just two men return, the Messenger and Xerxes; some others, indeed, have in fact returned to their homes in various parts of the empire, but 'not many' (510), nor will many return of the picked force that has remained in Greece (796–802).

The dead of Salamis and of the Persian retreat, of course, cannot feature directly in a drama unless they are either brought home as corpses or bring themselves home as ghosts. The latter is out of the question in *Persians*, since it would be a near-duplicate of the Darius ghost scene in form and of the Messenger speech in content; and the bringing home of bodies (or even of ashes, as in *Agamemnon* 438–44) is also out of the question, since fleet and army both 'took to headlong, disorderly flight' (480–1, cf. 469–70) without sparing time or thought for their dead comrades, who were left floating in the waters of Salamis or washed up on nearby beaches (272–7, 302–17, cf. 818–20 on the 'heaps' of Persian dead left unburied at Plataea). Rather the focus will be on the loss and grief of the bereaved survivors.

These survivors will preponderantly be women, children and old men. The Chorus of this play, consisting of old men, might therefore seem ideally suited to exemplify the sad truth that 'in peace sons bury their fathers, but in war fathers bury their sons' (Herodotus 1.87.4) – except that for these sons there was no funeral at all. This, however, is not the road that Aeschylus takes. His Chorus has much to say about the damage that defeat will do to Persia, but nothing whatever – not even when they are reproaching Xerxes – about any loss or harm suffered by themselves personally. For the purposes of this play, 'bereaved kinsfolk' means, most of the time, bereaved *female* kinsfolk, the wives and mothers[18] of those who had gone west with Xerxes.

These women-left-alone probably make their first appearance in the text at a very early point, in the second sentence of the Elders' opening chant. As transmitted in the manuscripts, this sentence reads:

> For all the strength of the Asiatic race
> has departed, and howls for a young man.
>
> 12–13

If this text is sound, it will have to be 'the strength of the Asiatic race' that is howling (literally 'barking'). Are they howling in confident anticipation, or in sorrow and anger – and how can the Elders possibly know about it, when they immediately go on (14–15) to note that no news of any sort has reached Susa from the army? It is more likely, as Page and Garvie among recent editors have seen, that the howling or wailing is being heard in Susa itself, and that it comes from those whom the army has left behind, to whom (as we shall presently see) attention will be specially drawn several times more in the choral *parodos* – the women left alone, and especially the young wives. In my Loeb edition (Sommerstein 2008: vol. 1), I accepted the view that a line had been lost from the text, indicated its likely content and (tentatively) its possible wording,[19] and translated:

> For all the strength of the Asiatic race
> is departed, and <in every house
> the woman left behind> howls for her young husband.

The motif reappears (59–64) at the end of the long passage in 'marching anapaests' that introduces the first choral song:

> Such is the flower of the men of Persia's land
> that has departed,
> for whom the whole land of Asia,
> which reared them, sighs with a longing that burns,
> and parents and wives count the days
> and tremble as the time stretches out.

And it reappears again, in considerably fuller form, at the end of the song itself (114–39), after the Elders have been reflecting (93–100)[20] on the possibility of 'guileful deception by a god' who may set a trap from which, as they say twice (93–4, 99–100), no mortal can escape:

> This is why my mind
> is clothed in black and torn with fear:
> 'Woe for the Persian army!' –
> I dread that our city may hear this cry –
> 'The great capital of Susiana is emptied of its manhood!' –
>
> and that the city of the Cissians[21]
> will sing in antiphon,
> a vast throng of women
> howling out that word 'woe!',
> and their linen gowns will be rent and torn.
>
> For all the horse-driving host
> and the infantry too,
> like a swarm of bees, have left the hive with the leader of their army....
>
> And beds are filled with tears
> because the men are missed and longed for:
> Persian women, grieving amid their luxury, every one loving and
>   longing for her husband,
> having sent on his way the bold warrior who was her bedfellow,
> is left behind, a partner unpartnered.[22]

Shortly afterwards the Queen enters, and for most of the rest of the play it will be she who dramatically represents these left-behind women – though she is more fortunate (or should we say, more privileged) than any of them, since not only is her son alive[23] but she will learn this very shortly (299), whereas the ordinary women of the empire will not know whether their menfolk are alive or dead until they return or fail to return with the remnant of the army.[24] She speaks and thinks throughout primarily as a mother. Very revealing is the contrast between the Queen and the Elders in the ways they speak of Xerxes. The Elders[25] normally call him either 'Xerxes' (five times[26]) or 'the King' (also five times[27]), or use some combination of one or both of these with an amplifying expression or expressions (five times[28]). They address him once as 'master', as if they were his slaves (1049); but they can also denounce him to his face as the man who has 'crammed Hades with Persians' (923–4) and 'brought great ruin to Persia' (1016). In speaking to the Queen, the Elders at one moment call Xerxes 'your child' (222) – echoing the Queen's own language, as we shall see – and at another 'a god' (157).

It is perhaps not surprising that Xerxes' royal parents, when conversing with each other (even with third parties present), do not use royal titles when speaking of their son. The ghost of Darius calls him 'Xerxes' once (832), 'Xerxes my son' once (782), and 'my son' four times;[29] the Queen, when addressing her husband, speaks either of 'Xerxes' (734) or of 'Xerxes the bold/rash' (*thourios*, 718, 754).

But everywhere outside the Darius scene, the Queen's profile in this respect is quite different. She refers to Xerxes thirteen times. Just once she uses his name (199); on all the other twelve occasions she speaks of him as 'my son' – *emos pais*[30] or *pais emos*[31] or simply *pais*.[32] Of these twelve passages, no less than five occur in the Queen's 39-line narrative of a dream and two omens (176–214), so that we are encouraged from the start to think of her less as 'the old Queen of Persia' than as 'Xerxes' mother' – which indeed is the first designation applied to her by the Elders when she arrives on the scene (151; 'mother' again in 156 and 157).[33] And she speaks for all the mothers – and fathers – of the empire when, after learning from the chorus-leader about the resources and past achievements of Athens, she comments, 'What you say is fearful to think about for the parents of those who have gone there' (245). Very shortly thereafter there enters a Messenger, and by his news the fearfulness is greatly augmented.

After the Messenger has finished his terrible narrative, the Queen soon departs to prepare offerings to 'Earth and the dead' (523–4), and the Elders, left alone, reflect on the disaster, highlighting first of all (532–49) the misery of the bereaved women:

> O Zeus the King, now, now by destroying
> the army of the boastful
> and populous Persian nation
> you have covered the city of Susa and Agbatana
> with a dark cloud of mourning.
> Many <mothers in a piteous plight>[34]
> are rending their veils with their delicate hands
> and wetting the folds of their garments till they are soaked through
> with tears, as they take their share in the sorrow;
> and the soft, wailing Persian women who yearn
> to see the men they lately wedded,
> abandoning the soft-coverleted beds they had slept in,
> the delight of their pampered youth,
> grieve with wailing that is utterly insatiable.
> And I too shoulder the burden of the death of the departed,
> truly a theme for mourning far and wide.
>
> For now all, yes all, the emptied land
> of Asia groans....

And as if this were not enough, the theme reappears later in the song (579–83):

> Bereaved houses mourn their men,
> and aged parents,
> now childless – *oaaah!* –
> lament their god-sent woes
> as they hear the news that brings ultimate pain.

After this the grieving wives and parents are not explicitly mentioned again, but we will not have forgotten them when the Queen – who had made her first entrance in a carriage, royally attired and attended – returns at 598 alone, on foot, plainly dressed and carrying in her own hands (presumably on a tray or in a basket) the requisites for her offering to the spirit of Darius; nor when Xerxes himself comes home at 908, likewise alone (cf. 1036, 'I am denuded of escorts'), likewise on foot, with his royal robes torn to rags (cf. 835–6), and carrying nothing but an empty quiver (1020–2), is met by a reception committee consisting entirely of old men – old men he knows well, his father's trusted advisers, some of whom must have had sons who went to his war and have not returned – and in shame and remorse cries out, 'The strength is drained out of my limbs when I see these aged citizens!' (913–14).

Let us hear the conclusion of the whole matter. The Persians came to grief not because they were Persian, but because they were human, with weaknesses that are part of human nature. If we had been in their position, we might very well have acted, and suffered, as they did.[35] And the pain of learning that a husband or a son is dead or 'missing in action', especially in a war that should never have been begun, is the same the world over.

Notes

1. Scholia to Aristophanes, *Frogs* 1028, citing the great Alexandrian scholar Eratosthenes.
2. Aeschylus may have made a god prophesy this victory in *Glaucus of Potniae*, the play that followed *Persians* in his Athenian production of 472 (note the mention of Himera in Aesch. fragment 25a); if so, he surely presented that play also while in Sicily. See Sommerstein (2012).
3. In this chapter Xerxes' mother will be so designated. Xerxes was actually the son of Atossa, daughter of Cyrus the Great, but it is doubtful whether Aeschylus knew this. He makes the Elders call the Queen 'wife of a god [Darius] and mother of a god [Xerxes]' (157), but not 'daughter of a god'; and the ghost of King Darius, addressing his widow and the Elders, mentions Cyrus with high praise (768–72) but does not call him 'your father'.
4. It has been suggested, notably by Page and Garvie, that a couple of lines have been lost from the Queen's dialogue with the Elders, in which reference was made to the Athenian fleet. This of course would destroy the effect argued for in the text above; Garvie argues that the information 'that ships ... [played] the decisive role ... will hardly come as a surprise to the theatre-audience'; but (if we reject the view of Page and Garvie) it *will* come as a surprise to the Elders. If the audience perceive that the Elders know nothing of the Athenian fleet, they will have the feeling of privileged knowledge that characterizes dramatic irony, and this feeling will be enhanced when the Elders mention the silver mines, since every Athenian knew what use had been made of their output in the late 480s.
5. I am assuming that the couplets 272–3 and 278–9 should change places in the text, as in my 2008 Loeb edition, since the Elders in 274–7 already know that the disaster has happened at sea; see Sier (2005), 410–14.
6. And also once on behalf of Xerxes' mother (150–1), who for her part once speaks of her deceased husband as a divinity (620–1).
7. *Augustus addiderat ... consilium coercendi intra terminos imperii* (Tacitus, *Annals* 1.11.4).
8. We are given the strong impression that Xerxes is in his twenties. In fact, being the first legitimate son born to Darius after he came to the throne in 521, he cannot have been much if at all under forty at the time of the invasion of Greece.

9 Aeschylus makes no attempt to portray Persian religion accurately. The Persians, like other 'barbarian' peoples, are assumed to worship the same gods as the Greeks; these gods may in their language have had different names, but in drama the Persians are made to speak Greek, and accordingly, just as they call a horse by the Greek word for it, *hippos*, so they call the god of the sea by the Greek word for him, *Poseidôn*.

10 Though soon afterwards, as David Stuttard reminds me, the Persians under Datis did destroy the temples at Eretria 'in reprisal for the temples burnt [by the Ionian rebels and their Greek allies] at Sardis' (Herodotus 6.101.3, cf. 5.102.1) – a plea of justification which, if it had any validity as against Eretria, would also have been valid as against Athens.

11 Darius' own bridging of the Bosporus and Danube (Herodotus 4.85–9) is conveniently forgotten, as is his unsuccessful invasion of Scythia in 852–907.

12 These chains or fetters must be metaphorical: Darius, whose knowledge of the whole bridging episode is limited to the Queen's brief statement at 722, cannot know of the story (Herodotus 7.34–5) that after a destructive storm Xerxes had the Hellespont flogged and real fetters thrown into it. Of course, if the story was already current, Aeschylus (not Darius) will here be alluding to it; alternatively, his words may themselves be the source of the story, if they were understood literally by some of those who heard or read them.

13 See Sommerstein (2010), 262–7, on what he calls the 'Maradona Principle'.

14 The word *barbaros* 'barbarian' was originally a term of disparagement meaning 'speaker of an unintelligible language' (cf. *Iliad* 2.867), but it had come to be the ordinary word for 'non-Greek', not necessarily with any pejorative connotation. In *Persians*, the Persians often use it in reference to themselves (or to themselves and their non-Greek subjects) (255, 337, 391, 423, 434, 475, 798, 844).

15 Where Xerxes is said to belong to the 'gold-begotten race', alluding to the unconventional method employed by Zeus to impregnate Perseus' mother Danaë.

16 Herodotus 6.54, 7.61.3, 7.150.2. The story must have been familiar to most of Aeschylus' audience (otherwise they could not have understood his allusions to it), though not mentioned in any earlier text that survives.

17 As expressed notably in the *Odyssey* where Odysseus, who had arrived at Troy with twelve fully manned ships (*Iliad* 2.637) and returns home all alone nineteen years later, and in Aeschylus' *Agamemnon* where Agamemnon, having sailed for Troy with a thousand ships (45), returns home not knowing if any ship but his own has reached port in Greece or will ever do so (658–73).

18 Sometimes the text speaks more broadly of 'parents' (63, 245), but when the mourners of an entire city are described as 'a vast throng of women' (123–4), it is evident that the poet has primarily female mourners in mind.

19 I suggested that the lost line might have been something like <λειφθεῖσα γυνὴ πάντα κατ' οἶκον>. (Angled brackets are the conventional markers of an editorial supplement.)

20 This stanza, which is an 'epode' (i.e. it is not part of a 'strophic par' of metrically identical stanzas), has by many editors been transposed so as to stand between lines 113 and 114; of arguments in support of this transposition (see Garvie 2009: 46–9), the most important is that 93–100 gives, as 101–13 does not, an immediately intelligible reason for the Elders then to say '*This is why* my mind is ... torn with fear' (114–15).
21 Cissia is properly the name of a region (the region whose capital was Susa), but Aeschylus evidently took it for the name of a city.
22 Literally 'yoked alone'.
23 Just as we are encouraged to suppose that Xerxes is considerably younger than he actually was (see n. 8), so we are encouraged to believe that he is the Queen's only son, or at any rate the only one who was with the expedition to Greece. In reality, Atossa had four sons serving on the expedition, but in Aeschylus' play the other three are ignored (the reference to 'your children' in 218 does not require there to be more than one son of military age).
24 And even then, their kinsfolk might hope – most of them in vain – that they had remained in Greece with Mardonius and would eventually return home.
25 The Messenger follows roughly the same pattern, referring three times to 'Xerxes', once to 'your son Xerxes' and once to 'the King'.
26 156, 550, 551, 552, 923.
27 58, 151, 234, 564, 918, cf. 8, 66. In 564 (a lyric passage), the word translated as 'King' is the archaic *anax*; elsewhere it is *basileus*.
28 'The lord King Xerxes son of Darius' (5–6, cf. 144–5), 'the Great King' (24), 'the bold ruler of populous Asia' (74), 'King of the land' (929).
29 739, 744, 751, 834. In 834, the possessive adjective is omitted and it is not clear whether one should translate 'my son', 'our son' or even 'the boy' (for the latter, compare the well-known prophecy of King George V, 'After I am gone, the boy [the future Edward VIII, then 41 years old] will ruin himself in twelve months').
30 197, 233.
31 177, 189, 211, 352, 473, 476.
32 227, 529, 847, ?850.
33 At 215, the chorus-leader actually addresses her as 'mother' *tout court*. This is the only passage in tragedy where the vocative *meter* is used without further specification in addressing a person who is not the speaker's actual mother.
34 Two distinct groups of bereaved women are described in this passage; the second group (541–5) are wives, so the first group (537–40) must be mothers, and a word or words making this clear must have dropped out of the text.
35 Athens was destined to prove this true, nearly sixty years later, in Sicily.

9

Atossa

Hanna M. Roisman

Introduction

Aeschylus' *Persians* was performed at Athens' City Dionysia in 472 BCE in a trilogy that won the first prize. While most tragedies were set in the distant past, depicting mythic events detached from the audience's lives, *Persians* is set in Susa, the capital of the Persian Empire, in the aftermath of a war that took place only eight years before the performance: Xerxes' massive land and sea invasion of Greece and his naval defeat at Salamis (480). Under these circumstances, Aeschylus' motivations in writing the play were to emphasize the extent of the Persian losses, while glorifying Greece and aggrandizing the Athenian victory. Therefore, his characterization of Atossa, the Persian Queen and other Persians, who would have been perceived not only as foreigners but also as aggressors in the recent war, presumably takes into account the sensitivities of the Athenian audience watching a play that depicted the fate of those who had dared to attack them.

In order to accomplish his aims, Aeschylus allowed himself artistic liberty when describing events that took place in the war.[1] His version differs from the accounts left by Herodotus on several points. Most critically for our purpose, it is Atossa, the Queen Mother, who appears to be in charge, instead of Xerxes' chief official Artabanus, who had in fact been appointed to govern the empire during Xerxes' absence (Herodotus 7.52). In other deviations from Herodotus' histories, in the play Xerxes orders the land forces to take immediate flight after the defeat, while the ships escape separately (468–70, 480–1). Accordingly, the Chorus describe to Darius' ghost the loss of the fleet and the land army as a 'twin failure' (676, cf. 719–20, 728). Herodotus, however, indicates that Xerxes actually left 300,000 troops under the command of his general Mardonius to fight a decisive land battle and attack the Peloponnese (8.102–3, 113, 9.32.2).[2] He also informs us that Xerxes himself remained in Sardis until the Battle of Mycale in the summer of 479 (9.107.3) and that the navy returned with the army and ferried the land forces across the Hellespont, since the bridges were down (Herodotus 8.115–20, 126; 13; 9.114.1).

Aeschylus, on the other hand, depicts the bridges as Xerxes' salvation (735–6), and returns him to Susa straight after Salamis. The only goal of these dramatic modifications is to heighten the nature of the disaster that befell the Persians because of their attempt to attack Greece and Athens in particular.[3]

By using Atossa as the hub of the play's action, Aeschylus created a dramatically intriguing character. Introducing her in this capacity smooths the way for Aeschylus' departures from the historical narrative; in addition, she serves as a plot device, used indirectly as a vehicle for glorifying Athens.[4] For example, Atossa's question to the Messenger as to whether Athens has been sacked, which it was, not only once but twice during the invasion (Herodotus 8.51–3, 65, 9.13.2–3; Thucydides 1.89.3, 2.16), gives the Messenger an opportunity to be inventive with the facts. He answers obliquely saying, 'While she has her men, her defences are secure' (349),[5] which hints that city's defences had not been breached, when in fact the entire city had been destroyed. The scene panders to Athenian sentiment, which would not tolerate any suggestion of Persian military success. While avoiding offending Athenian sensitivities, Aeschylus also enables the audience to turn their attention to the Persian losses.

If Atossa is mainly a plot device used for pillorying Persia while glorifying Athens, we might view her as a caricature, embodying a collection of foreign traits thought by Athenians to symbolize all that is inferior in Persian custom, while enabling other characters 'inadvertently' to sing the praises of democratic Greek culture. If, however, Aeschylus imbued Atossa's persona with characteristics that present a cohesive image of a credible woman, we may decide that she deserves to be considered a fully fledged character. Finally, bearing in mind that Atossa is the only female character in Aeschylus' extant tragedies that predates Clytemnestra, we might also look for hints in her persona of the magnificent queen who is to appear later on Aeschylus' stage. We will see that, while Atossa's persona does in some ways anticipate what is yet to come in Clytemnestra, the two women are also worlds apart. Atossa appears to have mastered the art of doing what she wants, while seeming to defer to the men around her.

It is easy to see that Aeschylus crafts aspects of Atossa to appeal to known Athenian prejudices about the Persians:[6] she has a strong interest in wealth, a short-sighted focus on big numbers and an assumption that despotic rule is the system that governs everywhere. However, Atossa's characterization may be more subtly complex than is immediately apparent. On a more careful inspection, we learn that Atossa's interest in the Persian wealth is not based on greed or due to wishes for an overly luxurious lifestyle, rather for her gold represents the welfare of her country. The issue of believing in quantity rather than quality is put in Atossa's mouth in a segment where she is used as a vehicle for the aggrandizement of Athens (230-1). Aeschylus may thus be catering to the predilections of some members of the audience while also creating a more nuanced character for those preferring a less black and white portrayal of Persians and Athenians.

Aeschylus' portrayal of Atossa as an apparently 'ignorant woman', as Sidgwick calls her (1903: x), asking surprisingly basic questions, such as where Athens is, how big its army is, how rich it is and who rules it (231, 235, 237, 241), could be thought to damage Atossa's credibility as a character. How can she not know anything about Athens? She is, after all, the daughter of Cyrus, wife of Darius and mother of Xerxes, all of whom went to attack the Greeks. How can she have such intimate knowledge of Xerxes' forces, as she exhibits later, and not know where they were heading?

It may therefore be thought that she serves simply as a plot device, with her questions enabling the Chorus to speak at some length of the glories of Athens, for the enjoyment of the spectators.[7] Answering her queries, the Chorus reveal that Athens has 'a silver wellspring. Their very land's a treasure trove' (238), that 'They're slaves of no man, no – nor vassals either' (242), and they seem to deliberately deflect Atossa's question about the size of the army to its quality, reminding her that that this army managed to destroy the large and splendid army of Darius (236-8, 244). Dramatically, however, Atossa's queries in fact make her a very credible character, true to a certain type of a woman.[8] When Aeschylus has her ask about the location of Athens, he shows her doing what 'real' people do when they are stressed and anxious, having difficulty deciding the correct course of action. She engages in 'a displacement activity', that is to say, she changes the subject of the conversation. She deflects attention away from the disturbing premonitions her dream has caused, to something less demanding of her emotional energy: the location of a faraway city her son went to sack.

In fact, many of the characteristics used by critics to find fault with Atossa's persona can easily be explained by the playwright's wish to please his audience when casting Atossa as the primary representative of a foreign people with whom they are at war. If Aeschylus was attempting to evoke some pity in the audience for his characters, the introduction of a grieving wife and despondent mother, in place of Xerxes, may have been a sound strategy. Since the invasion of Greece was Xerxes' idea, as Atossa herself attests (476-7), it makes little sense that the spectators would pity him. However, if the reigning view that Atossa represents Xerxes in this play is accepted,[9] the audience may have had similar difficulties in identifying with her since she would be a representative of the Persian ruling family. However, if Atossa is considered instead as a character in her own right, the audience could have empathized with her as a concerned mother, desperately worried about the fate of her son. Furthermore, Atossa could be emblematic of all mothers grieving the loss of their sons at war, a symbol that surely the Athenians could relate to.

However, in delving further into Atossa's characterization, we might ask whether she is indeed primarily a protective mother who cares greatly about her son, but manages to mute her worries as befits her role as caretaker of the empire during her son's absence. Since, chronologically, Atossa is the only female character in Aeschylus' extant tragedies who is fully portrayed and predates Clytemnestra, we might wonder whether instead of being primarily a concerned mother, Atossa is a prequel to the future dominant Queen of Argos.[10] Looking carefully, we do find indications that Aeschylus has created in Atossa a politically astute leader capable of making her own decisions.

It has often been assumed that Atossa prioritizes the well-being of her son over that of the Persian people as a whole, but challenging that view, we might ask whether Aeschylus does consistently frame Atossa as a concerned mother.[11] In an analysis of Atossa's reactions to Xerxes' behaviour, her attitude towards her son does not seem to be marked solely by pity or sympathy but rather by stark criticism, if not ire, at his hubris and lack of responsibility. Atossa's lack of firm personal attachment to Xerxes but deep concern for the country appear, for example, in her reply to the Chorus when they state that the Athenian force was strong enough to have defeated 'the brilliant and massive expedition force of Darius' (244). Hearing this, Atossa replies, 'What you say is fearful to think about, for parents of those who have gone there' (245, Sommerstein 2008). She is not singling out herself but uses the plural number 'parents', thus including all the Persian parents of those whom Xerxes took with him on the unfortunate campaign.

It is not easy to get a firm grasp on Atossa's personality. However, as we follow her engagements with the Chorus, Messenger and Darius, we do detect several attributes hinting at what is still to come in Aeschylus' characterization of Clytemnestra. From what she tells the Elders, it is clear that Atossa has a deep sense of foreboding following her most recent dream, and has already seen ominous portents. However, in accordance with the behaviour expected of her gender, she presents herself as needing confirmation from the Elders of what her own senses tell her. She does later reprimand the Elders for not having taken her dream seriously, even though, in contrast to her successor, she had nevertheless dutifully gone off to perform the sacrifices as instructed, despite being aware of the futility of these acts, as she could not avert what had already taken place.

When Darius' ghost appears, he knows he can count on Atossa's perspicacity, knowledge of details and ability to communicate clearly, when the Chorus seem incapable of expressing themselves in his presence. However, once Darius has assessed the situation, she also makes no objection to exiting the scene for Xerxes to take centre stage on his return. She obeys Darius' bidding when he sends her off to perform the wifely and motherly duty of preparing new clothes for her son, yet, as an independent thinker, makes her own decision not to be the first person welcoming Xerxes on his arrival. Altogether, Atossa's treatment of Xerxes anticipates Clytemnestra's treatment of her children. She only calls him by name once (199), describing his misfortune in her dream, and then only in her conversation with the ghost of Darius, when she has to differentiate Xerxes from his brothers and can obviously no longer refer to him as 'my son', as she did in her conversation with the Chorus (718, 734, 754).[12]

Xerxes is at war, and as a mother she would be expected to worry about his well-being. However, we find her more concerned about the results of his actions for her country and by extension for her and her other children. As we analyse her references to her son, we shall see that her attitude toward Xerxes in some ways foreshadows Clytemnestra, for whom Iphigenia becomes almost a pretext for the revenge she takes on Agamemnon. Even though Clytemnestra tells the Chorus that she murdered her husband because of his sacrifice of Iphigenia (*Agamemnon* 1412–18, 1431–2), the audience never see or hear the Aeschylean Clytemnestra proclaiming any love for the girl, as we witness, for example, in Euripides' *Iphigenia at Aulis* (e.g. 1171–6). For the Aeschylean Clytemnestra, Iphigenia became a tool whose fate justifies the revenge, an excuse, not much more. For Atossa, too, her child may be little more than a means to an end. If he serves his purpose well, he will be lauded. If, however, he fails in his duties, he will be severely criticized. It is possible to see in the play's ending without the presence of Atossa, that in spite of her words to the contrary, she is indeed prepared to abandon her 'beloved' son in times of trouble (851).

Ultimately, we will argue that Atossa combines traits of independence, leadership and clear thought with a pragmatic acceptance that she needs to at least appear to bow to the conventions of both motherhood and her gender. She appears to have mastered the art of allowing the men around her to believe she is deferring to their 'superior' masculine acumen, while, in fact, she does what she deems best. She displays an intuitive intelligence, enabling her to negotiate her path without rebelling against the society within which she lives.

We will analyse Atossa's appearances and engagement with three characters: the Chorus, the Messenger and Darius, and ask at the end the most revisited question: Why isn't she allowed by the playwright to come and greet her returning son?

Atossa and the Chorus

The audience first encounter Atossa after the entrance song of the Chorus of Persian Elders, in which they proudly describe the wealth and antiquity of the Persian empire, Xerxes' royal power, and their confidence in the invincibility of the sizeable Persian forces. It is often assumed that *Persians* presents a double tragedy, the suffering of Persia as a whole and that of the individual, Xerxes. The Chorus of Persian Elders evince the suffering of the people, while for most of the play it is Atossa's distress that represents the personal torment suffered by Xerxes. While it is true that the Elders represent Persia, they are not alone. Atossa is stricken by the losses of her country and her people. She does not so much 'represent' Xerxes, but, as we would expect, is concerned about his safety and well-being. However, the Queen may also represent all of the mothers and the wives of the soldiers who went with Xerxes, whom the Chorus mention early in their *parodos* (59–64). Although in some of her speeches, she ultimately mentions her son, as a member of the ruling family, Atossa also maintains a keen interest in the success of the army and in Persia as a whole, and is very aware of her own status.

Atossa's female diffidence is introduced in her first sentence. Despite being the Queen Mother and the only governing monarch present in Susa while Xerxes is away heading the expedition against Athens, she underscores her own status and power by emphasizing that she was the wife of Darius: she has left the palace, she says, and 'the rooms I shared with Darius' (160). Next, she focuses on Persia's wealth. She fears not only that 'this great wealth of ours will blind us, bring an end to the prosperity that – with god's help – Darius amassed' (163–4), but she expresses two supplementary fears suggestive of the fall of the whole of Persia: she fears that wealth 'without men is useless, while without wealth – no matter that a man is strong – good fortune will not shine on him' (166–7). This will be in fact Xerxes' and by implication Persia's position after the defeat. Wealth without men to defend it is not to be honoured. Persia's power lies in the wealth that Darius' amassed, but now without the army or the navy, Xerxes can be overthrown, along with his entire empire. All of a sudden, Atossa retracts her concern: she says that the Persian wealth is ample, and only then expresses her concern 'for *him*, the apple of my eye, who lights the palace with his presence' (168–9). Xerxes becomes here almost an afterthought, following her consternation over the Persian wealth.

Atossa does not offer her reason for coming to see the Elders until her next speech. She tells them of the dream and her subsequent encounter with an eagle attacked by a hawk. In the dream Xerxes appears to be toppled from his chariot by a woman dressed in Doric garb, an image symbolizing his utter military defeat resulting from his attempt to enslave the Greeks. Next, seeing his father standing and pitying him and realizing the depth of his disgrace, Xerxes rends his clothes in a sign of mourning for his defeat.[13] Xerxes managed to squander the wealth his father had raised, the riches which Atossa has been just praising. Atossa's dream does not focus on Xerxes' safety or fortune, but on the well-being of the throne and Persia. Xerxes has endangered Persia by wasting its great wealth. The following image repeats the dream's message. Atossa, speaking as a Persian, sees her son as the King of Birds, the eagle and metaphorically Persia, while the hawk, second in status to the eagle, must be representing the Greeks.[14] The bloody victory of the hawk over the eagle clearly symbolizes the defeat of Xerxes, that is to say of Persia.[15]

The dream therefore reflects Aeschylus' political motivations of criticizing Xerxes and lauding Athens. It also depicts Atossa as being aware of the damage which her son has caused to the throne and to Persia. The dream conveys to the audience for the first time that the Persians, or at least Atossa, may be critical of Xerxes' actions. His misguided attempt to assemble his campaign and set out to destroy Greece has caused her constant nightmares (176–8), not because of the risk to him as much as because it emptied the coffers which Darius had filled. No wonder then that she is afraid for the throne and warns the Elders:

> What I saw – it alarmed me, and it's right that I should tell you. You're all
> aware that if my son succeeds he would be heroized, but if things should turn
> out badly ... The state cannot hold him accountable. If he is saved, he shall rule
> Persia as he always did.
>
> 210–14

The message to the Elders is clear: Xerxes is not accountable to the state. What is also important to realize is that, by extension, neither are she and her other three sons. The throne remains in the hands of the monarchical family. Xerxes has become an instrument of potential destruction and peril for her entire family as well as for Persia. Her insistence that he cannot be held responsible by the state for the defeat of his army is not necessarily only to save him, but to save the power of those whom he put in danger by his rash act.

Atossa's dream serves to criticize Xerxes but also to flatter the Athenian ego. She saw two women, one dressed in Persian attire and one 'as a Dorian

Greek' (182–3). Atossa's comment on the Greek woman's robes as 'Doric' stresses the simplicity of the Greek garment versus the sumptuousness of the Persians as Sommerstein (2008: line 183) suggests: 'Aeschylus chooses to dress the woman representing Greece in "Doric" rather than "Ionic" style, not because he is imagining her as a Dorian (e.g., a Spartan) – both styles were in use in the Athens of his day – but because the Doric *chiton* ... symbolized Greek simplicity, in contrast to Persian luxury, more effectively than the Ionic.' However, in spite of the simplicity of attire of the Greek woman, she struggles against the leather straps Xerxes put on the necks of both women, and 'with both hands tears apart the chariot's equipment and – once freed of her reins – she drags it off by force and snaps the yoke straight down the middle. My son is thrown, and Darius, his father, stands beside him full of pity. When Xerxes sees him, well, he rips his robes to rags' (194–9). Athens, in other words, cannot be enslaved. It might not be as luxurious as Persia is, but it struggles against subjugation, and successfully fights for its freedom. Even before the Chorus tell her that Athens does not have one man governing it, the dream tells Atossa that freedom is the most important good the Athenians will fight for and that the Greeks will not be subdued by Xerxes. They are of free spirit and able to go on the offensive.

Can we also deduce a more universal implicit message behind the dream, however modern it might sound? The two women depicted are not entirely strange to each other. Both of them are of 'flawless beauty and are sisters of one family' (κάλλει τ' ἀμώμω, καί κασιγνήτα γένους ταὐτοῦ, *kallei t'amōmō, kai kasignēta genous t'autou*, 185–6). Indeed, mythically the Greeks and the Persians were related.[16] Is Aeschylus striving to make a connection here beyond their 'historical' kinship? The playwright underscores their affinity by the grammatical dual form (see above). Greek has a grammatical system to indicate a dual number in addition to singular and plural, often used of pairs that the speaker considers a unit. It does not have to be employed for two persons instead of the regular plural, so we may assume that Aeschylus uses the dual here purposefully. It emphasizes the essential similarity between the two women so as to give the differences of their homeland and behavior a more striking impact. Why is he doing this? Is he using Atossa's dream to indicate to the audience that the split between 'them' and 'us', i.e. Greeks and Persians, causes intense suffering, and that underneath their robes, the Barbarians and the Greeks are the same; they are 'Sisters'? Although the Athenians were not the aggressors, and they should rejoice in their defensive victory, they should also acknowledge that there is blood shed on the other side, with a multitude of their enemies, who are as human as they are, lying dead. The heavy loss on the Persian side is symbolized by the encounter Atossa sees after waking up from her sleep.

She sees a hawk attacking an eagle as it flees for refuge to the altar of Apollo. The hawk tears the eagle's head with its talons, while the eagle does nothing 'except cower ... and surrender' (209–10). As the bird of Zeus, the eagle should not seek refuge at the altar of Apollo. In fact, it should not seek refuge at all. It is the eagle that is usually described as tearing its prey with its talons, and it should not be overpowered by a hawk, a bird of a lesser status. It is thus once again intimated that Xerxes' expedition against Greece was ill-conceived. Atossa, then, while associating her son with the king of birds, sees that he is overpowered by what she would consider a lesser opponent, that is to say, Athens. The Athenians might not like to be seen as the 'underdog', but they surely must have enjoyed being portrayed as mightier than a seemingly invincible opponent.

The Chorus avoid committing themselves as to whether Atossa's fears about the country are justified. They give her some general advice to approach the gods and pray for them to avert anything sinister in her dream but to fulfil whatever good there was for her, her children, and the state and for anyone about whom she cares. This advice is rather unhelpful because Atossa has already tried to do this, with disastrous results (201–4). The second part of their advice seems more helpful: to pour drink-offerings to the Earth and to the dead and propitiate them, asking that Darius send up to the light blessings but keep under the earth whatever is contrary to them (219–23). It makes sense that Darius would be interested in the welfare of his family and country. They end their advice in a quasi-dismissive way, for which she will call them out later:

> From what we've heard
>   our judgement is
> that this will bring
>   in all respects
>   a good conclusion.
>
>   224–5

The first encounter with the Chorus shows Atossa as a woman who does not really trust herself but who has good intuition. Having been left in charge of the throne while the King is away, she carries out the duties a monarch should perform by consulting the Elders, who in fact were chosen by Xerxes to oversee the Persian territory in his absence, but their attitude to Atossa rather belies their sense of their own importance (5–7). She wants their assurance that her fears are justified, but is left with no clear answer. She does not ask about her son per se, but about the welfare of the country. She has already done half of what the Chorus advised her, on her own initiative, by supplicating the gods. She leaves saying she will see to their second piece of advice. The response of the Chorus however is a precursor of the Argive

Elders' treatment of Clytemnestra, when they disbelieve her report that Troy has been taken and accuse her of the womanly tendency of listening to gossip and seeing a mirage (*Agamemnon* 274–80, 479–87). Atossa's reaction will also serve as a prequel to Clytemnestra's response.

After the Messenger's report, when the magnitude of the defeat has been described in detail, Atossa scolds the Chorus, who, she claims, did not take her dream seriously enough (520), just as Clytemnestra will scold the Argive Elders (*Agamemnon* 587–97). As noted above, they were rather dismissive of her fears and claimed that if she followed their advice of making offerings and supplicating Darius, things would turn out well for her in every way (225). Atossa's rebuke is noteworthy because in reality even if they had taken her dream as a serious message about the defeat, it would have been too late to change or prevent anything anyway. However, it shows Atossa as a self-aware person who does not like to be ignored or dismissed, insisting on being taken seriously. Nevertheless, in accordance with the contradictory features of her persona, she is about to follow the advice they gave in 216–25, that is to pray to the gods. She goes back to the palace to bring a rich libation, as a gift to Earth and the dead (522–4). She understands that these libations are being offered after the event, that is to say after the defeat, and cannot prevent it; however, she will pour them as 'perhaps such services will mean the future might be better' (525–6).

Before she leaves, she gives a general warning to the Elders that they should debate honestly about what has occurred and offer trusty counsels to her. This directive may reflect on the rebuke she previously gave them. However, her second charge is more peculiar: 'if my son comes here before I return, comfort him and escort him home, for fear that he may add some further harm to the harm he has suffered' (529–31, Sommerstein 2008).

Why is Atossa following the Chorus' advice, despite any criticism she may have of them? The vagueness of her explanation that her sacrifices will allow for a better future seems uncharacteristically sweeping and vacuous for a person who demanded such precise and detailed accounts of the battle.[17] Somehow, she seems eager to leave. Is it because of Xerxes' possibly imminent arrival? This would explain her second directive to the Chorus about Xerxes. We should note that again she fails to mention him by name. Her directive together with her sudden departure are usually explained as indicating the playwright's wish to surprise the audience.[18] That is to say, the spectators expect Xerxes to arrive, but instead Darius' ghost appears. This might be true, but one cannot deny that this sudden departure for no good reason also sheds some light on Atossa's motherliness.

Atossa seems to have a double fear. First, as Wilamowitz suggests, she is aware that there is a threat of revolution and is concerned about Xerxes passing through the streets alone; thus she asks the Chorus to accompany him to the palace.[19] This kind of thinking is characteristic of a political ruler, which she is. Second, it seems clear that she is concerned about Xerxes' mental condition. She recognizes that Xerxes is crushed by his defeat and might even consider suicide. Such a threatening mental condition requires a gentle touch, which she acknowledges as she tells the Chorus to calm him. Would not it be more fitting, however, for a mother to respond to such a situation directly, rather than relegating it to others? Is this motherly warmth and devotion? Should we explain her prompt departure by her feeling of obligation to obey the Chorus, to obey what men tell her to do? Her obedience to men, and almost automatic response of following directives given by them, anticipates her immediate rush to prepare new robes for Xerxes upon Darius' order. If this is the case, it shows how a woman who is perfectly capable of fulfilling manly tasks while standing in for the absent ruler feels obligated to do what men tell her to do, whether the action makes sense or not. This feeling of obligation somehow surpasses what one would expect of a mother. If Aeschylus wished to portray the Queen as a mother stamped by fathomless worry for her son, would he remove her from the scene at this critical point?

The first stasimon fills the interval between Atossa's departure from the stage and her return. The Chorus present a picture of the mourning into which the great Persian cities and indeed the whole empire are now plunged. They hold Xerxes responsible for this catastrophe and contrast Xerxes' disastrous naval venture with Darius' wise and unblemished rule. They note that Xerxes has hardly made his way home through Thrace, and that the best-born Persians are left perforce behind, tossed by the sea and gnawed by fishes. Finally, they express a fear of open rebellion now that the King's authority has been undermined. What is remarkable in their song is that unlike the Messenger and Atossa, they don't divide the blame for the disaster between Xerxes and the gods, but hold Xerxes solely responsible for it. They do not comment on Atossa's possible fear of Xerxes being attacked while on his way to the palace, but do bring up the possibility of Persia's subjects refusing to continue to pay their tribute. Atossa's hope that the defeat would not have an impact on her son's status as expressed in 213–14 is obviously seriously disappointed. All that once was Persia is left behind at Salamis. One should note that had Xerxes indeed arrived at this point in the play, while Atossa was away, the Chorus were clearly not the right choice for calming him, whom they see as culpable for the calamitous state of affairs in Persia. The Elders do not offer any extenuating circumstances for what he has done. How would they have been able to soothe him?

Atossa re-enters on foot and unattended, bearing in her hands due offerings for the dead: milk, honey, water, wine; also, a branch of olive and flowers tied in garlands. Her words follow the maxim of *pathei mathos*, learning by suffering, stated more explicitly in Aeschylus' *Agamemnon* (177):[20]

> Whoever has experienced great crises knows that, whenever a great tidal wave of crisis washes over mortal men, they tend to be afraid of everything. But when, thanks to good fortune, all goes well, they think the
> same good fortune will ease their way to happiness forever.
> 598–602

As a result, she is now full of apprehension for the future and brings the promised offerings to Earth and the dead (523). She asks the Chorus to summon the ghost of Darius with auspicious songs while she pours the libations.

What is missing? We know she was expecting Xerxes to arrive, but there is not a word about him. The audience have just heard the Chorus gravely blaming Xerxes for the defeat. Had Aeschylus wished to underscore her motherly affection for her son, he could have allowed her to utter some concern that Xerxes has not arrived yet, or musings on how devastated he must be by the terrible misfortune. Yet the audience hear nothing of the sort, and are left with the choral assessment of his blame, which will shortly be confirmed by Darius. Furthermore, in their following prayer to the gods of the Netherworld to send Darius' soul to the light, the Chorus repeat and dwell on the death of the Persian young men, the loss of the land army and all the navy's ships (670, 674–80), while emphasizing that Darius did not cause great loss of life and the army's destruction through catastrophic wars (652–3), all of which allude to the antithetical activities of his son.

In sum, in her engagement with the Chorus, Atossa seems to be torn between how she is expected to behave as a woman, and what she feels is right and proper due to her status. On the one hand, she behaves obediently as expected; on the other hand, she rebels against being taken lightly. As far as Xerxes is concerned, she calls him the apple of her eye (168), but does not express any foreboding for him specifically, but rather for what happens to Persia due to his actions. It is possible that in her motherhood she also is torn, between loving her son and being critical of his rash behaviour. This will be discussed further below.

Atossa and the Messenger

The scene between the Messenger and Atossa fortifies the view that Atossa is a capable woman who acts as a responsible and skilled leader of the empire, and that she should be seen as representing not only Xerxes, but rather the overall Persian interest, as the Chorus do.

Critics are highly disturbed by the fact that during the first 41 lines (249–89) of the epirrhematic (i.e. mixture of spoken and lyric) exchange between the Chorus and the Messenger, Atossa is silent. Some attribute her silence to her remarkable self-control, her queenly dignity, her aloofness, or her high-mindedness; others to Aeschylus' early challenge in integrating a second actor, or to the fact that Atossa starts speaking only when her concern is personal about Xerxes.[21] However, Atossa's silence is well understood in the text. The first 41 lines of the Messenger are rather unclear in their information beyond saying that the Persian army suffered defeat; he is short on detail. Atossa herself explains her silence:

> I have stayed silent until now, in mourning, crushed by this catastrophe. Yes, this disaster is so overwhelming that I don't know what to say or what to ask you. Still, mankind must endure the suffering gods give us. So. Compose yourself. Tell us the full extent of the disaster – even if you do 'groan' at our misfortunes. Who is not dead? Which of our generals should we be mourning? Which of our commanders died and left his post deserted?
>
> 290–8

As a competent commander-in-chief, Atossa was waiting for specifics and intervened only when she was not given them. The audience will witness a similar scenario occurring when the ghost of Darius asks for specifics and the Chorus continue with their incoherent lament. He eventually turns to Atossa and says: 'my venerable queen ... dry your eyes and stop your weeping and speak to me in terms that I can understand' (704–6). Atossa needs specifics and clarity, just as her husband, Darius, the former great king and commander, will need clarity if he is to help.

The Messenger's immediate answer to Atossa's query 'who is not dead?' is: 'Xerxes is alive ...' (299), as he assumes that this is what Atossa is asking about. In reality, the fact that the Messenger has not announced from the start that Xerxes was dead must have indicated to Atossa that he is alive.[22] Had the playwright wanted to portray her as an overly concerned mother, he would have allowed her to ask about her son specifically, which would have been perfectly natural for a mother to do. In refraining from doing so, he actually indicates that this was not a feature of Atossa he meant to highlight. Atossa acts now as a commander-in-chief, and as such she needs more specific information. When instead of telling her how the various generals died, the

Messenger simply gives a list, she swiftly and plainly reins him in and insists he tell her not 'a litany of grief' but

> ...go back to the beginning. Tell me this: how large was the Greek fleet, to let them think they could do battle, turn their ships' rams on the Persian navy?
>
> 333–6

Aeschylus uses Atossa to reinforce the view that the high-quality troops of free Greeks defending their land could not be defeated by a force just because of its superior numbers (Herodotus 8.101–3; 7.208–10). Once she learns that Athens has not been sacked (see above) and that the Athenians had about one third as many ships as the Persians had, Atossa demands to know whether Xerxes started the battle first, being 'too confident because he had the larger fleet' (350–2). All Atossa's questions attempt to force the Messenger to give a systematic account from the beginning. She needs to assess and understand exactly what happened, so she can make sense of it, exactly as Darius will want to understand what has happened. While the Chorus cry over the losses announced by the Messenger, Atossa acts as a statesman. She does not lose her head but demands a specific and factual report from the Messenger, not a general description of a catastrophe. Had she been only interested in the fate of her son, once she was told he was safe, she would have stopped querying, but this was *not* her goal. As a monarch and commander, she has to figure out what happened: more specifically, how much of the defeat was her son's fault. Xerxes might not be accountable to the state, but he is accountable to his mother, who is far from forgiving.

After hearing how Xerxes was deceived by the Greek strategy and how once he saw the destruction of the navy in Salamis and the slaughter of his forces on Psytaleia, he tore his robes and 'wailed – a high-pitched wail', which characterized female lamentation (468), Atossa reacts. However, her first comment is not about her son's misfortunes, as the losses of Persia take priority in her mind. She blames a cruel divinity that 'deluded us Persians!' (472–3). Xerxes comes second. She does not pity or sympathize with him. Like the Messenger, while she blames the hateful demon for his deceit, she acknowledges that it was Xerxes himself who in his misjudgement decided on the fatal expedition (361–2, 373, 454). Wishing to avenge Darius' defeat in Marathon, 'my son plunged himself in so much misery' (476–7), she says. It is noteworthy that she does not ask what happened to Xerxes after he tore his robes, or where he is now, but rather wants to know: 'What happened to the ships that got away? Where did you last see them? Can you give an accurate report?' (478–9). Again, it is the fate of the Persians as a whole that she is interested in.

The Elders, on the other hand, no longer express any interest in the details provided in the Messenger's account. Their only response is their typical exclamation of sorrow: 'You demon! You black demon! You've swooped, too heavy, on us Persians!' (515–16). Atossa whole-heartedly joins the grief: 'The whole army gone' (517). She does not utter one word about her son or his tragedy.

Atossa and Darius

The audience learn more about Atossa's views of Xerxes during her encounter with Darius' ghost. She repeatedly calls her son 'headstrong' (718, 754) and has very little to say in his favor. Darius censures their son for his attempt to chain the Hellespont, and his ill-thought-out expedition to Greece, which squandered the wealth that he, Darius, had amassed. Only when Darius attributes Xerxes' behavior to his youthful rashness, lack of counsel, and mental disease (744–52, cf. 725, 829) does Atossa intercede. She feebly tries to excuse Xerxes' deeds by claiming he was under the influence of bad men who taunted him for not having achieved as much as his father, Darius, had done (753–8), but she does not seem to forgive him either. After all, this excuse does not apply to his acts elsewhere, for which only he is responsible.[23] She seems completely in agreement with Darius' harsh words about their son's lack of thinking in attacking Greece and especially Athens. Atossa's lack of attentiveness as a mother, however, comes into focus when Darius asks twice about the well-being of his son. First, he wants to know if there is any hope 'that he is safe' (735); then he ascertains that his son reached the continent safely and insists on verifying that the information is reliable (737). Atossa, on the other hand, has never asked the Messenger about Xerxes outright. What also stands out in the details Atossa gives her husband about the return of Xerxes is the fact that she claims that 'to his relief he reached the bridge that yokes both continents' (736). This information was not given by the Messenger, who only insinuated in 510–11 that Xerxes and the remnants of his army have already reached Persia. Atossa's insistence on the bridge and Xerxes' rejoicing on reaching it so he could cross the Bosporus to the continent is difficult to understand, unless she knew that chaining the waters of the Hellespont would not please Darius, and would only make him angrier at the thoughtlessness of his son (743–51).

After hearing the sorrows and misfortune that Xerxes caused Persia, Darius gives two directives before departing back to the land of the shadows, one to the Chorus and one to Atossa. Both orders revolve around Xerxes. The Elders are trusted with keeping the young man on the straight and narrow, giving him well-reasoned guidance that should prevent the rash leader from further angering the gods by his conceit and arrogance (830–1). In other words, their concern should be with Xerxes' general attitude and policy in the future, when Xerxes will be in 'a fit state to listen to them' (Broadhead 1960: on 838). Atossa's concern is more mundane and relevant to the immediate situation:

> And you, my dear, Xerxes' revered mother, go back inside the palace. Fetch robes appropriate for royalty. And prepare to meet your son. He is tormented by the scale of the catastrophe. He has torn his robes – his rich-embroidered robes – to tatters. Soothe him with gentle words. You are the only person he will listen to, the only one whom he will respond to.
>
> 832–8

At the end of this play, after Atossa has shown her perspicacity, her concern for the well-being of the entire country, her ability to act as a commander-in-chief on whose knowledge of detail Darius came to rely once the Chorus disappointed him with endless lament (which would be rather the characteristic of women), Atossa is brought back by her husband to the only function she had while he was alive: mother to his children. It is an honourable and responsible role and task, but why couldn't she be trusted with both: taking care of Xerxes' immediate needs but also making sure his attitude in the future would change? Has Darius forgotten that in their emotional upheaval the Elders were unable when asked to give him the details of the disaster that came upon Persia? He blamed them for being paralyzed by 'atavistic fear' (703).

However, this directive to Atossa to act as a mother does brings the audience back to the theme of her motherhood, as displayed throughout the play. This theme is not particularly well developed, although Aeschylus obviously wanted the audience to pay attention to it, by having Atossa refer to her son in her first entrance as 'the apple of my eye' (168). This would have had the effect of making spectators expect further displays of the affection of a mother for her child, which they will never see; indeed, if they had entertained such expectations, they might have been sorely disappointed. In fact, Aeschylus is using Darius' open affection for his son to highlight Atossa's lack of it.[24] Darius' parting injunction to his wife that she 'soothe him [Xerxes] with words' because he must be 'tormented by the scale of the catastrophe' emphasizes the fact that although Atossa not only knew how upset Xerxes might be upon his return and even expected him to commit suicide, nevertheless she chose to absent herself from his expected imminent arrival and gave the charge of calming him down to the Chorus (529–31).[25] Absenting herself from his meeting with the Elders would allow her to avoid the awkward situation of scolding and criticizing her son in the presence of the Elders, to whom a united front of the monarchy needed to be exhibited. However, it is noteworthy that while the Queen says she will adhere to Darius' injunction to bring Xerxes new clothes, she says nothing about calming her son. Darius' words are intended to ensure that now that the King is returning, Atossa will resume the female, motherly role she fulfilled before Xerxes left and before he, Darius, died. Thus, by the end of the play, Atossa is returned to a position thought suitable for a woman. Despite this ending, the play as a whole shows the audience the abilities of a woman who can rule effectively, without the ruinous effect that in future Aeschylus' upcoming Queen of Argos will display.

Atossa's reply to Darius' order to fetch Xerxes new clothes reveals a new person:

> God! All the suffering is tearing *me* apart, but most of all this one. Misfortune cuts me to the core – to hear the ignominy of my son dressed in rags. So. I shall go. I'll bring his regalia outside from the palace, and I'll try to intercept my son. I'll not abandon my beloved son in times of trouble.
>
> 845–51

We know from Herodotus (3.66) that rending one's clothes is a marker for Persian mourning.[26] According to Sancisi-Weerdenburgh (1983: 29), the person wearing the royal robe is the king, and no one else is allowed to do this because the royal robe equals kingship. Xerxes' torn clothes therefore symbolize not only his personal misfortune and the defeat at Salamis, but might also indicate his loss of the empire, as the Chorus foresaw by suggesting there might be a rebellion against the central rule (584–97).[27] Atossa's focus on replacing the robe might therefore not only indicate being preoccupied with the misfortune of her son, but might also symbolize her continuing concern for Persia as a whole. At the same time, the tenor of her words and her immediate wish to obey Darius do indicate a more personal concern for her son. Hearing her words, one could justifiably wonder how, after all that has happened, could she possibly seriously mean that what upsets her most is that Xerxes' clothes are in tatters.[28] She herself dreamt this earlier (199)! With these words the political figure we have seen up to now, the proud representative of Persia's monarchy, the commander-in-chief who asserted her agency over the Messenger, who was concerned about the entire country, has vanished. On the face of it, we are presented a dwarfed version of the former imposing Queen. Here, she is a wife who obeys her husband's bidding. Until this point Aeschylus has not portrayed Atossa as a woman who was solely concerned with her family and its appearance. Nowhere until now was Atossa concerned with family alone, other than wanting the power to remain in the current royal hands.[29] Aeschylus has given Atossa political power and elevated her to a statesman's status in her dealings with the Chorus and the Messenger, but now he seems to forcefully return her to the embrace of her family, and she seems to accept this role. She is not a disruptive female figure as Clytemnestra will be: she knows how to yield to male power.[30] However, Aeschylus also allows her to have the last word. She will never appear in person as a mother consoling her son with the new clothes.[31]

By denying Atossa a final appearance at the end of the play to re-clothe Xerxes, Aeschylus denies political and moral rehabilitation to Xerxes after the young King's terrible defeat. The audience leaves Xerxes with his torn robes reliving his ignominy and symbolizing the crowning catastrophe of a crushing Persian defeat.[32] Had Atossa returned with new raiment, the debacle would have been in a way erased, with a promise of a new beginning. Xerxes would have been restored to his former status, as the politically savvy Darius had hoped.[33] With the play's ending, Xerxes remains tarnished and defamed: this is what the Athenian audience wanted to see, and what Aeschylus with brilliant dramaturgy delivered to them.[34]

In conclusion, Atossa is a woman with political power, but she is not subversive, as Aeschylus' Clytemnestra will be. Did Aeschylus mean to show that while in some cases a woman wielding political power could pose a threat to the established order, a woman who knows when to retreat to her traditional role should not be viewed as incapable of ruling? Although Atossa possesses some features of the future Clytemnestra, she also knows how to show the men around her that she excels in the trait they value most in women: obedience. It is Atossa's ability to appear obedient, yet retain an independent mind, that lies at the heart of her characterization. This is the source of her strength and the positivity of her persona. Although some of her characterization by Aeschylus can be seen as serving to flatter the ego of the audience, one can also deduce from her portrayal a general message about the Queen: she is a capable, resourceful, and intelligent woman who can tell when her son goes wrong. Even though she must have loved her son unconditionally, as a mother would,[35] she could not forgive his impetuousness and foolhardiness, and therefore chose to absent herself at the end.[36] The more positive her image is, as an obedient woman and wife, the more this absence undermines the standing of Xerxes, which is exactly what would have delighted the Athenian audience.

Notes

1 For a discussion on whether Aeschylus conceived the composition of this play as a historical duty and thus would try to stick to the facts, see Harrison (2000), 25–30.

2 The ghost of Darius somehow knows about these remaining forces (796–7, 800–4).
3 Torrance (2013), 234 with n. 174, discusses the split in the interpretation of the *Persians* between 'a patriotic celebration of Greek supremacy over the disgraced Persians, or a tragedy of profound *pathos* where the audience is asked to identify with its own mythological "historical" victims' (ibid.). Avery (1964), 173, suggests that Aeschylus wanted to glorify Athens, but also to make his contemporaries aware of the Persian power and potential for aggression in the future.
4 Hall explains the introduction of Atossa in two ways. In (1989), 95, she suggests that this evolved simply 'because it was a "law" of Greek ethnography that the more barbarian a community, the more powerful its women'. In (1993), 121, she suggests that this is part of Aeschylus' feminization of Persia. On the ethnographic view that Persia excelled in powerful women, see also Sancisi-Weerdenburgh (1983).
5 The statement echoes Themistocles' rebuttal of the taunt of the Corinthian Adeimantus who claimed that Themistocles has no right to take part in council because he was a man without a city. To this, Themistocles answered that the Athenians had both a city and country as long as they had 200 ships fully manned; for there were no Greeks who could beat them off (Herodotus 8.61).
6 Hall: 'the Asiatics of Greek poetry and art were invented by the Greek imagination' (1993: 108).
7 For the view that Aeschylus presents Atossa as an ignorant woman, see Garvie (2009), on 231. It should be stated that the name Atossa does not appear in the play, where she is addressed only as 'queen'. Various explanations were proposed; Wilamowitz (1914), on 159, for example, suggested that her name, undoubtedly known from Herodotus, was transferred from the scholia into the list of characters.
8 For the view that this display of ignorance underscores Atossa's helplessness and paints her as 'a respectable secluded matron rather than a woman experienced in public life', see McClure (2006), 82. Is that view dramatically credible though?
9 For the Chorus representing the Persian people and their tragedy, and Atossa as a representative of Xerxes' tragedy, see Garvie (2009), xxxiv–xxxv, 145 and *passim*.
10 Cf. Antigone's and Ismene's very brief appearance at the end of *Seven against Thebes* performed in 467 BCE.
11 Many view her as such. E.g. Broadhead (1960), xxvi, Alexanderson (1967), 9, and Dworacki (1979); Sancisi-Weerdenburg (1983), 24, sees her as 'a model of motherly care for her son Xerxes'. See also McClure (2006), n. 4.
12 Atossa bore four sons to Darius: Xerxes, Achemenes, Masistes and Hystaspes. Darius' sons are mentioned in plural by both Darius and Atossa (717, 754).
13 Both Persian men and women rend their robes in a sign of mourning (537–8); see Prickard (1917), line 199. Conacher (1974), 154, cf. 165, points

out 'the relation of raiment to Persian pride and Persian ruin' (199, 832–6, 846–51, 1030, 1060).
14 Cf. Moreau (1992–3), 46.
15 It seems misleading to interpret Atossa's words to the Chorus after hearing their positive interpretation of her dream and vision that they have 'found a good interpretation *for my son and all my family*' (226–7) as a proof for Atossa's narrow interest in her family's private matters with no regard to the Persians. Atossa responds here to the Elders' encouraging words, which mention the *polis* only once, while mentioning the good that will turn out for *her* three times, which she obviously understands as meaning her family (218–19, 222, 225). See, however, Dominick (2007), 437.
16 See Garvie (2009), on 185–6.
17 It may well be that the spectators understood her remark about the future as a reference to Plataea and knew that her prayers would not be fulfilled, but Atossa herself obviously could not know the future, as the ghost of Darius will in line 807.
18 For the three dramatic surprises in the play, see Garvie (1978), 67–71.
19 Wilamowitz-Moellendorff (1914), 44.
20 For a brief discussion and bibliography see Rabel (2014).
21 For the various explanations and bibliography, see Garvie (2009), lines 249–531.
22 Of course, Atossa wants to know whether her son is alive, as is usually assumed, e.g., Dworacki (1979), 104, but her general question is not necessarily the proof for this assumption.
23 Cf. Michelini (1982), 150.
24 733, 735, 737, 744, 750–1.
25 For considering these instructions of Atossa as an attempt at 'maternal characterization' by the playwright, see Broadhead (1960), xxxvii. Alexanderson (1967), 9, sees in Atossa's reply to Darius' directive also an attempt 'to characterize the queen: she has a mother's concern for her son'. Taplin (1977), 92–3, prefers to see Atossa's injunction to the Chorus as keeping the imminence of the defeated Xerxes' return in the spectators' minds, while 'characterization can be allowed, at most, an incidental function in these lines'. See, however, Conacher (1996), 34–5, for the objection to considering either the directions about Xerxes given by Atossa in 529–31 or Darius' injunction to Atossa at 837–8 as characterization devices. He explains her exit as dramatic convenience: she needs to make some preparations for Xerxes' return.
26 This is why Darius knows that his son must have torn his robes, not from the prophecy (739–52) as suggested by Dworacki (1979), 106 n. 8.
27 Cf. Taplin (1977), 121, who states that Xerxes' telling (upon recalling Salamis 1013) how he rent his clothes 'stresses the connection between Xerxes' robes and the whole state of Persia'. Cf. Avery (1964), 179. This is why Xerxes ought to appear in his rent clothes, to show the complete and devastating defeat of Persia. *Pace* those who doubt he would remain in his torn robes from

Salamis to Susa; for discussion of this view, see Alexanderson (1967), 6–7. Avery (1964), 182–3, suggests that Xerxes changes clothes in the middle of his return scene (1038), where Xerxes is in complete command of the situation. He no longer seems ashamed, and the Chorus meekly follow his commands. The clothes could have been brought by the Queen as a silent character. The purpose of this change of clothes is an intimation to the Athenians of the Persian revived power (see n. 3 above).

28 Taplin (1977), 94–8, sees these lines and Atossa's disappearance from the final scene as a possible 'clumsy dramaturgy' for which he suggests an emendation by moving 529–31 after 851.
29 *Pace* Schenker (1994), 287–9.
30 Cf. Foley: 'Despite her august status, she displays a largely traditional role in following male instructions and performing religious duties' (2003: 143–4).
31 For a summary of views on why Atossa does not appear in the last scene with Xerxes, see Dworacki (1979), 101–2. They range from dramatic necessity, with the consideration that the two roles of Xerxes and Atossa are played by the same actor, e.g., Anderson (1972), 174 n. 2; that there is no dramatic need for Atossa any longer, e.g., Wilamowitz (1914), 46; that the dignity and wisdom that Atossa has displayed throughout the play disqualify her from appearing in the disgraceful scene at the end, Taplin (1977), 120; that her absence 'is of no particular importance, however it has a dramatic value', e.g. Dworacki (1979), 101–8. For the view that once Xerxes arrives on stage, Atossa loses her dramatic relevance and thus disappears, see Garvie (1978), 68, and Schenker (1994), 290 and n. 26. See also more recent bibliography in McClure (2006), n. 52.
32 Cf. Garvie (1978), 69–70.
33 McClure (2006), 74, 79. At 95 compares the intended reclothing of Xerxes to Thetis' rearming of Achilles. She maintains however 'this finery does not embody Xerxes' *kleos* but rather represents a womanish attempt to cover up his disgrace'. I disagree with this statement. It is not Atossa's idea to re-robe him, but the command of Darius, and Atossa has already stated that Xerxes will not be accountable.
34 This view is somewhat concordant with McClure's (2006), 88, 93–6. However, she also thinks that Xerxes is effeminized both in Atossa's dream and at the last scene, among other things because of the use of the word *peplos* for Xerxes' attire; on the latter, see also Hall (1993), 19. It is unlikely that the spectators would necessarily associate the use of this word with femininity. Were it so, Xerxes would have not used it for his own robes, as he does in 1030. Indeed, *LSJ* s.v. *peplos* II.3 states that it is a less frequent term of *man's* robe, especially for a 'long Persian dress' (cf. Xenophon, *Cyropaidia* 3.1.13). Xerxes' clothes are interchangeably indicated by *peplos* (199, 468, 1030), *kosmos* (833), *esthēmata* (836, 848), *stolē* (1017). Furthermore, *peplos* is used for male garments on the tragic stage in other cases, for example for the robe in which Agamemnon dies (Aeschylus, *Agamemnnon* 1126), or the gown Deianeira sends Heracles (Sophocles, *Women of Trachis* 758).

35 Cf. Aristotle *Nicomachean Ethics* (viii.8.28–33), Aristotle states that a mother's love is especially valuable because it does not derive from self-interest.
36 Notice her cagy reply to Darius' injunction: 'and I'll try (*peirasomai*) to intercept my son' (850).

10

Theatrical Ghosts in *Persians* and Elsewhere

Anna Uhlig

Aeschylus' *Persians* begins with a striking juxtaposition of presence and absence. The chorus of Persian elders, assembled before the royal palace, declare themselves the loyal council of those Persians who have gone forth to campaign in Greece (1). The chorus, whose song the audience now hear, have remained and are present on behalf of those who are gone and no longer present. This simple assertion encodes the stage with a critical spatial binary – establishing the 'here' of the space conjured in the theatre against the 'there' of a distant land.

For nearly every Greek audience that Aeschylus might have imagined for his play, thinking of 'here' as the Persian capital would have represented an unsettling prospect. At the play's premiere, it would have required a perfect inversion of the audience perspective, since, for the assembled Athenian theatregoers, it is the 'here' of the play, the royal palace of Susa, that would have represented a faraway place of the imagination. By contrast, the unknown land 'toward the setting sun' would be the place that they call home. 'I'd like to find out,' Queen Atossa reflects almost rhetorically once she has made her way to the stage '– where is Athens?' (231). Such invocations of spatial dynamics establish the category of distance, and its changing perception from different perspectives, as one of the key themes of *Persians*.

The contrast with which the Persian elders introduce the play is not simply a question of geography. Or, rather, not a question of simple geography. It contains within it the seeds of a more complex notion of distance – of separation by means that are temporal and existential as well as spatial. The soldiers who have *gone* to Greece have not merely left Asia but, as Aeschylus' marked use of the Greek verb *oichomai* suggests, they have passed out of the land of the living; they are, in the colloquial sense, 'goners'.

The chorus' opening lines establish a parallelism between the literal geography of (what we would call) the 'historical' martial conflict between Greeks and Persians with that of (what we would call) the 'mythical' or 'religious' world of the dead. This connection – part metonymy, part allegory – is a crucial facet of this unusual play, since it permits Aeschylus to treat events recently experienced by himself and his fellow Athenians in a manner normally reserved for mythical narratives from the days of yore. In other words, to take what is temporally close and hold it at a remove. And nowhere is Aeschylus' fusion of the worlds of myth and history more strongly marked than when he brings the ghost of Xerxes' father, the dead king Darius, back to life.

The appearance of Darius on stage is something of a surprise; a 'coup de theatre'. As Taplin has underlined, despite the fact that 'Darius has been repeatedly named in the first half of the play, and called to mind as the one among the dead who may be particularly relevant to the present,'[1] the dead king's return still introduces an unexpected and unsettling element of the supernatural into an otherwise relatively realist drama.

In retrospect, of course, the ample foreshadowing of the play's spectral imagination is apparent. Darius' first significant introduction within the play comes in Queen Atossa's portentous dream, where he stands beside his son 'full of pity' when Xerxes is thrown from the chariot that he is unable to control (197–8). The chorus respond by urging Atossa to call upon the dead king for aid, outlining the very steps they themselves will later enact.

> ... pour libations
> to the earth and
> to the dead.
> Talk to your husband,
> gently, sympathetically –
> Darius
> (you tell us that you saw him
> in the night).
> Ask him to send
> good fortune
> from beneath the earth
> into the light ...
>
> 219–22

Later, when Atossa learns of her son's defeat at Salamis, she recognizes that the disaster foretold in her dream has come to fruition. But she holds fast to the chorus' advice and renews her intention to make offerings of food as 'a gift for Earth and for the dead' (523).

Atossa's preparations take her offstage while the chorus lament the great loss of Persian lives. When she returns, her instructions to the chorus are more explicitly necromantic than hitherto:

> So, friends, as I offer these libations to the dead, lend your support with solemn chanting. Summon up the ghost of Darius, while I pour these oblations for the soil to drink in honour of the gods beneath the earth.
>
> 619–22

The chorus comply, undertaking a virtuosic performance that succeeds in recalling Darius from the underworld into the light of day and the centre of the theatre.

The return of the dead king to his erstwhile kingdom is a rare concession granted by the gods of the underworld; a sign of the power that Darius is afforded even amongst the dead (691). In this regard, Darius marks a contrast with the countless fallen Persians whose deaths have ensured that they will never return to their homeland. The dead king's haunting presence is a metonym for the physical absence of the Persian troops from Aeschylus' drama, the 'departed' whom the chorus long to see. But Darius also presents us with an alternative to the other 'successful' revenants of *Persians*: the Messenger, whose dire report precipitated Darius' recall, and Xerxes, whose subsequent return to Persia will stand as a mark of the catastrophe that his expedition has brought upon the army and empire.[2]

The incommensurability of father and son, a critical theme throughout the play,[3] is repeatedly emphasized in the chorus' necromantic invocations and by Darius himself. The chorus praise Darius' unique excellence ('Persia's soil has never held another man like him' 645–6) and celebrate his avoidance of disaster, in contrast to his son ('he never caused destruction to his men through reckless catastrophic wars' 652–3).[4] Emerged back into the light, Darius expands upon the chorus' sentiments, cataloguing the royal lineage from which he descended in order to mark out the aberration of his son's martial defeat ('the greatest devastation ever to strike Susa since Lord Zeus ordained that one man should rule all Asia with its teeming flocks, and wield the sceptre of authority' 760–4).

The political consequence of Darius' posthumous pronouncements is a prohibition of future Persian campaigns against the Greeks (790–2). But, within the dynamics of Aeschylus' drama, the effect is felt in the resulting diminution of Xerxes when the defeated king finally makes his way onto the stage. Though still claiming his place amongst the living – one of the few 'departed' who is permitted a return – Xerxes appears as if already dead. The rags that disgrace his body (847–8; 1017) cover limbs that have lost their strength (913). The description of the latter, voiced by Xerxes himself, echoes the language used by the Homeric narrator to describe the limb loosening death of heroes in battle. So diminished, with the weight of countless dead upon him, Xerxes wishes that he too had died: 'Zeus!' he cries 'So many men gone! I only wish death's destiny had shrouded me with them!' (914–17). Even more than his father, who still retains his power and regal nobility in death, Xerxes is a ghostly figure within the theatre.

It is through the combination of these two spectral bodies, father and son, that the play is able to conjure into presence the great loss of life with which it is ultimately concerned. Following the success of the chorus' necromancy, the solitary arrival of Xerxes, shrouded in failure and haunted by his absent troops, sparks a dirge that will comprise the remainder of the play. In contrast to the chorus' earlier invocation of Darius, their subsequent song of lament finds response only in the paired lament of Xerxes himself. The ruined king entreats the chorus to 'look at me now - *oioi*- and weep' (931). And so they do, singing that they will greet his homecoming with

> a lamentation
> > fraught
> > > with evil omen
> >
> > fraught
> > > with evil destiny
>
> 935–40

The news of the defeat has been known since the Messenger's arrival, but the chorus are only now moved to full-fledged lament as they behold their defeated king, returned home in rags. Yet it is not for him alone that their mourning voices are lifted. The ruin of Xerxes' regal appearance – 'so little left out of so very much' the chorus will observe – serves as a proxy for the massive loss of life that he has caused.

The chorus' song looks beyond the man standing before them to catalogue the men whose day of return has been lost.

> where are the rest
> > of all our friends and
>
> where are those
> > who stood
> > by you
>
> men such as
> > Pharandakes
> > Susas
> > Pelagon and
> > Dotamas and
> > Agdabatas
> > Psammis and
> > Susiscanes
> > > who set out
> > > from Ecbatana
>
> 956–61

where is
> Pharnuchus and
> brave Ariomardus

where is
> the lord Seualces
> noble Lilaeus
> Mephis
> Tharubis and
> Masistras
> Artembares and
> Hystaechmas

967–72

In naming those who have perished far from home, the chorus inscribe the theatre with an unseen landscape of loss. The complexity of distance first sketched in the play's opening song is now definitively mapped onto the geography of death, in which departure has significance beyond mere spatial separation.

It has often been noted that the chorus' listing of the dead, like that of the Messenger before them (302–30), echoes both the catalogues of Homeric epic and Athenian war dead, both of which would have been quite familiar to a fifth-century Athenian theatre audience. And yet, the rhythmic, almost incantatory patterning of foreign sounding names would have struck a Greek audience as quite distinct from the types of catalogues they were accustomed to hearing. And, in this regard, there is an undeniable flavour of necromancy to the chorus' invocation of Persian dead. The chorus cannot fathom that their dead soldiers have not made their way back; are not *revenants* like their king Xerxes, or their king Darius.

> I'm stunned
> I'm stunned
> that they're not
> > here now
> > in your entourage
> > behind your
> > covered carriage.

1000–1

These men are truly 'gone', as both Xerxes and the chorus are quick to assert. There is only so much that theatre can blur the line between living and dead.

Paradoxically, this insight into the irreversibility of departure in death – the lesson of unmitigated sorrow which is conveyed through the chorus' mourning – is made palpable only through its flagrant denial earlier in the play. Unlike other tragedies, in which the lives of individual heroes trace the boundaries of human emotion, *Persians* seeks to comprehend mass human suffering on a heroic scale. To do so, it asks us to see what is 'here' as predicate to what is 'there'; to recognize that, like distance, loss can only be rendered comprehensible when it is measured against what remains. Darius' presence in *Persians*, like that of his son, invites us to contemplate the nature and cost of return; to gauge our desire for those who are absent against the harrowing spectacle of the one who has been summoned *back*. It is hardly a coincidence that, after all their work to raise him, the chorus cannot bring themselves to address Darius once he has arisen (694–702). In this respect, it is Darius' return that transforms *Persians* from simple Athenian political propaganda into a profound meditation on the limits of human understanding and the boundlessness of our suffering.

The puzzle of how these two Persian kings – one dead yet returned amongst the living, one living yet bound to the dead – both delineate and confuse the boundary between life and death within Aeschylus' play is itself a distillation of a more general question that tragedy poses to its audience: how can the exalted lives lived out in the theatre represent the experiences of those in the audience whose exploits are far less lofty but whose emotions are no less keenly felt. For ancient Greek audiences, especially those in Athens, watching this play in the years following the defeat of Xerxes' forces, the challenge of identification would be particularly pointed. Rather than present simple equivalences, Aeschylus plunges the theatre ever deeper into uncertainty. The relationship played out by the two kings on the stage offers a doubled perspective on the fraught relationship between actor and spectator, presence and absence; as so often, tragedy compounds one uncertainty by exposing another.

It is the return of Darius that prompts us to consider this play of past and present, dead and living; that brings these questions palpably into presence. And yet, from another perspective, Darius' presence within the theatre is the very thing that renders him, and the play of which he is a part, most distant; for it is Darius' unusual ability to return, both as a ghost and as a ghost on stage, that situates him in a 'here' that is markedly theatrical, a space that is distinct from the world outside of dramatic conventions. To return to life through the particular necromancy of dramatic re-enactment is to partake, albeit in a somewhat different fashion, in the immortal fame after which all heroic warriors seek. In this regard, the theatrically charged appearance of Darius' ghost in *Persians* is matched by similarly conspicuous revenants elsewhere in Aeschylus' extant works.

Most familiar to modern audiences is the apparition of Clytemnestra's ghost, calling for the Furies to avenge her murder at the beginning of *Eumenides,* the third play in Aeschylus' *Oresteia* trilogy. In certain respects, Clytemnestra's return in *Eumenides* presents us with a striking contrast to that of Darius. Rather than serving as the centrepiece of the play, arriving after elaborate incantations, the ghost of Clytemnestra is a self-generating presence whose early appearance on stage is the catalyst for the subsequent action of the play. Unlike the relatively passive Darius, she acts, as Robert Cioffi has observed, as a kind of 'chthonic chorêgos' on the tragic stage, directing those around her in accordance with her plans for vengeance.[5] Darius may have power in the underworld, but his role in *Persians* is to prophesy and advise. Clytemnestra, by contrast, is still possessed of her own agency, wielding sway within the theatre much as she did in the trilogy's two earlier plays, while still in living form.

Yet, for all of the dissimilarities between the two revenants, there is a certain common ground demarcated by the embodied presence of both of these figures within their respective dramas. Although they are distinguished in their particulars, both of these ghosts call attention to the unsettling nature of dramatic re-enactment and its uncanny ability to conjure the past into presence.[6] For a modern reader of ancient tragedy, it can be easily forgotten that drama (still a relatively new type of performance in Aeschylus' time) uses actors in costumes and masks to bring bodies from the mythical and historical past back – back to presence, back to life – within the conjured world of the theatre.

The Clytemnestra of *Eumenides* is 'dead'; like Darius, she is present in a spectral form that transcends the normal limits of human ability. In this regard, her 'return' to the stage marks a contrast with her husband (and murder victim) Agamemnon, who did not appear on stage in the trilogy's second play, *Libation Bearers,* despite an extended necromantic *kommos* invoking his aid in that play's revenge plot. But the Clytemnestra of *Eumenides* is also, markedly, a contrast with her own former self. In her condemnation of the Furies, she points to the ways that her body has been disfigured by her son's violence (*Eum.* 103), simultaneously calling attention to the fact of her murder and the insistent presence of her body in the theatre, in seeming contradiction of her death.[7]

This blurring this blurring of life and death is hardly limited to the *Oresteia* trilogy's final play. We might also note that Clytemnestra's murder was accomplished by someone thought to be dead; as Clytemnestra is herself informed 'the dead are killing the living' (*Choe.* 886). Likewise, in *Agamemnon,* Cassandra is able to perceive (through sight, hearing, and smell) the dead of the past as well as her own imminent demise. If, as Cassandra is well aware and

Clytemnestra makes manifest, the 'living' bodies of the stage are little more than placeholders for the dead bodies that they will soon become (displayed like trophies on the ekkyklema), then these living characters are distinguished from their future ghostly selves only by the time at which they appear.[8] Moreover, from the perspective of the audience – who look towards the spectacle of tragic drama as if to a time machine – the mythical heroes from days of yore are all long dead, brought back to life in the theatre through the bodies of actors trained to function as vessels for actions that are not their own.

Fragments of other Aeschylean dramas suggest that the playwright populated the theatre of Dionysus with ghosts on other occasions as well. The clearest example, and the most fulsome embrace, of spectral drama in the surviving fragments comes from the aptly titled *Necromancers* (*Psychagogoi*). The play is a dramatization of Odysseus' journey to the underworld, the so-called *nekyia* of Homer's *Odyssey*, in which the wayward hero seeks insight into his future from the long-dead prophet Tiresias. The few fragments that remain of Aeschylus' *Necromancers* suggest that the action of the play lived up to its ghostly title, with a chorus instructing Odysseus in the proper rituals for summoning the dead – including the possible slaughter of a live animal on stage (fragment 273a Radt) – as well as, one imagines, supplying incantatory prayers similar to those of the *Persians* chorus.

The fragments of *Necromancers* do not tell us which spirits Aeschylus allowed Odysseus to meet with, beyond that of Tiresias. It is possible that he encountered a parade of dead,[9] from his own past and from the time before his birth, as Homer so vividly depicts in the *Odyssey*. But even if they do not confirm such a panoply of spectres, the fragments hint that Odysseus' own mortality – the ghost that he will soon become – played an important role in Aeschylus' drama. In a fragment recording a portion of Tiresias' prophecy, Odysseus is warned that he will die from the sting of a sea-creature, which will 'rot his aged and balding skin' (fragment 275 Radt). The description of Odysseus' future body, decaying as a result of age and the sea-creature's venom, strikes a note of contrast with the virile and hirsute body that (we must imagine) he inhabited on the Aeschylean stage. Through his prophecy, the ghostly Tiresias thus conjures – in words if not in body – the form that Odysseus will take when he once again approaches the threshold between living and dead; the very location which Aeschylus has asked the theatre to represent.

Another, even more fragmentary Aeschylean drama entitled *Weighing of Spirits (Psychostasia)* hints at a more central and confounding presence of ghosts on stage. Almost nothing of Aeschylus' text remains, but ancient discussions of the play make clear that the 'spirits' in question are those of Achilles and Memnon, two heroes of the Trojan War, though on opposing sides, and both sons of goddesses. Before their encounter on the battlefield,

Zeus undertook a literal weighing of their spirits to determine which of these mortal fighters would live and which would die.[10]

Although one might first presume that the 'spirits' of the play did not correspond to embodied actors on the stage, some ancient evidence suggests that the warriors might, in fact, have been represented by actors as ghostly apparitions. In describing the spectacular elements of the play, the ancient scholar Pollux describes not only how Zeus and the other gods were arrayed on the *theologion* above the stage, but how the goddess Eos employed the theatre's crane (*mechane*) to 'snatch the body' of her son Memnon (4.130). The meaning of this detail is far from certain, but it may suggest that the 'spirits' being weighed in the play were portrayed as bodies neither fully living nor yet dead. Such an inference is further supported by Plutarch's inclusion of this play in a discussion of implausible poetic depictions of the underworld.[11]

If Aeschylus did, indeed, include the 'spirits' of Memnon and Achilles amongst the *dramatis personae* of *Weighing of Spirits*, the effect would be an even more exaggerated version of the temporal uncertainty we have seen Aeschylus explore through his other ghostly apparitions. With both heroes of *Weighing of Souls* still 'alive', their future ghostly forms would appear on the stage so that the gods could determine which would cross permanently into the world of spectres sooner. Ultimately, both men must take their place amongst the shades of the underworld, but the play centres on the moments before that transition, when each must offer a preview to ensure that the timing is right.

Viewed in concert with these other Aeschylean revenants, Darius' ghostly appearance in *Persians* can be understood to form part of a broader program on the part of the playwright to explore the distinctive spatio-temporal properties of dramatic re-enactment. Ghosts, insofar as their presence is always out of step with those around them, call attention to the way that all bodies in the theatre claim a presence that is in some way out of time and place, standing at a distance from the 'here and now' with which the audience are themselves familiar.

Necromantic and otherwise spectral elements continued to be employed by tragic playwrights after Aeschlyus' death, such as in Sophocles' *Polyxena* or Euripides' *Hecuba*. But it was in the comic theatre that the connection between ghosts and the haunting produced by dramatic 'returns' was most exuberantly explored. On the comic stage, it was the playwrights themselves who returned in ghostly form to contemplate the fate of their city and its theatre after their deaths.

The most famous of these hauntings, in fact, coincides with what is often considered the founding text of scholarship on Athenian tragedy:

Aristophanes' *Frogs*. In the hands of the comic playwright, the shades of the two dead tragedians compete for the underworld 'chair' in tragedy: an honour amongst the dead not unlike those claimed by Darius and desired by Clytemnestra. The importance of the underworld setting of *Frogs* can easily be underestimated. The playwrights are dead, after all; where else should the drama be set? But the significance of the location, and more pointedly of the spectral appearance of the duelling playwrights, is evident when one considers the frequency with which other comic playwrights 'brought back' dead from Athens' recent past or the fact that *Frogs* was not the first time that Aeschylus 'returned' to the theatre in the form of a comic ghost.[12]

It is in the light of such later, more explicit reflections on the connections between ghosts and theatre that we might reconsider the terminology of 'necromancy' (*psychagogia*) employed by Aeschylus to describe the lamentations by which the chorus are able to raise Darius (687).[13] At some point, whether before or after Aeschylus' time we cannot say, the Greek term for necromancy came to be applied to the powerful effect that theatre could have on its audience. So, in Aristotle's *Poetics*, the philosopher notes that the plot (*muthos*) of a tragedy has the power to 'necromance' (*psychagogein*) and that the visually spectacular elements of tragic drama (*opsis*) represent a distinctively necromantic (*psychagogikon*) 'facet of the form'.[14] In this latter detail, we can perhaps detect the influence of the 'coup de theatre' of Darius' unexpected arrival on stage and its exaggerated celebration of drama's ability to bring the dead back to life. By setting the ghostly appearance of Darius within this broader frame, we are able to appreciate how this tragedy – so unlike the majority of others that have been preserved down to our day – contributed to one of the most exciting ancient theorizations of theatre production.

But it is not only ancient theorists who are drawn to the link between ghosts and drama. In recent years, theorists of contemporary theatre and performance have been developing a 'necromantic' outlook not dissimilar to that of the ancients. In his influential work *The Haunted Stage*, Marvin Carlson has argued that 'everything in the theatre, the bodies, the materials utilized, the language, the space itself, is now and has always been haunted, and that haunting has been an essential part of the theatre's meaning to and reception by its audiences in all times and places'.[15] Carlson's 'haunting', as he himself would undoubtedly recognize, can be seen as the far-removed progeny of Aristotle's tragic 'necromancy' and of Aeschylus' as well. The haunted theatre that Aeschylus envisaged through the revenants of his stage continues to be practiced to this day. Perhaps never more so than when we bring his ancient dramas back to life.

Notes

1. Taplin (1977), 114–15 who discusses possible staging in detail.
2. On Xerxes' guilt, see the excellent discussion of Hopman (2009), 365–8.
3. Saïd (1981) and Griffith (1999).
4. Darius' own martial failures are all but forgotten in Aeschylus' drama.
5. Cioffi (2015).
6. I explore the connection between ghosts and theatrical re-enactment in greater detail in Uhlig (2019).
7. So, recently Worman (2021) argues that Clytemnestra inhabits a place between living and dead.
8. Their 'hour upon the stage', as Shakespeare would later put it.
9. This seems to be the implication of the term 'swarm' in fragment 273a Radt, so Mikellidou (2016).
10. On the theme of weighing the dead in Aeschylean theatre, see Rehm (2016).
11. *How to Study Poetry* 17a, on which see Hunter and Russell (2011), 92–3.
12. On comic ghosts, see Story (2003), 123; on Aeschylus in comedy, see Hanink and Uhlig (2016), 51–3.
13. This may be the scene praised by Dionysus in a difficult to interpret line of Aristophanes *Frogs* (1028).
14. Hunter (2009), 37, and Bassi (2017),144–9.
15. Carlson (2001), 15.

11

Words and Pictures

Carmel McCallum Barry

Aeschylus' *Persians* is the earliest Greek tragedy surviving to us and in modern times has often been regarded as static and unstructured with no action and no focal point; there are as many interpretations as there are critics. However, the judges of the dramatic competition in 472 BC awarded it first prize as they did his other extant plays, so what could make it enthralling and exciting for the huge audience in the theatre of Dionysus?

This was an audience of listeners, as well as spectators, in a society where the spoken word was the principal way to communicate ideas. Aeschylus was born towards the end of the Archaic period and poetry had traditionally been the medium for airing important opinions about politics (e.g. Solon, Alcaeus), life and love (e.g. Sappho, Mimnermus), even invective (Hipponax). Verse was more compact than prose speech, as well as being pleasantly rhythmical to hear and remember.

Critical judgments closer to his own time can give some clues about what made Aeschylus successful. The comic poet Aristophanes at the end of the fifth century parodies some typical features of Aeschylus' dramatic style (as well as that of Euripides) in his play *Frogs* (405 BC), where Dionysus, the patron god of drama, goes down to the underworld to take back the recently dead Euripides to Athens because he misses his smart and clever plays. There Dionysus is made to judge a contest between Aeschylus (d. 456 BC) and Euripides over who has the best claim to the throne of tragedy in the world of the dead, currently occupied by Aeschylus. As the two poets prepare for battle the chorus inform the audience that words will be the weapons here (814–21). The opponents criticize specific aspects of each other's style of construction and versification until it is decided (1365–8) to bring in a set of scales and weigh individual lines, each man in turn choosing one of his verses to say into the scales! Aeschylus naturally wins this section of the contest because his words are more imposing and weighty, just as the chorus described him earlier 'first of the Greeks to build up towers of portentous words to adorn his tragic babble' (1005–6). Aristophanes makes fun of the typical features of both dramatists, in characterization, staging and language.

In Aeschylus' case (Euripides is the speaker) he targets his unusual words, strange compounds and the predominance of warlike themes in his plays, as well as characters who come on stage and stay silent. Naturally Aeschylus ridicules aspects of Euripides' works in turn. Dionysus cannot decide between the two because he likes both, but eventually chooses Aeschylus because he wants to bring back the poet who can give the best advice to the city and also make sure that the city can continue to put on plays (1419–21). At this time, Athens was in crisis and close to defeat in the war with Sparta, and the god's decision is one based on the old fashioned values that he says the dramas of Aeschylus can encourage, so on moral rather than on literary grounds.

The contest of words (literary criticism made fun) occupies almost half of the play and its success as comedy depends on the audience's recognition of the use of metre and language by both poets and of popular lines, otherwise no one would find it funny. We have no other complete comedies apart from those of Aristophanes, but fragments show that literary topics were used frequently by other comic poets so audience recognition remained important

One other (non-comedic) work that should be considered is Aristotle's more scholarly examination of tragedy in his *Poetics* in the middle of the fourth century, when tragedy was still being written and performed, and with access to critical thinking and other assessments on tragedy that are now lost to us. Aristotle takes a scientific and philosophical approach in his observations on tragic poetry, defining it (as imitation) and analysing its important elements (development, construction, performance and language). He sees a progression in its development, beginning from choral song performance, with new elements gradually being introduced until it reaches its familiar form in the fifth century. Only epic and tragic poetry are serious or worthwhile (*spoudaios*), as they depict worthy men and their actions (not menials or absolute villains) and his primary focus is on the Attic tragedians and on Homer, who made his imitations not only good but dramatic (Ch 4 1448a).

Aristotle tells us that Aeschylus was the first to bring on a second actor and reduce the role of the chorus so as to make speech the main element ('the leading role'), that Sophocles added a third actor and introduced scene painting. His brisk summary of the development of tragedy suggests that Aeschylus was an innovator at an early stage in the formation of this genre, which was changing and accepting new elements during the fifth century. Aristotle lists the essential components of tragedy as plot, character, style, spectacle, thought and song (Ch 6 1450a), and for him plot structure is most important.

This essay will focus on the two elements of style (*lexis*) and spectacle (*opsis*), which are closely connected in Aeschylean drama. Aristotle says very little about them in *Poetics* and seems to have little interest in them, but is more forthcoming when dealing with prose style in his *Rhetoric* where he is concerned with how an orator (*rhetor*) can be effective. An orator must compose his speech and delivery so as to bring events and places 'before the eyes' (*pro tōn ommatōn* 1411b), that is he must prompt the audience to visualize in their minds what they cannot see physically in front of them. Oratory, whether political, in the public assembly, or in the law courts is after all another form of acting performance where one must keep the audience's attention and good will.

Spectacle (*opsis*) denotes sight, both what we see and how we see it, and a dramatist must encourage his listeners to 'see' (make a picture of) what is sung or narrated before them. That this is possible without any theatrical aids is attested by Plato who was so well aware of the power of poetry that he banned it from his ideal city, except for hymns to the gods. In his short dialogue *Ion*, the rhapsode Ion is interrogated by Socrates about his skills. A rhapsode was a professional reciter of poetry (here Homer) at public festivals and games around the Greek world, who recited in front of large audiences for prizes. Under questioning, he tells Socrates that when he recites a pathetic passage his eyes fill with tears, when he recites something terrifying his hair stands on end and his heart pounds – 'what about the audience?' asks Socrates. 'I can see them from my stand, weeping or looking fierce, as the case may be,' replies Ion.

Most important for Aeschylus in stimulating the visual imagination of the audience is his choice of words, that will create rich mental images and provide the scene painting. He uses flashbacks to past action and the linguistic devices that Euripides later ridicules in *Frogs*, such as strange exotic names, ornate compounds, long speeches and bold metaphors. We know that there was no scenery so the few visual aids available to him – costume, props, the movement of actors and chorus – are all made to work with the words towards the audience's vision. Listening was the audience's role in the drama if they were to appreciate and enjoy it, and they were accustomed to pay attention to the words and translate words into images. Aeschylus also liked to reinforce the words with visible and often startling stage effects.

When *Persians* was produced in 472 BC Aeschylus had been presenting plays for some time; his first entry in the dramatic competition was in 499 BC and his first victory in 484 BC, so he had been able to observe the reception of his and other dramatists' works by the audience and judges at the festival of the City Dionysia, and knew what would be popular. An earlier invasion of Greece in 490 BC during the reign of Xerxes' father, Darius, had been defeated by a mainly Athenian force at Marathon. Aeschylus himself had fought in the battle, so he and his contemporaries were familiar with Persians in their world. Not many tragedies were composed on non-mythical subjects but the Persian Wars had already assumed the feel of heroic myth.

Throughout *Persians*, the chorus provide the main emotional power. In their lyrics they reflect on what has been said or reported and speculate on what is to come and create a mood or atmosphere around the protagonists' usually more measured speeches (Xerxes later is an exception). The chorus deliver the first words of the play as they stride on chanting, to set the scene. They are old men, left behind as guardians of the royal palace 'rich in gold', (*poluchrusos* 8) when the younger men went to war. The wealth as well as the power of the Persian empire is part of their picture, even the army gleams with gold. They break off briefly to mention their anxiety because there has been no news of the army, before resuming their account of the departure. The huge extent of the empire is evoked in the lists of commanders with strange names from faraway cities and they prompt listeners to visualize the hordes of men on foot, on horseback, in chariots and in ships, all eager 'to cast the yoke of slavery on Greece' (50). The image of the yoke as a symbol of violent compulsion appears twice in this opening song because the army has crossed the Hellespont by 'a yoke cast on the ocean's neck' (72). It is a key image for Aeschylus in establishing the character of Persian rule and contrasting it with Greek freedom. Even though the army is irresistible and the king is warlike they are still worried: what if . . . ? Aeschylus gives their feelings an emotional emphasis using a bold compound word of the kind parodied by Aristophanes, literally, 'my heart dressed in a black tunic is torn apart' ('my mind is dark with fear' 115). The mood of dark misery continues as they think of the women left behind; wives and new brides are left desolate in empty beds, in the city of Kissia the women tear their fine robes in distress, Persia is empty of men (120–36). The elders sit down to think, wondering has the Persian army conquered ('the drawn bow' 147), or the Greek ('the sharp pointed spear' 147)?

Queen Atossa, Xerxes' mother is approaching and the chorus prostrate themselves and greet her obsequiously. Her appearance picks up all the themes in the previous chorus lines; she too is worried, and echoes their musings on the precariousness of royal wealth in gold. She is anxious for her son, for if things go wrong the common people may not be willing to obey their king. Atossa is especially disturbed by a dream she had the previous night in which she saw her son trying to control a chariot with two women yoked to pull it. One of the women wore Persian dress and was blithely submissive to the yoke, the other, a Greek, fought against it. As they struggled, Xerxes lost control and was thrown from the chariot, an unsettling picture. Xerxes saw that his father Darius was watching this happen and in shame tore his royal robes. In the morning, as the queen made offerings to the gods she saw an eagle, the king of birds, attacked by a hawk, a much smaller bird. Both her amazing dream vision and the familiar bird omens are profoundly disturbing and introduce the idea that a powerful force could be defeated by a smaller, an idea that an Athenian audience could easily accept as a people that had banished tyrants and then repelled the first Persian invasion at the Battle of Marathon.

The chorus try to reassure the queen and advise her to give offerings to the gods and to her dead husband to ask for good fortune for Xerxes (preparing for the appearance of Darius later) (219–23). Atossa then asks them about Athens, where it is, have they many men and much gold, who is their supreme ruler. Critics have commented on this strange ignorance, but her questions serve to strengthen the contrast between the Greek and Persian states, as Greeks are free, and do not acknowledge a supreme ruler. Her second question on Greek fighting methods reintroduces (from 147) the difference between bowmen who fire from a distance and armed men who fight at close quarters, both of which will be relevant when listening to the messenger's numbing report of Persian misfortunes.

The messenger enters, and immediately announces that Persian wealth and prosperity have been destroyed at one blow, the flower of their young warriors have fallen, perished. He continues with a longer account, the first part dealing with the naval battle around the island of Salamis, in which the Athenian ships played a large part. He begins with five two-line pieces of information that give an overview of the scene and the chorus respond in lyrics with laments and wails of misery. He stresses that he was an eye witness, inviting the audience to see it with him. Most striking is the news (272–3) that the waters and shores around Salamis are filled with the bodies of Persians who died in the battle and in responding the chorus easily provide their own vivid picture of corpses floating in the water with their full Persian robes drifting around them (lit. 'wandering', 274–7). Since the ships were packed tightly in the narrow channels Persian soldiers were helpless, unable to use their bows and their ships were broken up by the enemy rams.

Atossa has been silent since the messenger's entry but now tells him 'Compose yourself' (295) and asks for more details, wanting to know which of the leaders died in the battle, avoiding a direct question about her son. She is reassured that Xerxes is alive, which brings a bright day after a dark night and recalls her words earlier that the presence of the king 'lights the palace with his presence' (169). The messenger begins his account of the casualties, listing the fallen commanders by name with a short but vivid picture of each man and how he died, to prompt the audience to 'see' them. Dadakes was hit by a spear and made a dainty leap from his ship (305); Matallos' bushy ginger beard changed colour when he fell into the blood-filled water (316–17).

Atossa wants to know how big the Greek fleet was that it could disable the huge Persian force. Numbers made no difference, he says, even though the Greeks had only three hundred ships whereas the Persians had at least one thousand. It is a reminder of her dream where the eagle was torn apart by a hawk, a great king's strength overcome by a smaller force. When the queen asks how the battle began the messenger begins the longest part of his report, a tour de force on the part of the actor (perhaps Aeschylus himself).

The action lasts a full day from the night before the battle until the end of the next day, and is marked by images of the sunset, darkness and brilliant dawn. The messenger's detailed account of the engagement could hardly fail to stir the audience to visualize the scene as many of them must have taken part in the battle eight years before and told and retold the story to others (as old sailors do). Xerxes was tricked into believing that the Greeks would try escape overnight, so he arranged his ships in the narrows to trap them, warning that if the Greeks did get away then all his ship commanders would be beheaded, adding more colour to the picture of an absolute ruler. The night passed with no movement from the Greek fleet, but as soon as the brilliant day spread over the earth a loud clear shout came from the Greeks, as they rowed on at speed. The scene is full of noise, a trumpet urges them on, they sing a battle hymn (paean) and someone shouts patriotic encouragement, 'Onwards, sons of the Greeks, free your country, free your children, your wives, the graves of your fathers ...' (402–5). The sequence of events is vivid and exciting, we can imagine a very emotional audience. The large numbers of Persian ships, crowded in the narrow channels, were vulnerable when the more agile Greek force surrounded them and attacked. It would take little effort to visualize the scenes of carnage, the sea covered with upturned ships and bodies. The vocabulary is brutal, direct and familiar; men who fall overboard are speared and gutted with splintered oars, like fish (413–27). Atossa responds to his gruesome account with a lament maintaining the nautical theme, 'a great sea of troubles has broken over the Persians' (433–4), but there is yet more disaster to be told. The élite Persian troops whom Xerxes had stationed on the little island of Psyttaleia, supposedly to kill any Greek survivors, were surrounded and trapped by Greek hoplites landing from the mainland who attacked them with stones and arrows, then butchered them like animals. Once more the language is violent and brutal (*kreokopeō*, cut up meat, 463).

Xerxes was watching the battle from Mount Aegaleos on the mainland and when he saw the disastrous events he screamed (465, 468), tore his robes and rushed away with his land forces. The messenger reports more briefly on the fate of those who were left. The ships sailed away and many of the foot soldiers died of hunger and thirst on the trek back through northern Greece.

Aeschylus here displays his fondness for geographical detail in describing the route of the retreat. Many more men were lost in Thrace when they were crossing the frozen River Strymon. Some, including the messenger, were able to cross, but the ice began to melt as the sun came up and 'made a passage through the middle' (505). It is easy to picture the men falling into the icy water. Those who died quickly were fortunate, and only a few survive to come home. The gods, as in every other particular, are hostile to Persia.

The queen leaves to bring offerings for the gods and for her dead husband Darius to ask them to send good fortune in the future. When she goes, the chorus sing a dirge which is an emotional, disconnected version of the information in the messenger's speeches. It recalls the miseries suffered so far, the countless dead and the women weeping and mourning for the men who will not return. As earlier, they sing of women tearing their veils, grief stricken and longing to see their husbands and enjoy the soft sheets of the marriage bed. They blame Xerxes: because of him, the land of Asia is now empty of men (548–9); he led them away to die and drown in the waters of Salamis. Their final thought is that now the people will speak freely against the king when the 'yoke of power has been loosed' (594).

This emotional lament mirrors themes introduced in their entrance song and in the messenger scene. Most prominent are the many references that point to the differences between the Greek and Persian way of life, which are elaborated with more details as the play continues.

When Atossa returns her appearance is markedly different from that of her first entrance when she appeared as a symbol of royal power, in a chariot, wearing rich clothing and adornments. Then she was greeted by the chorus, who prostrated themselves before her as 'the light from the eyes of the gods', now she is shaken and afraid, she comes on foot with no royal trappings and there is no mention of chorus prostration. On this appearance she represents the defeat and failure of Persian power, what we see is the visual confirmation of the messenger's verbal report.

She is carrying offerings suitable for giving to the dead and the gods below and she orders the chorus to call up the spirit of Darius. Their ritualistic incantation is strange and unsettling; in keeping with Aeschylus' frequent use of unusual effects. They call upon the dead king, 'do you hear me?' and upon the deities of the underworld in turn, 'allow him to come to me'. They sing his praises, too, as a beloved king who did not destroy armies; they beg him to appear in his royal clothing, yellow slippers and tiara, presenting a striking picture of how a Persian king should be dressed, before we see Xerxes arrive in rags. The rhythm of their song is like a litany, with short prayer like lines and frequent repetition. The chorus behaviour is bizarre, as we learn from Darius himself when he appears. 'the earth groans, is beaten, torn up' (683) and 'you are lamenting, calling on me piteously, shrieking with spirit raising cries' (*psychagōgois goois* 686-8). The sight of their movements as they stamp and scratch at the ground, and the noise of their crying and wailing would be shocking for an Athenian audience, for whom such behaviour was unthinkable, since in Athens public lamentation was only done by women. However, it is sufficient to awaken the dead, for Darius appears, the first ghost in extant Greek tragedy. The chorus are afraid to speak, so he asks Atossa to say why they have summoned him from below the earth.

The queen tells him about Xerxes' expedition, his bridging of the Hellespont and how most of the great army and naval force has been destroyed. In their exchange Darius and Atossa emphasize the totality of the disaster, with many compound words formed from Greek *pās* ('completely, all, wholly'). As did the chorus, Darius blames Xerxes for the disasters. No previous king caused such grief for the Persians.

The chorus now have courage to speak and take over from Atossa, asking Darius how to act. His advice is never to invade Greece again and he tells them that even the forces now left in Greece will be slaughtered the following year in the battle at Plataea. Persian misfortune and suffering will be punishment for their impious and violent behaviour towards the gods (*hubris*) because Xerxes bridged the divine waters of the Hellespont and in Greece the army desecrated temples and shrines of the gods, looting their riches. The lesson is that men should not desire, 'lust after' other men's riches (826) and in doing so, lose their own. It is a strongly moral sermon against violence and impiety towards gods and men, for which Zeus will punish them (808-28). Darius' final words are more prosaic, but not for a king; he knows that Xerxes has torn his royal robes, so before he returns to the world below, he tells Atossa to bring clothing suitable for a king. The dire prophecies delivered by her dead husband are agonizing for Atossa, but the news that Xerxes is dishonoured by having ragged clothing causes her most distress, so she leaves to collect royal clothes for him. Once more the chorus sing the glories of the Persian Empire under Darius who conquered many cities, ruled wisely and brought his armies home safe again. Aeschylus takes the opportunity for a geographical catalogue, as they list the cities and islands around the Aegean that Darius brought under Persian rule, many of them Greek settlements, which had been freed by the time that *Persians* was produced.

At last Xerxes enters, returning from war, not as his father did, but lamenting for himself and the men he has lost. Even more so than Atossa he is an image of fallen power, he is in rags and in a curtained carriage (lit. 'wheeled tent') instead of a war chariot, without any symbols of royalty, he is not even properly armed. They begin the *kommos*, a dirge sung between an actor and the chorus (931) 'the longest and wildest in extant Greek tragedy' (Hall 1996: 169). Xerxes first commands attention, 'Look at me', ordering the chorus to wail and cry with him. His words are allusive and his version of the sea battle is impressionistic and emotional, 'Ionian Ares robbed me with his fences of ships, cutting through the plain of the night sea and the fatal shore' (950–4). The chorus respond with cries of grief 'Oioioi', and they ask where are the various commanders of the army, calling them by their strange exotic names, names which make up the major part of the poetic lines. To each query, Xerxes answers with news of their deaths (955–1001).

Their last question leads to Xerxes himself and his appearance, 'there are others missing, why are they not following your carriage?', referring to the high-ranking men who would serve as the king's royal escort, but they too are dead (992–1002). Xerxes now takes over, and shows them and the audience his final disgrace. 'Do you see what I have left?' (1017), he makes them look at the royal robes he has torn into shreds, he shows them his empty quiver, he does not even have his bow. So, the symbol of Persian fighting strength is useless, with no defences when both men and weapons are lost. What the audience see completes the words of the previous scenes. After this demonstration the laments become more frantic, they sing short staccato lines punctuated with shrill cries and wails, with Xerxes directing them. He tells them 'Row with your arms, . . . tear out your beard, . . . beat your breast black, . . . tear your robes' until, having exhausted all modes of grief, finally they escort him home. The passage of this procession out of the orchestra acting space has still dramatic force as the chorus promise to escort him 'with harsh sounding cries'; visually, the last movements of the actors out of sight suggest a funeral, a picture of the death of the Persian empire.

The treatment of Persians is far from historical, but it is dramatic. Aeschylus creates a picture of what Persians are like in appearance and behaviour and of their sufferings in defeat. The first words of play establish that Persia has great wealth that comes from a prosperous empire stretching from the Aegean well into Asia, the catalogue of the troops' departure emphasizes its extent. The palace is rich in gold, the army glistens with gold, the king is born of the golden race, i.e. godlike (79–80). King Xerxes is an absolute ruler, his subjects are not free in a way that Greeks would accept; they must prostrate themselves before the god-like king and his mother. The queen's questioning of the chorus makes clear that Persians fight differently from Greeks, their customary weapon is the bow, which dictates their method of fighting – from a distance, whereas the typical Greek warrior in the fifth century was the hoplite who carried a spear and sword and fought hand to hand. The most forceful passages that arouse the visual imagination are used to depict Persian sufferings, the most obvious example in this play being the verbal re-enaction of the Battle of Salamis from the Persian point of view. In picturing the deaths of the ship commanders who fall into the water the language is poetic and colourful. Dadakes leaps from his ship, Matallos dyed his beard in the bloody water. More violent and brutally graphic are the deaths of the numerous men who fall from the wrecked ships, and of those trapped on Psyttaleia, described with imagery of gutting fish and the butcher's block. There are no mentions of Greek casualties or combatants, only the cheer raising exhortation as the battle commences. The focus is on Persians, what they look like and how they behave. Aeschylus' treatment of Persian personal characteristics is important and he builds up a picture of their appearance and behaviour throughout the play, starting in the chorus entrance song which begins with a picture of the invincible army setting out, but when the elders voice their anxieties about the outcome ('my mind is dark with fear', 115–16) the visual emphasis moves to the women left behind in cities empty of men. The chorus imagine their own cry or lament, 'oa', echoed by the women of Kissia, as they tear their fine linen gowns (125). A fuller description of the women grieving and lamenting (also imagined by the chorus) comes after the news of defeat (537–45). These lines are dense with the vocabulary of femininity, building a picture of softness, luxury and excessive grief which is portrayed in wailing and clothes tearing early in the play. The clothing that the women tear is the *peplos*, a long, full, draped gown, which in Greece was only worn by women, but Persian men also wear full robes, for which the same word, *peplos*, is used. All the details fit the Greek perception of Persians as soft and effeminate.

Lamentation and wailing make up a large part of the chorus lines, especially in the *kommos* with Xerxes, where they and the king take part in a highly emotional dirge, bruising themselves with repeated blows and tearing their hair. In tragedy the emotional lament was usually performed by women, so in presenting this forceful and unusual depiction of male behaviour he is inviting the audience to identify it with the female. The fullness of Persian 'female' dress makes possible the striking visualization of the corpses at Salamis floating along, buoyed up in their full robes. The robe that Xerxes tears in grief at his disasters is *peplos* (468, 1028) and the word used for his shrill cries is one usually only used for women (*anakōkuō*, wail, scream aloud, 468).

Clothing plays a significant part in the visual side of Aeschylus' planning in *Persians*, as a marker of status and of changes in fortune. It is particularly meaningful in the play's depiction of royalty, since their clothing denotes a special godlike status; the great king must look different from other men. We get a glimpse of the unique appearance of a great king from the chorus, as they sing their spirit raising song. They beg the dead king Darius to come to them wearing his yellow slippers and royal tiara (660–1), so when Xerxes tears his robes he acknowledges that in defeat his royal status has been diminished. We have only a brief mention of what Xerxes' robes actually looked like from the ghostly Darius, who speaks of them as 'rich embroidered garments' (837). The importance of the royal dress is why both Darius and Atossa are anxious that Xerxes should have new and appropriate robes, he must have them in order for him to reclaim his status as king.

The clothing motif appears throughout the play and is a vital part of the image of the Persians and their empire. The descriptions of the women left behind prepare the audience for the application of the same vocabulary to Persian men in battle and in defeat. Atossa's two very different appearances, with and without her royal splendour, mark the changes in Persian fortunes. The ghost of Darius in royal robes is also in dramatic terms the ghost of Persian power as the chorus pictured it at their entrance and all of these lead up to the appearance of Xerxes in rags and unarmed. The play is anything but unstructured, as all the descriptive elements come to completion in the final scene.

Persians is a *nostos* drama, about a warrior's homecoming (Gk *nostos*) from war, and of those who wait for his return. The most famous *nostos* story in Greek story telling is the *Odyssey* of Homer, the story of Odysseus' adventures and setbacks as he tries to make his way home after the fall of Troy. In *Persians* the mother of Xerxes and his subjects are waiting for him and his army to return from their expedition against Greece, but as depicted by Aeschylus his *nostos* is a failure.

In Aeschylus' final dramatic work, the *Oresteia* trilogy (458 BC) dealing with the family of Agamemnon, the *nostos* theme is also prominent. By this time many of the problems facing a dramatist who has to make scenes 'visible' to his audience have been resolved, a third actor had been added and there is a stage building (*skēnē*) with doors which enables more dramatic entrances and exits as characters no longer are compelled to enter by the long side passages. In the first play, *Agamemnon*, the *skēnē* represents the palace at Argos where Agamemnon's wife Clytemnestra and household wait for his return (*nostos*) from the war against Troy. Clytemnestra is a powerful woman who has been ruling Argos in her husband's absence and although she pretends to care for her husband, she intends to revenge herself on him for sacrificing their daughter, Iphigeneia, in order to be able to sail to Troy.

A brief look at words and images that Aeschylus uses in *Agamemnon* to heighten tension and mood in the play will show some that are familiar from *Persians*, enduring characteristics of his individual style. As the play opens the scene is set, not by the chorus, but by a watchman on the roof of the palace, a bold novelty. He is watching for signal fire from a beacon that will announce the fall of Troy, and it appears as he speaks. The chorus enter and in their song tell the story so far. In order to have favourable winds for Troy as the army set out Agamemnon sacrificed his daughter to Artemis, putting his duty as leader before his duty as a father. The theme of compulsion, using the vocabulary of taming animals is frequent early in the play. Agamemnon's reluctant decision to sacrifice his daughter meant that he put on the halter of necessity (216); men bound (bridled) the girl's mouth before the sacrifice (237–8); later a herald announces that Agamemnon in victory has cast the yoke upon Troy (529).

The beacon signal has been arranged by Clytemnestra to relay news of the fall of Troy all the way across the Aegean; she boasts of it to the chorus in an excited speech listing places it touches, (Aeschylus' much favoured geographical catalogue). Still speaking to the chorus she imagines the scenes of destruction in Troy, but pauses to think 'if only they revere the gods and their shrines and do not *desire* to plunder what they should not take, conquered by greed' (338–42). The pattern of action that she imagines is identical with what Darius' ghost censures in *Persians* as the reason for the deaths of Xerxes' soldiers. Violent and impious actions towards gods and men are *hubris* and will be punished. Later in the play, the chorus blame Paris, son of king Priam of Troy for the ruin of his city because he took Helen from her husband Menelaus; Troy has been destroyed because '*hubris* loves to breed' (763).

When he returns Agamemnon enters in a royal chariot accompanied by the Trojan princess, Cassandra, who is his war prize and also a prophetess. Clytemnestra welcomes him, telling a rather sceptical chorus how she loves her husband and has longed for him in his absence. She calls to her attendants to spread purple embroidered cloths for him to walk on, 'let Justice lead him home' (911). The king is reluctant to tread on such rich, expensive fabrics – 'do not treat me softly or fall on the ground before me as if I were a barbarian' – as she prostrates herself before him. Troy in Asia Minor can easily be identified with the luxury and servility that characterized Persian society.

The scene that follows is a battle of wills in which Clytemnestra is the winner. She persuades Agamemnon by asking what he thinks king Priam would do if he had been victorious. He thinks that Priam would walk on the embroidered cloth. Her victory comes as she asks him to surrender to her as she is only a woman. So, he walks on the purple-dyed fabrics towards the palace doors, even though he hesitates to offend the gods by trampling the wealth of the house. In his wife's eyes he has done so already by killing his daughter, and after a speech of triumph Clytemnestra follows him inside. Eventually Cassandra moves towards the palace, but stops suddenly, crying out to Apollo, the god of prophecy. A long scene of her madness and possession by the god follows during which she has a vision of the murders in this family, past, present and future (1070–330. Agamemnon's murder is told in riddles, which the chorus do not understand: the wife bathing her husband, stretching out her hand to throw the net over him, and 'she takes him by trickery in the robes' (1126). Finally, her ravings calm down and she foretells vengeance for Agamemnon's death and hers. The mad scene is a theatrical shock as the sound and cries from the possessed woman, together with her barely intelligible words and restless movements add horror to the already unsettling scene.

Cassandra enters the palace knowing she too will die, and we soon hear the death cries of Agamemnon from inside the palace. There follows one of Aeschylus' most spectacular scenes as the palace doors open and Clytemnestra is seen with the bodies of Agamemnon and Cassandra (1373). She boasts of her deed, 'I cast an inescapable net over him . . . I put it all around him, an evil richness of clothing . . . I strike him twice and then again, his blood spurts over me.' The horrified chorus attack Clytemnestra accusingly until her lover Aegisthus arrives, who threatens the chorus and orders them away, and he and Clytemnestra enter the palace together.

This powerful play displays Aeschylus' style at its peak with bold visual effects in the unusual opening by the watchman, the mad scene and the tableau of the murderess exulting over her victims. In *Persians* clothing was important as a signifier of royal status, as well as a way contrasting of Persian life and character with that of Greeks. In *Agamemnon* there is also a focus on cloth and its significance and Aeschylus uses a variety of vocabulary for the fabrics. Clytemnestra calls the cloths laid for Agamemnon to walk on 'embroidered cloths laid down', and 'a purple strewn path' (909–10), so he will walk on costly fabrics, that also are the colour of blood. In her vision of the king's murder Cassandra sees him trapped in a net thrown over him, but also says he is caught in robes. The accumulation of words to signify cloths that can also be traps comes to a climax in Clytemnestra's exultant speech to the chorus over Agamemnon's body which includes two more ways to describe what she used. 'I surrounded him with a casting net, as for fish, . . . a richness of clothing' (1383–4) and she brings the whole together in colour as she speaks of the blood spurting out over her like a shower of dew (1390).

Aeschylus has not spent such graphic images on this one play, as they will come home in the following play (*Libation Bearers*) with the deaths of Clytemnestra and her lover Aegisthus. Her son, Orestes, will have his *nostos* when he comes back to Argos to avenge his father's death, but for Xerxes in *Persians* there will be no avenger.

12

National Theatre Wales: *The Persians* (2010)

Mike Pearson

1.

In August 2010, the newly founded National Theatre Wales (NTW) presented Aeschylus' *Persians* in a version of the text by Kaite O'Reilly that subsequently received the Ted Hughes Award for New Works in Poetry (2010).[1] In the company's opening season – dedicated to 'located-ness', with twelve productions at twelve different places in Wales – it felt appropriate to mount the earliest drama in the Western canon recorded in anything close to completeness – from before the very notion of nation – as a site-specific work. Site-specific practices were amongst established, independent – though dormant – approaches to devising theatre in Wales[2] that NTW artistic director John McGrath deemed worthy of recovery and enactment in altered circumstances – within both the opportunities and the constraints afforded by a highly funded national institution.

The Persians was created and staged in a replica village constructed by the British Army on the Sennybridge Training Area (SENTA), close to the Brecon Beacons National Park in South Wales, an area from which the inhabitants were evicted in 1942 and never allowed to return. Cilieni[3] – or in its Army appellation FIBUA (Fighting in Built Up Areas) – is a cluster of houses and other buildings, with steel shuttered doors and windows. Outwardly German in appearance, it was designed at a time when the Third World War, if non-nuclear, was foreseen as a major tank battle in northern Europe. Almost diagrammatic in aspect, it is a collection of simple architectural shapes, forms and unadorned facades, that can – as required – stand in for any 'elsewhere': Northern Ireland, Kosovo, Iraq, Afghanistan . . .

Cilieni provides the daily setting for war *games*, though what usually happens here is a serious business. Occupied temporary by different casts – sometimes passing through to theatres of war elsewhere – it is a place of simulation: a configuration of streets and rudimentary structures in which to rehearse urban warfare, to test scenarios and manoeuvres and, as a consequence, to train and fashion the military body. A place of continual vigilance and stress where others are frequently – figuratively – trying to kill you.

Here, darkened rooms have trapdoors and hidden tunnels. But interiors lack vernacular details – the traces and patinas of human occupancy. There are no signs of domestic habitation – no paint, wallpaper, furniture. There is no plumbing; the barn bears no marks of agricultural labour; gravestones bear neither names nor dedicatory verses. In such spartan conditions, everyday life would indeed be tough. However, the milieu has to be real enough to convince the trainee soldiers who visit; there must needs be a threshold of credibility. Though unostentatious and muted – as just the barest of outlines – it speaks for itself, in complex and shifting ways: with burned out tanks, it might resemble an abandoned community – in Bosnia *after* the conflict perhaps.

But its *emptiness* is profound: it is in this latency that potential resides. Cilieni awaits and anticipates all that might be brought to it, and read onto and into it: actions, engagements, imaginaries. What could this place be for you, it demands. Anything might be said or done here: military certainly, and – for the first time in *The Persians* – theatrical.

From the outset, the decision to conceive and devise *The Persians* for and at this specific location – in a restricted zone – provided opportunity and difficulty in equal measure, as we exploited and dealt with the potentialities and impediments inherent to the place. In a fine balance between desire – enacting artistic ambitions for the production – and necessity – tackling the concrete realities and restraints of the site – Cilieni informed both conceptual (strategic) and directorial (tactical) procedures. Responding directly to its characteristics and specificities – spatial, architectural, environmental and acoustic – required the implementation of both programmatic and pragmatic approaches to the possibilities and problems enshrined there. Outside the controlled ambit of the auditorium, it offered new creative prospects, whilst also necessitating the application of extended techniques of production management: to address, enhance and moderate its unique attributes; and to attend to the needs of performers and audiences alike – ensuring effective expression and its reception in a context where the usual conventions and techniques of theatre-making and exposition were in abeyance or insufficient to the task.

Cilieni is already in a quasi-theatrical mode; daily, it is a scene of performance. Early, we realized that any impulse to theatricalize it further – by scenically 'dressing' it, by decorating it to represent a particular period or locale; by using its domestic buildings domestically; or by explicitly indicating this or that feature – would be detrimental, serving as a counterproductive form of over-coding. It needed to remain as it is, affording the same stimulus it does for the troops that engage it, with its ground-plan and buildings suggesting layouts and locations for performance: informing processional routes, the placement of episodes, the sequencing of entrances and exits ...

The Army decides what is permissible at Cilieni, and thus we further perceived that – beyond the reach and remit of those regulatory bodies that normally license public events – anything might enter the orbit of theatre: that which might be impossible, illegal or dangerous in the auditorium – the use of vehicles, the mass movement of audiences ... In this originary drama, in an embryonic institutional initiative, off the beaten track was an occasion to rethink the contracts of theatre: spatial, scenic, rhetorical ...

2.

The Persians is a drama of anticipation and consequence, of reportage and repercussion: a warning against reckless adventurism. Its principal concerns are *hubris* and ensuing *nemesis*. As revelation follows revelation, the only possible outcome is grief and chaos. But there can be no cathartic resolution, for this concerns foreigners. It is then cautionary – of the threat to establishment – rather than triumphalist.

In Kaite O'Reilly's version, there is no attempt to modernize the text; it is peppered with anachronistic talk of spears and chariots and quivers. Certainly, no direct equation of antique and contemporary individuals or circumstances is inferred: figuring Saddam Hussein as a latter-day Xerxes, for instance. Her tenor is direct and robust, as much as poetic;[4] the words issue easily – despite the archaic names of people and places – from modern mouths.

In *The Persians* at Cilieni, it's reasonable to assume that the juxtaposition of text and military site would be some direct allusion to, or allegory for, particular current world events. Instead, the production attempted to lay bare the perennial nature of vaunting human ambition – through the collision of ancient and modern, in the coexistence of, or frictions *between*, performance and location: drawing out themes of the cult of personality, the collapse of old order, the threat of regime change, and the incipient danger of reversion to barbarism and ritual.

In the conceptual phase – and then as a means to schedule rehearsal – the text was divided into five phases or movements, each presaged by an arrival or departure: Prologue, in which Chorus and Queen are introduced – '*Most reverent of women, our first Lady of noble birth,/consort to Darius, the God of Persians/and mother to a god* too' – and the scene is set; Premonition, in which Queen and Chorus await intelligence of the conflict with gathering apprehension – '*I feel the canker-fret of care*'; Revelation, in which the Messenger brings news of the defeat at Salamis – '*Everything is lost*'; Recrimination, in which Darius is summoned from beyond the grave and consulted –'*You hooked me with your words and hauled me up*'; and Chaos, in which events spin out of control following the return of Xerxes –'*I grieve and I mourn/I mourn and I grieve*/Ieh, ieh!/ io, io!/Yay yay, yooh yoh!*'*.

A preparatory period of two weeks was spent in a studio space in Cardiff. This experience was problematic for performers in two ways. First, simultaneously and in close proximity to each other, they were tasked with preparing texts and actions that at site – though synchronous – would be widely distributed both horizontally and vertically; and only there differentiated and rebalanced to stress their relative dramatic import. As activities inevitably jostled for attention and primacy in the studio, taped outlines on the floor – that in conventional practice demarcate elements of the *mise-en-scène* – were insufficient to describe the complexities of site, and to prevent frustrating clashes in delivery. Second, there was no directorial expectation that an overarching interpretation would be gradually revealed and emerge solely through trial and error in rehearsal. With only ten days of access to Cilieni, the dramaturgical, choreographic and scenographic frameworks – within which the performers' preliminary renderings would be set – had to be precisely envisioned and meticulously pre-planned. The objective of this first phase then was to develop performative propositions, sketches, fragments and prefabricated elements that would be brought to site and there modified, expanded and refined as performers learned, adapted to – and to make sense of, inhabit and capitalize upon – the ambiance and full extent of their new sphere of activity; and to manage its in-built arrangements and material resistances.

Crucially, only at site were key elements of technology and media introduced: variously integrated into – and determining – the patterning of movements and interactions. For the underlying operational conceit of *The Persians* at Cilieni – undisclosed in promotional releases – was of a televised event happening in real time with a bussed-in audience. That goes terribly wrong.

3.

The first quandary for the production was how to shepherd and organize the audience, and get them to an isolated site that few, if any, would have visited before.

At 7 p.m., spectators assemble at the Army's administrative base in Sennybridge, where the range's permanent staff is housed. Here, they are issued with waterproof, windproof ponchos, for it's always going to be wet on a Welsh hillside, even in August. And – in a critical Army regulation – they are given stern warnings by uniformed officers not to touch anything on the ground, littered as it is with spent munitions: establishing an immediate sense of anticipation, and level of apprehension ... They are then transported by coach on a twenty-minute journey, across an unfamiliar and disorienting landscape, accompanied – as an intimation of things to come – by a discordant, unsettling pre-recorded musical soundtrack on the tannoy.

As they disembark at Cilieni's boundary chicane, a martial anthem plays in the distance. They are led through the seemingly unoccupied village, passing wrecked vehicles and cloistered dwellings. Is it half-built, or half decayed? With few clues as yet, they might wonder: 'What is this place?' A community without men, with women and children closeted safely out of sight of visitors? A threadbare country stripped and bankrupted by war effort? A dismal 'victory museum' displaying the captured detritus of past wars, as in North Korea? An abandoned community in a military 'no-go' sector? A deserted film set? War-ravaged Athens? Disconcertingly, the streets have Welsh names.

And who are we, assigned a sort of contingent collective identity, in our matching khaki garb? A procession, demonstration or cortège? A group of tourists, weapons inspectors or refugees? The straggling survivors of conflict? Persian prisoners? Greek theatregoers, in a setting redolent of Athens in 472 BC, when the sacked temples – still in ruins and left as a reminder of the city's ordeal – were the backdrop for the premiere of Aeschylus' drama?

It's perplexing, the usual decorum and expectations of the auditorium already upset and confounded. How to behave here, to comport oneself? With so little to go on, anything might indeed happen. Though soon, theatre will supply much-needed orientation ...

They arrive at the central square where, in front of the mock church, there is a temporary dais with flags, three chairs, three megaphones, and a large portrait photograph that will eventually be disclosed to be Darius: this is the only independent scenic element emplaced for the production. There is also a small 1950s Peugeot van with mounted loudspeakers – that had previously avoided the walking audience, travelling on a different route through the village – from which the anthem repeatedly and remorselessly issues. And a single male figure.

Suddenly, there is the sound of a blaring car horn and a heavy, black Rover 100 saloon – also from the late 1950s – approaches, driving straight into the middle of the crowd and coming to rest. An anachronism hinting at a society mired in tradition, or already past its best? The Chorus – three men in cheap suits – emerges, kissing the ground, waving, shaking hands, embracing spectators: the inspiration here is of images of the arrival of Radovan Karadzic at some secret meeting in Pale, Kosovo. A modern *parodos*?[5] The waiting figure – who ran to meet them, jogging beside the car – is now revealed as one of their number, though he will remain silent throughout. These are Darius' men – *'understudies to power, rulers by proxy for the warring Xerxes'* – though as much nightclub bouncers or secret service agents as junta: intimidating and menacing, their forceful entry and proximate energy already too large to imagine confined in the auditorium. They are media men, too. As preening and pompous as Mussolini, they know how to create an impression for an outside broadcast (OB) camera and operator that immediately focuses them. In motion, they aim for barely restrained power and taut masculinity; at rest, for compositional precision and rigour.[6]

They ascend the dais – clapping, saluting the crowd – and begin their oration, using the crude amplification. They are assertive, bullish, bombastic: describing the departure of Xerxes and his armies – a rollcall of passing military might, of what 'we' witnessed 'on this spot'. They foresee the triumph of formidable force –of overwhelming size and strength – with extravagant mimetic hand gestures and poses that might, as with their Athenian forbears, be understood by visiting foreigners – *'Victory is inevitable / Failure is not in our language.'* This then is a rally to celebrate anticipated military success, the audience cast unwittingly as Persians. Such is the fervour generated that many applaud. But the atmosphere is disturbing, out of kilter. Anything might happen here.

The speeches reach a climax – *'There is no resisting this force/as futile as fighting a hurricane, the sea.'* A procession of loudspeaker van, Chorus carrying the portrait, and audience forms up and proceeds to the singular Skills House: a three-storey, concrete-block building with pitched roof but no façade, that resembles an open-fronted, life-sized doll's house. Surprisingly, there is a projecting forestage. And a small grandstand stands opposite, facing it.

The troops that usually gather there can see into rooms two deep, into exposed staircases and basement. It is a precisely controlled context in which to demonstrate military operations and to provide a viewpoint for their appreciation, as they observe trainers and colleagues attacking and defending the structure, all sallies and repulses manifest for their inspection and instruction. A place of acute observation where, under normal circumstances, a detailed appreciation and understanding of behaviour and response may eventually be a matter of life or death.

The Persians identified and aligned itself with this function, providing unimpeded views of contacts and exchanges, whilst – in times of dramatic confidentiality and stress – also redressing the building's unhelpful transparency, and shielding events from scrutiny.

Designer Simon Banham and Mike Brookes modified the Skills House to a degree: all safety rails – a prescribed facet of health and safety practice even in Army training – were removed; though all windows and doorways were left as empty openings. In the main interior spaces, mobile walls were installed – galvanized metal on one side, wood on the other – that fitted the room-sized apertures. Suspended on overhead, front-to-back tracks, they could be shifted forwards and backwards, angled and rotated. Their manipulation during performance conspired varying spatial configurations – temporary rooms, short-lived passageways. And combinations of their different surfaces offered reordered backdrops and refurnished social contexts. Their articulation facilitated new juxtapositions of 'on' and 'off', between public and private. Laying bare – and masking – moments of dramatic tension and conflict and offering kinetic counterpoint to weighty passages of text. Some equivalent of the Greek *periaktos*[7] perhaps?

The Skills House is made for performance – *orchestra*, *theatron* and *skene*[8] combined? It was illuminated from inside by discretely placed weatherproof halogen lamps and neon strips hung on convenient architectural projections: no light was ever beamed from outside. These were operated by performers as they entered or left rooms, as a natural part of their function, from the very outset: as darkness fell, the 'House of Darius' almost imperceptibly began to light up.

The seating rake of the grandstand was extended but left unroofed to accommodate the one hundred and forty spectators on wooden benches: the ponchos dispensing individual rather than communal protection from the elements. With the option to withdraw exposed sequences of the performance back into the house at will, weather became an active and affective component of dramaturgy and of reception – most strikingly in prospects riven by diagonals of beating rain, or part-obscured by intervening moorland mist, or of the house topped by black clouds. On some evenings, the scene included distant mountains, rainbows, vivid crimson sunsets, a large moon; on others, little could be perceived beyond the immediate edifice.

The main aim of the production was to preserve the stark and inherently dramatic coexistence of two these distinct architectural entities: grandstand and house. The key question was how to link them: outdoors, on a windswept moorland. The solution: through the extensive, though discreet, application of sophisticated digital technology in this sparest of locations.

At Cilieni, *The Persians* was highly mediatized: the experience of war was reimagined in the era of 24-hour news, of images of far-off populations and countries whose names barely register. And of constant media attention and intrusion into both public and private affairs. Hence, there was an unexpected proliferation of screens: at eight strategic interior points, there were wall-mounted video monitors; below the eaves, the uppermost, third-floor opening was sealed by a projection screen.

'What is this place and why are we gathered here?' the now-seated audience might wonder. A continuation of the victory rally? A celebration for the dedication of the 'Darius Memorial Home for War Veterans'? An annual gathering at his shrine or tomb? Or an assembly to witness the recommencement of work on a half-finished, speculative construction, familiar from present-day Greece?

As the Chorus holds the portrait of Darius aloft, the audience witnesses not only that gesture but also shots of themselves in cutaway reaction, greatly enlarged on the upper screen: the OB camera is now revealed to be radio-linked. The Chorus also appears, in strange, distorted close-ups on the video monitors. Only gradually is it apparent that their non-speaking member is wearing a small camera on his wrist, conveying shots from the very midst of their confidential groupings.

The Chorus hangs the picture on an interior wall. There is an *impasse*. As they impatiently await the Queen, they begin to express doubts concerning the state of affairs[9] – '*Is it a trick?/Have we walked into a trap*.' But *sotto voce*. Yet they are heard clearly, for all performers wear radio-microphones: all spoken text is amplified. The audience will be privy to intimate thoughts, whispered asides, private misgivings, privileged conversations from individuals and knots of performers at different locations in the house, without the need for unnatural vocal projection – here, outdoors and in unstable conditions of weather. The array of audio speakers is located in, around and beneath the grandstand. The effect is to keep the words close and the quality constant, though performers may be distant or even unseen: as the production increasingly turns away from those watching, into the interior of the house – as the initial public-facing aspect is superseded by momentous events that impact upon the procedural workings of the royal household, and core of government.

The audience sits within a sonic envelope in which the words are combined with a continuous, prerecorded musical soundtrack by composer John Hardy, known in Wales for his film and television scores, that variously complements, extends and challenges the tone, dynamic and meaning of the spoken text. Significantly, given its focused reach, the performers hear little of the soundtrack, lessening any temptation to follow its tempos, or to try to equal or outperform its shifting volumes. The mixing of words and music – that constitutes the intended dramatic effect of the production – is achieved externally: continuously modulated and rebalanced to accommodate changing ambient factors.

The Queen finally approaches in a matching white Rover saloon,[10] picked up by the OB camera for the audience even before the Chorus registers her arrival. Two Chorus members rush across the grass to meet and escort her, whilst their associates police the audience closely – for intimations of dissent, or at least lack of enthusiasm. She acknowledges the crowd – she might bring purpose and meaning to this congregation – but she is too distracted to address them directly. Whatever should have happened here is compromised. She has been disturbed by a dream; as she relates her terrible premonition – *'And when Xerxes saw his father's piteous gaze/he tore at his clothes, destroying them'* – the animated reactions of the Chorus behind a wall appear on the monitors. The Queen herself is seen throughout on the large screen, her red costume and blond hair striking at scale in the fading light, her slightest facial responses apparent; from now until the end, the OB camera will pursue her relentlessly, paparazzi-like.

In the house, she touches nothing. As she begins to question the Chorus about Athens – *'How great is their force, the numbers?'* – they reposition walls to create shifting 'corridors of power'. Glimpsed in their roving, classified conversation by the two cameras, appearing and disappearing on the various screens, though their voices remain clear.

The situation is disturbed by the appearance of the Messenger breaking through on the video monitors as if by satellite-link from a war zone, with extended news of crushing defeat at Salamis – *'I was there, an eye-witness.'* As the Chorus pushes back walls to ensure the visibility of all monitors, the Queen is sequestered in a closed second-floor room. The audience witnesses her private enquiries and increasingly distraught responses at the news of Xerxes' defeat only as a magnified, projected image from the ever-attentive OB camera, which occasionally and incidentally also catches shots of the Messenger on one of the monitors – *'Everything from the expedition – utterly destroyed.'*

The Chorus is now dispersed, watching and addressing the Messenger from several positions simultaneously: engaging in silent solo and joint actions that respond to, and then increasingly appear to echo and enact the account of the battle and subsequent disastrous retreat – *'I could still hear the sounds of slaughter/ Thousands upon thousands. Their screams in the dark.'* A frenzy of acts and liaisons compartmentalized and framed in the open-fronted rooms.

The audience is now watching a complex interplay of live and mediated action and pre-recorded video: activities of different orders and intensities, with perfect attendant sound, that include extreme close-ups of considerable scale. The OB camera offers candid footage as well as staged oration and 'direct to camera' interjections: the audience is always aware of the presence of the crew, constantly apparent as it goes about its business.

The footage of the Messenger was recorded huddling against concrete Second World War anti-tank defences on a pebble beach in South Wales. He spoke directly to camera with increasing urgency – in a single take, the text scrolling on an autocue on a smartphone taped above the lens – whilst leaving pauses of appropriate estimated length for the verbal responses of Queen and Chorus – '*So tell us of the battle, how it began, this naval disaster.*' Filling these gaps successfully in performance – to create the illusion of a live dialogue – would prove to be one of the most challenging aspects of on-site rehearsal. But the video assured a similar dynamic drive night after night and the melding of heightened, highly charged acting by the Queen with the televisual style of the Messenger proved to be a revelation of the production.

After an admonition to do their duty and prepare for Xerxes' return, the Queen exits – '*If my son returns, comfort him/and guide him to my door.*' The Chorus is now racked with unease. The empire is in danger, their rule under threat – '*What remains of Persian might/is washed up in the tide/alongside our dead.*'

The Queen reappears in a black robe, hair in disarray, lamenting but defiant. As she descends to the forestage, so the Chorus retreats to the basement where with incantatory voices and flagellant actions, they summon their dead master Darius: suits discarded, the veneer of enlightenment cracked, they resort once more to ritual – '*Lord of the dead, earth itself/let him ascend from forgetfulness.*' As they open their shirts to disclose white body armour – their own insecurities at their provisional hold on power betrayed – beating their chests and raising their arms in invocation, materialize he does, the 'Eternal Leader'. His over-sized head and shoulders appears in a prerecorded, back-projected video in the upper storey, his highly amplified voice booming and echoing across the hilly landscape – the only sound ever to issue directly from the Skills House. Technology here addressing a key question in staging *The Persians*: how to represent a ghost.

One danger was that the pre-recorded sequences of video would set an inflexible dynamic. The rapid, rolling delivery of the Messenger and the more measured tones of Darius forestalled this, as did the concentrated and compensatory intercourse of the live performers with recorded imagery that remained, by definition, unresponsive.

As the Chorus adopts a number of friezes – extreme graphic physical compositions – against a lower concrete wall, so a stratified stage picture is contrived – Chorus, Queen and at the apex, Darius. Isolated on the forestage, the Queen never looks up at the looming image above. She always faces front, in a conversation with Darius that is initially antagonistic – '*The fool! Did he attempt this madness by land or sea?*' Sustaining of the illusion of being pursued in real time – '*What became of the men, to make you grieve so?*' '*Destruction on land; destruction at sea.*' And then conciliatory – '*You're wise, my friends, so counsel Xerxes/Explain this to him, correct his pride/Heaven has warned him.'* Darius fades – *'But I must go, returning to the dark, below/ forgetfulness.'*

The Queen retires to prepare for Xerxes' return, and there is a hope of welcome, resolution, reconciliation. But the Chorus is now racked with unease: their rule is under threat. They remain agitated, taking stock, counting what has been lost – *'And now the reversal/Crushed. Drowned. Conquered.'* Increasingly disturbed – pushing, grabbing each other, cannoning around a small room – the endemic violence of this society is laid bare.

Xerxes is first heard panting for breath in the amplified soundscape as he runs from a distance across adjacent fields where the OB camera eventually picks him up. He arrives alone, having lost or abandoned his retinue. He enters the basement through a side entrance and calls up through the house, which is now fully illuminated and glowing in the dark. He appears in anachronistic dress, in distressed body armour and kilt. The Chorus comes to him like rabid, snarling dogs, their reversion to barbarism almost complete. He is herded out onto the forestage. It is a rough and accusatory homecoming – *'slain by Xerxes / who crams Hell's jaws with our thousands dead'* – the consequences of over-weaning militarism now fully internalized within this royal edifice, this House of Darius. Half-built, or already half-destroyed?

He is remorseful – *'I did it. My fault'* – but forthright, eventually expressing his own state of trauma having witnessed the massacre of his friends. As the soundtrack swells, he becomes more assured: his grief is to be shared in a scene of increasing mayhem. The Chorus engages in extreme actions, spinning dervish-like in closed spaces, seen only on the monitors. Smoke pours through cracks, as their acoustic, chanting voices become wordless, as language splinters and runs out – 'Otototttotoi! O-toto –toto-ee!'. Xerxes reaches a crescendo of exulted grief, and finally collapses – 'Ehhh-ehhh-ehhh-ehhh! *The men the ships destroyed.'* The Chorus – now resembling penitents – carries him up the staircases, extinguishing lights as it travels – 'Home, now; home, now.'[11] As they enter the Queen's closed room on the second floor, there is sudden blackout and silence, as if the power plug of the production has fallen out of the socket.

The performance appears to end. But as the audience walks back to the coaches through the shadowy village, there is a disturbing coda: keening female voices seem to emerge from distant houses.

What started as a premature victory parade ends as constitutional crisis . . .

With no pre-conditions for the nature of theatrical exposition at Cilieni/FIBUA, *The Persians* was a *hybrid* of dramatic stage traditions as exemplified in the performance of the Queen, Darius and Xerxes; of practices of physical theatre and devised performance apparent in the work of the Chorus; and of multi-media installation. In sum, it resembled a live film, which the specific configuration of the village and specifically the Skills House suggested, accommodated and made possible. A production particular to one place and in one moment, with no further life possible elsewhere.

Performers: Queen – Sian Thomas; Darius – Paul Rhys; Messenger – Richard Harrington; Xerxes – Rhys Rusbatch; Chorus – Richard Lynch, Richard Huw Morgan, John Rowley, Gerald Tyler; Lady-in-Waiting – Rosa Casado. Direction: Mike Pearson; Conceptual design: Mike Brookes; Scenic design: Simon Banham; Music: John Hardy; Video: Pete Telfer.

Notes

1. Kaite O'Reilly's *Aeschylus's Persians* is published by Morda, Oswestry: Fair Acre Press, 2019. All quotations are from this volume.
2. Twenty years previously, Welsh company Brith Gof had created a series of large-scale site-specific works, including *Gododdin* (1988–9), *PAX* (1990–1) and *Haearn* (1992) at disused industrial sites and in public buildings in Wales and throughout Europe. See Pearson (2010).
3. For images of Cilieni/FIBUA, see: https://www.coflein.gov.uk/en/site/268123/images (accessed 7 April 2022).
4. '... the iambic drumbeat of English blank verse, and a long-lined lyricism that befits an epic lament', Gillian Clarke, on the rear cover of the published edition of O'Reilly (2019).
5. In Greek theatre, a large passageway giving access to the stage, and the entrance song of the chorus.
6. The inspiration here was the performance of Toshiro Mifune in Japanese director Akira Kurosawa's film *Throne of Blood* (1957), and the group compositions in the video works of US artist Bill Viola.
7. In Greek theatre, a revolving device for displaying and rapidly changing scenes.
8. In Greek theatre, performing space, seating area and scenic backdrop.
9. In the NTW production, the opening phase of O'Reilly's text – from p. 17 line 2, 'The bloom of the Persian land is gone', to p. 20, line 11 '... the abject loneliness of their days' – is inserted here, at p. 27, line 7, prior to 'But look the Queen approaches, radiant.'
10. Both cars were bought and resold online.
11. The inspiration here was Spanish artist Francisco Goya's painting *A Procession of Flagellants* (1812–19).

Aeschylus' *Persians*

translated by David Stuttard

The Characters of the Drama

In order of appearance

Chorus	Persian elders
Queen (Atossa)	Widow of Darius and mother of Xerxes
Messenger	A member of Xerxes' army
Darius (Ghost of)	Former Great King of Persia
Xerxes	Great King of Persia

Non-speaking roles include Atossa's Attendants, the Driver of her carriage, and the Driver of Xerxes' covered wagon.

The play is set in front of the stepped entrance to the Persian royal palace at Susa in the immediate vicinity of the grave mound of Darius.

Persians was the second play in a tetralogy comprising two other tragedies (*Phineus* and *Glaucus*) and one satyr play (*Prometheus*) staged at Athens' City Dionysia in 472 BC, when it won first prize. Only fragments of the companion plays survive.

Stage directions do not appear in manuscripts of *Persians* but many may be surmised from the text. To aid the reader some suggestions (printed in sans serif font) are given in the following translation.

Enter the **Chorus.**

Chorus   we are assembled

    the loyal council of the persians
        campaigning out in greece
    custodians of the treasury
        and palace riches
    men whom our lord himself
        king xerxes
        son of darius
    chose
        hand-picked
        for our seniority
        to oversee
        his empire

    concerning their return
    however
        (his –
        the king's –
        his richly kitted army's)
    i feel
    extreme foreboding   10
        a premonition of disaster

    all asia has left us
        on campaign
    all asia cries out
        for her young men
    and still no messenger
        no horseman
    comes here to the persian
        capital

    they left behind them
        susa
        and ecbatana
        and ancient kissa
            all so strongly fortified

    they set out on campaign
        on horseback

                    or in ships
                    or massed
                        as infantry
                        in close-packed ranks
                        for war
                men like
                    amistres
                    artaphernes
                    megabates and
                    astaspes
                all kings
                    yet subjects
                    of the great king

                they make good speed
                    these men
                    who oversee
                        our mighty army
                each an accomplished archer
                    an accomplished horseman too
                        intimidating
                        terrifying
                            in battle
                        for his steely spirit
                            and his force of personality

                the horseman
                    artembares and
                    masistes
                and the lethal bowman
                    noble imaeus
                and pharandakes
                and the man who spurs his horses
                    sosthanes

                the fruitful stretching nile
                sent others
                    sousiskanes
                    pegastagon
                        a native-born egyptian
                    great arsames
                        the potentate

             of sacred memphis
and
      the governor
      of ancient thebes
ariomardus
and so many expert oarsmen
      from the marshes
that you could not count them   40

next follows a contingent
   of louche lydians
who rule over the peoples
   of the western coast

      metrogathes
      and arctaeus
         royal commanders both

and sardis
   glittering in gold
sent them to war
   in countless
   four- and six-horse chariots
a terrifying sight

and men who live
   near sacred tmolus
vow to cast the yoke   50
   of slavery
on greece –
   mardon
   and tharubis
      proof against any spear
and mysians
   the masters of the javelin

babylon too
   glittering in gold
sends snaking lines
of men from many lands
   in ships
      as mariners
      or deadly bowmen

and sabre-wielding persians
from every part of asia
follow in the terrifying procession
   of the king

these are the men
   the flower of persia
who set out on campaign

all asia
   reared them
all asia
   sighs for them
      in quenchless longing
while wives and parents
   count the days
and tremble
   at the lengthening
      of time

already the royal army
   that turns cities
   into rubble
has reached
the far shore –
   europe –
bridging the greek hellespont
on a pontoon raft
   a fleet of ships
      bound taut with cables
   a hobnailed road
   a yoke
      cast on the ocean's neck
as the lord of teeming asia
   unbridled
   drives his herd
      his superhuman herd
      to conquer the whole world
in two divisions
   land and
   sea
   placing his faith in
      chiselled

       tough commanders
a shining man
a godlike man
   whose race is spun
      from gold
   whose eyes flash
      with the clouded glare
         of a marauding dragon
         bristling with infantry
         and mariners

he races onwards
   in his syrian chariot
leading
   a slaughtering mass
   of archers
against men
   the world knows
   fight with spears

no mortal is so strong
he can resist
   so great a surge of people
or staunch
   the sea swell
      which cannot be staunched
   with powerful barricades

no
persia's army
   cannot be withstood
her men
   are fearless

by god's will
fate
has ruled
   since ancient times
and has predestined
   for the persians
the pursuit
of war
   towers toppling

        the clash of chariots
        and cities stormed
           and conquered

and they have trained themselves
to view
    the mystic waters of the sea
        unflinchingly
    when raging storm-winds
        turn its waves
        to hissing foam
and put their trust
    in artifice
        in fine spun ropes
        to give their people
        passage

but then
what mortal man
can flee the will of an
    impenetrable
    guileful
    god

who is so agile
that he can outleap
    god's hunting nets

for até
goddess of infatuation
    so attentive to our wants
lures mankind deep
    inside her snare
and no-one can escape
    unbroken

and so my mind
    is dark with fear
o-á!
    foreboding
    for the persian
    expedition force

i fear

that persia might discover
that her capital
   great susa
has lost all her men

i fear
   great susa
   will re-echo
o-á!
   to the howl
   of crowds
   of weeping women
      beating breasts
      and ripping
      their soft linen dresses
         into rags

for all our cavalry
and all our infantry
   like swarming bees
have left us
   with their general
and gone
   across the bridge
   that yokes
      two continents

in marriage beds
wives weep
   with longing
   for their husbands
every persian wife
who watched
   her husband
   seize his spear and
   rush to war
lamenting for him
   in her grief
   and longing
abandoned
   like a horse
   that's lost its yoke-mate

140   but come now
             persians
         we must take our places
             here
                 on the ancient palace steps
         and give some careful
             serious
                 consideration
                     since our need is
                     great now
                 to how king xerxes
                 son of darius
         is faring

         has persia's bow
             won victory
         or greece's spear

Enter **Atossa**, *sumptuously dressed in a royal carriage with much pomp. As she descends, the* **Chorus** *prostrate themselves before her.*

150 **Chorus** but now –
         light
             like the
         light
             that blazes
                 from gods' eyes –
         the mother
             of our king
         our queen

         i prostrate myself
             before her
         and as etiquette demands
         we must salute her
         with a loyal address

         queen
         greatest of all
             persia's elite women
         xerxes'
             august mother
         darius'
             wife

    we salute you
        wife
            of a persian god
        and mother
            of a god –
                unless its former fortune
                has deserted
                our campaign force

Atossa Which is why I am here now.
    Which is why I left my golden palace
        and the rooms I shared with Darius.   160
    I, too, am worried.
    You are my closest confidants.
    I can confess to you
        that I am not without some apprehension
        that this great wealth of ours will blind us,
        bring an end to the prosperity that –
            with a god's help –
        Darius amassed.

    Which is why I have been struggling
        with this contradictory concern:
    that wealth without men is useless,
    while without wealth –
        no matter that a man is strong –
    good fortune will not shine on him.

    As for our wealth, we have no need to worry.
    But I fear for *him*, the apple of my eye,
        who lights the palace with his presence.

    Which is why, since things are so, you must advise me,   170
        Persians,
        my most trusted, my most senior advisors.
    Yes, I am pinning all my hopes
        for sound advice on you.

Chorus Be reassured, Ma'am,
        that you need not ask us twice to say or do
        whatever might be in our power to help you.
    You have summoned us as your advisors
        in these matters.
    We are your ever-willing subjects.

Atossa Ever since my son assembled his campaign force and set out to destroy Greece, I have been plagued by constant nightmares – but I never saw a vision quite as vivid as last night's. I shall describe it.

I dreamt two women stood before me, sumptuously attired – the dress of one was Persian, and of the other Dorian Greek. Both were more tall, more striking than the women of today; their beauty flawless: two sisters of one family. As for their homelands, Chance had settled one in Greece and one in Persia.

They were quarrelling, or so I dreamt it, and when my son found out he kept on trying to stop them and placate them. He yokes them to his chariot. He fastened leather straps around their necks. One of them preened and postured in her new accessories, her mouth subservient to the reins. But the other struggled, and with both hands tears apart the chariot's equipment and – once free of her reins – she drags it off by force and snaps the yoke straight down the middle. My son is thrown, and Darius, his father, stands beside him full of pity and, when Xerxes sees him, well, he rips his robes to rags. That was my dream, my vision.

When I got up, I washed my hands in pure spring water, and approached the altar to make sacrifice. As ritual demands, I wanted to give sacred cake as offerings to those spirits who deliver us from evil.

But then I see an eagle fleeing in terror to Apollo's fire-pit. I was frightened. Friends, I stood there, speechless. And then, a hawk – I see it swooping, wings outstretched, and tearing with its talons at the eagle's head. And it – the eagle – it did nothing. Except cower . . . And surrender.

What I saw – it alarmed me, and it's right that I should tell you. You're all aware that, if my son succeeds, he would be heroized, but if things should turn out badly . . . The state cannot hold him accountable. If he is saved, he shall rule Persia as he always did.

Chorus Mother, we should not wish to make you
   either overly afraid or overconfident
      by what we say.
   However, if what you saw
      unsettled you
   approach the gods
      in supplication.
   Pray they deliver you
      from evil

and bring matters to a
>good conclusion
>>for yourself and
>>for your children,
>>for Persia,
>>for all that you hold dear.

Then you must pour libations
>to the earth and
>to the dead.

Talk to your husband,
>gently, sympathetically –
>>Darius
>>>(you tell us that you saw him
>>>in the night).

Ask him to send
good fortune
from beneath the earth
into the light
>for you and
>for your son
and that the opposite –
bad fortune –
>be fettered
>>in the darkness of the earth
>>and fizzle out to nothing.

That's my advice.
>I'm saying it as I feel it.
>Sympathetically.

From what we've heard
>our judgement is
that this will bring
>in all respects
>>a good conclusion.

Atossa You are the first
>to have interpreted my dream
and you have done so
>with good will.
You have found
>a good interpretation
for my son

220

and all my family.
So, may all turn out well.

230 When I go back inside the palace
I shall perform the sacrifices
to the gods
    that you suggest
and to my family
    beneath the earth.
Meanwhile, though – friends –
I'd like to find out –
    where is Athens?

Chorus Far to the west
    toward the setting sun.

Atossa And yet, my son – he really was obsessed
    with taking it?

Chorus Yes. That way all Greece would become vassals
    of the king.

Atossa And their army – is it very large?

Chorus It is such ... that it has caused the Persians
    much suffering.

Atossa Are they good archers, then?

Chorus No, quite the opposite. They stand firm,
    fight with spear and shield.

Atossa And what else do they have?
    Enough resources in their palace?

240 **Chorus** They have a silver wellspring.
    Their very land's a treasure trove.

Atossa Who herds them into place?
    Who wields his will over their army?

Chorus They are not slaves of any man –
    nor vassals either.

Atossa So how can they withstand
    an enemy invasion?

Chorus Well, they destroyed Darius' glorious and monumental
    expedition force.

Atossa   Your words bring fear to any parent's heart
          whose son has gone to war.

Chorus   I think you'll soon find out
          the truth of the whole story.
    Look! Someone's coming –
          running like a Persian courier.
    Good or bad,
          he clearly brings important news.

Messenger   Persia! Cities of all Asia! A haven of such luxury and wealth! 250
With one blow our prosperity, our happiness has turned to dust. The flower
of Persia lies fallen. *Omoi!* It's bad to be the first to bring bad news. And yet...
I have no choice. Persians, I must give a full account of the catastrophe. You
see, the Persian expedition force in its entirety has been destroyed.

Chorus   disastrous
          disastrous
    so sudden
          and so cruel

   aiai

   weep
          persians
   weep
          to hear
          of such disaster

Messenger   It's over. It's all over. I did not think that I would ever see the 260
light of home.

Chorus   we are old men
          so old
          so many years
    and now
    to hear
    such news
    we never thought
          to hear

Messenger   Yes. I was there. I did not hear the news from others. Persians, I
can describe the tragedy that overwhelmed us.

Chorus   *otototoi*
          a storm of arrows

>   and a multitude of men
>   and yet
>   they marched
>   to greece
>   from asia
>   in vain

Messenger The coasts of Salamis and all the nearby shores are choked with corpses of our men – such cruel death.

Chorus *otototoi*
>   you're saying
>   the corpses
>   of our families
>   our friends
>   are drifting
>   bobbing
>   washing
>   in the current's
>   ebb and flow

Messenger Our bows were useless. Our whole army was destroyed, lost in the shattering of ships.

Chorus raise loud
>   the sad lament
>   for persians
>   killed so cruelly
>   wiped out
>   destroyed
>   *aiai*
>   our army
>   gone

Messenger I hate the very name of Salamis! *P-heu*! The very memory of Athens makes me groan.

Chorus yes
>   athens is abhorrent
>   to her enemies
>   and we
>   we must remember
>   persian wives
>   widowed

> persian mothers
> robbed of their dead sons

Atossa I have stayed silent until now, in mourning, crushed by this catastrophe. Yes, this disaster is so overwhelming that I don't know what to say or what to ask you. Still, mankind must endure the suffering gods give us. So. Compose yourself. Tell us the full extent of the disaster – even if you do 'groan' at our misfortunes. Who is not dead? Which of our generals should we be mourning? Which of our commanders died and left his post deserted? 290

Messenger Xerxes is still alive…

Atossa Well, that news brings a ray of light into my house, a white dawn following the darkness of the night. 300

Messenger But Artembares, the commander of ten thousand cavalry, is being pummelled on rugged coast of Salamis, while Dadaces, who led a thousand men, struck by a spear, dived like a dancer from his ship, and Tenagon, the best of all the native Bactrians, is drifting past the island home of Ajax, sea-washed Salamis. Lilaeus, Arsames and (third) Agestes are all rolling in the current, always butting up against the stony shore, alive with doves. And Arctaeus, who lived beside the waters of Egyptian Nile, and Ardeues and (third) Pharnuchus the shield-bearer – all three fell from the one ship. And Matallus of golden Chrysa, leader of ten thousand men, died, drenching his long tumbling beard, staining it blood red. Arbarus the Magus, died there too, and Bactrian Artabes who led the thirty-thousand-strong Black Cavalry, a settler in a savage country now. Amistris, Amphistreus, who cut a swathe of devastation with his spear, and the noble Ariomardus, whose arrows rained down suffering, and Mysian Seisames, and Tharybis who led five squadrons each of fifty ships, a Lyrnaean by birth, a handsome man, is lying in squalid death, all his good fortune gone. Syennesis, the Cilician commander, was conspicuous for his courage. Alone he caused the greatest suffering for the enemy, and he died gloriously. Those are the generals I can remember. Our losses were so many. I cannot recall them all. 310 320 330

Atossa *aiai!* What I am hearing? The most unthinkable disaster. Disgrace for every Persian. A litany of grief. But go back to the beginning. Tell me this: how large was the Greek fleet, to let them think they could do battle, turn their ships' rams on the Persian navy?

Messenger If it had been simply down to numbers, our navy would have won. You can be sure of that. Yes, the entire Greek navy numbered just three hundred ships, together with a handpicked squadron of ten more. Xerxes – I 340 know this for a fact – commanded a good thousand, of which two hundred and seven were the fastest ships at sea. So much for the resources. Did you think that we were simply outnumbered? No! It was some divine agency that tipped the scales and wrecked our army. The gods protect the city of Athena.

Atossa   You mean Athens has not yet been sacked?

Messenger   As long as she has men, she is impregnable.

350 **Atossa**   But tell me, how did the sea battle start? *Who* started it? The Greeks? Or was my son too confident because he had the larger fleet?

Messenger   Some demon out of nowhere, some spirit, some vindictive Thing began the butchery. A Greek man – from the Athenian army – came to your son, Xerxes, spun a tale how, when night fell and darkness, the Greeks would not stay put. No, they would scramble for their rowing benches, try to
360 save their lives by slipping out to sea, unseen, scattered in all directions.

Xerxes did not understand the Greek man's cunning or the gods' resentment – so as soon as he heard this he passed the word to each of his commanders: as soon as the sun's last rays had faded from the earth and night bathed all the sky, they must draw up their ships in three lines, watch every exit closely and the thundering straits, and position others in a circle around Ajax's island. And if any Greeks escaped their death, discovering some way out for their
370 ships, unseen, he proclaimed that every one of his commanders would be beheaded. It was because he was so confident, he said it. He did not know what the gods had in store.

Our crews, well disciplined, obeying orders, prepared supper, and each oarsman looped his oar around the thole pin – snugly. And when the sunlight faded and night fell the oarsmen, to a man experienced, and the marines,
380 all seasoned warriors, embarked onto their ships. Squadron by squadron the long ships raised a cheer, and so they set the course that each had been assigned, and all night long the captains kept their vessels – manned and ready – cruising back and forth across the straits. And night drew to an end, and still the Greek force had made no attempt to slip out of the bay unseen.

But when day broke blazing over all the earth – the clouds were like white stallions in the sky – the first thing we heard: a cheer, a shout of triumph – optimistic, sacramental – loud from the Greek camp, and at once an echo
390 from the island's cliffs returned the war cry amplified. And terror gripped the Persians – every one of us – our certainties undone. You see, the Greeks were chanting now – a sacred battle hymn – not like a fleeing rabble but like men

racing into battle, confident, inspired. And then the trumpet call ignited their whole army. At once the order came and, out from shore now, they began to sweep the water with well-measured strokes of oars as every ship shot into view.

Their right wing led, well-disciplined, a tight advance, and then the whole fleet was approaching us, and as it did we heard a shout – huge, roaring: 'Forward, Greeks! Set free your fatherland! Set free your wives and children. Set free your fathers' gods, and spirits of your ancestors. The contest is at hand and it is all to fight for!' 400

We answered, bellowing our Persian war cry. The time had come – no holding back – ship smashing bronze ram into ship. It was a *Greek* warship that attacked first, slicing the ornamental stern-post from one of our Phoenician ships. Then another captain drove *his* ship like a missile into one of ours. At first the tide of Persian vessels kept firmly in formation, but with our huge fleet crowded in the narrows, not able to help one another, crashing into one another with our bronze-toothed rams, and splintering whole banks of oars, the Greek ships seized their moment, circled round us and attacked, capsizing ships until the sea became invisible, a dense mass of shipwrecks and the bodies of the dead. 410

420

The coastline and the shoals were choked with corpses as – with no thought now to keep in tight formation – each vessel in the Persian navy tried to row to safety, while they – like we were tuna or fish netted in a fishing net – they kept on clubbing us with broken oars and bits of splintered wreckage. Screams and groaning blanketed the surface of the sea until black night came down and hid it all from view.

But as for the full scale of the disaster – even if I spoke for ten days straight, I still could not tell you everything. One thing's for certain, though. Never before on one day have so many men – so many, many countless numbers – died. 430

Atossa   *aiai!* A great sea of troubles has engulfed all Persia and all our people.

Messenger   So much for the battle. But you've not yet heard the greater part of our catastrophe – so overwhelming a disaster that, after what had come before, it pressed down twice as heavy.

Atossa   What could have happened that was even worse? What are you saying? Tell me! What new disaster could be even greater than what went before? 440

Messenger   Those Persians at pinnacle of life ... the most brave-hearted ... the highest born ... the best ... and always first to earn the king's confidence ... they met the most dishonourable, most squalid death of all.

Atossa   Such a disaster. Friends, I'm overwhelmed. How did you say they died?

Messenger   There is an island lying off Salamis – a little island, no good anchorage at all. It's sacred to the god, Pan; he loves to dance there through
450   the surf. That's where he'd stationed these crack troops, so that, when shipwrecked Greeks sought refuge on the island, they could dispatch them easily, while at the same time saving allied comrades from the sea.

But he misjudged it badly. You see, no sooner did the god give victory in battle to the Greek ships, than they disembarked, bronze-armoured, and encircled the whole island, so that our men ... they had nowhere to turn. A
460   hail of stones and slingshot pelted down on them, and deadly arrows found their mark. Then – in the end – the enemy with one long endless roar rushed at them, cut them down, kept hacking at their limbs and butchering those poor unfortunates, 'till every one of them was dead.

As he watched the full extent of the atrocity unfolding, Xerxes groaned – he'd established his command headquarters high up on a headland that overlooked the sea with unobstructed views of every element of our armed forces. And he ripped his robes and wailed – a high-pitched wail – and he issued the command
470   to his land army to turn and flee immediately with no concern for order.

So mourn this, too, our second catastrophe.

Atossa   (*looking to the skies*) You – what? A god? No! No, you, demon! Oh, how you deluded us Persians! The cruel vengeance that my son was planning for that starry city, Athens, has turned on him instead. The Persians that Marathon destroyed were not enough! No! Now in his attempt take revenge for those men's deaths my son has plunged himself in so much misery.

(*to* **Messenger**)   But you – tell me. What happened to the ships that got away? Where did you last see them? Can you give an accurate report?

480   **Messenger**   The captains of whatever ships were still intact scrambled to escape wherever the wind took them, no thought of keeping in formation. As for the rest of the land army ... Some died in Boeotia from thirst as they searched unsuccessfully to find a river or a spring, while the rest of us exhausted, lungs on fire, pushed through to Phocis, Doris and the Malian Gulf, where the River Spercheius floods welcome water through the plain, before, with no provisions left us, the broad lands of Achaea and the towns of
490   the Thessalians received us.

But still many of us died of thirst and hunger, which by now were plaguing us…

Then, onwards to Magnesia and Macedonia, the ford over the Axius, and Bolbe's reedy marshland, and Mount Pangaeus in the land of the Edonians.

But in that night the god unleashed an early winter, froze the sacred River Strymon solid. And any man who up 'till then had shown the scantest of respect for gods now prayed and begged and offered ritual prostration to the gods of earth and sky. Then, after they had finished calling on the gods, the troops began to cross the ice-bound river, and those of us who started early – before the sun's rays bathed the earth – we got across to safety. But then the fireball of the sun, bright, blazing, baking, melted the ice midstream, and one by one our men began to sink – and blessèd was the man who died most quickly. 500

The survivors – there were very few of us – pressed on for safety, struggling through Thrace and countless hardships 'till we reached our own land and salvation. 510

So Persia's capital will mourn in longing for her country's youth, the best, the most beloved of men. What I have told you is the truth, although there's much I've left unsaid – such horror did the god unleash against the Persians.

Exit **Messenger**

Chorus You demon! You black demon! You've swooped, too heavy, on us Persians!

Atossa The whole army gone. Horrendous. The sleep-vision that came to me so vividly last night – you laid the whole catastrophe before me; you made it all so clear.

(*to* **Chorus**) And you – your glib interpretation was so shallow. Still, you did recommend the first thing I should do was make prayers to the gods, so pray I shall. Then I shall come outside again – out of my palace – with consecrated offerings of food, a gift for Earth and for the dead. What's done can't be undone – I know that – but perhaps such services will mean the future might be better. And you – you must debate honestly, my honest councillors, about all that has happened. 520

If my son arrives before I do, be comforting. Bring him inside the palace. Stop him doing anything to hurt himself to add to all the hurt that we've already suffered. 530

Chorus   zeus
        king
        you have wiped out
        the persian army
            countless men
            so confident
        you've plunged
        our cities
        susa and ecbatana
            in leaden grief

        so many women
            bruised with sorrow
        share our anguish

            soft hands
                tear veils

540   tears fall
                on tear-soaked dresses

        persian wives
        are wailing
            longing
                for their husbands
            abandoning
                their marriage beds
                    so soft
                    so sensuous
                the scene of
                    so much pleasure
                    in the sensuality of youth
        and their grief
            their weeping
        knows no end

        and i too
            mourn
            with all my heart
        the fate
            such grief
            such overwhelming grief
        of the men who have gone
            who have left us

now all the land
all asia
   abandoned
   desolate
is mourning

xerxes   550
   led them
      popoi
xerxes
   lost them
      totoi
xerxes
   organized it all
      so carelessly

      launching
      river barges
      out across
      the ocean

not like his father
   darius
      the archer king
      unscathed
      unconquered
and the men of susa
   loved him

the infantry and
crews of ships
   sail-winged with
   dark-eyed prows

warships   560
   led them
      popoi
warships
   lost them
      totoi
warships
   rammed to smithereens
      in the greek onslaught

men
  cut down
  by greek
  hands

and our king
  we hear
only just managed
  to escape
    across
        the icy tracks
    across
        the plains of thrace

the first to meet their deaths
   p-heu
abandoned by necessity
   e-é
are dragging in the sea
   o-á
along the coast of
   salamis

groan
   in your grief

bawl loud
your sorrow
   to the skies

   o-á

scream loud
the lamentation
   of your suffering

ripped by the racing waters
   p-heu
they are torn apart
   e-é
by voiceless creatures
  of the sacred sea
   o-á

the house
  robbed of its master

>   groans
> and parents
> old now
>   robbed of sons
> weep for the fate
>   the demon
>   gave them
> as they learn the
> full convulsion
> of their sorrow

> the peoples of
> the land of asia
> will not remain for long now
>   under persian rule
> or pay the tribute
>   forced on them
>   by persian masters
> or prostrate themselves
>   in reverence
>   before the king
>   now that the king's power
>   has been demolished

> no more will tongues
>   be guarded
> now the people
>   have been freed

> they can
>   speak freely
> now the yoke
>   of power
>   has been destroyed

> the blood-soaked soil
>   of salamis
>   ajax's
>   wave-washed island
> now houses everything
>   that once
>   was
>   persia

Enter **Atossa** *on foot, perhaps with attendants, bearing jugs and trays of offerings and flowers.*

Atossa Friends! Whoever has experienced great crises knows that,
600 whenever a great tidal wave of crisis washes over mortal men, they tend to be afraid of everything. But when, thanks to good fortune, all goes well, they think the same good fortune will ease their way to happiness for ever. For me the situation now seems full of fear. Gods' hatred stares me in the eye; my ears are ringing with a rushing sound, a baleful sound – I am confounded by catastrophe.

I'm frightened.

So, I've come back – on foot, without the pomp and ceremony of before. I've
610 brought soothing libations to offer my son's father, libations to appease the dead: white milk – delicious– from an unblemished cow; glistening honey drawn from dripping blossom by the bees; fresh-flowing water from a pure virgin spring; and, from the fertile hills, pure, unmixed wine crushed from an ancient grapevine. I have, too, the fruit – sweet-smelling – of the grey-green olive tree, that lives for ever in its fecundity of leaves, and woven flowers sprung from the fertile earth

So, friends, as I offer these libations to the dead, lend your support with
620 solemn chanting. Summon up the ghost of Darius, while I pour these oblations for the soil to drink in honour of the gods beneath the earth.

Chorus queen
lady
most revered of all
   the persians
send your libations
   to the chambers
   deep below the earth
while we
   with chants
will beg
   the guides and
   guardians
   of the dead
   beneath the earth
to look on us
   with kindness

*As the **Chorus** prays, some of its members may start whirling in circles, while others beat and scratch at the earth with increasing urgency.*

Chorus   now
    sacred spirits
        of the underworld
  earth
  and hermes
  and you who rule as sovereign
    of the dead
  send his soul back   630
    into the light

  if anyone can know
    a remedy
    for our catastrophe
  he is the only
    mortal man
  to tell
    how to
    dispense it

  does our king
    our blessèd king
    our godlike king
  hear my words
    my woven words
    my endless words
  mouthed in his
    persian language
  or
  must i bawl
    my pain
  more loud
    my never-ending pain
  that he might
    hear me

  can he
    hear me
    from the underworld

  you   640
    earth

and you
   you others who
   hold sway
   beneath the earth
hear
   my prayer

grant
   that his proud spirit
   persia's god
   born here in susa
may leave his
   present home

send him
   back up
   to earth

persia's soil
   has never held
   another man
   like him

we reverenced
   the man
we reverence
   his tomb
we reverence
   the qualities
   entombed there

650   aidoneus
aidoneus
you
   who lead spirits
   back
   to earth
let darius
return
   our god
   our king
     e-é

he never caused
   destruction
to his men
through
   reckless
   catastrophic
   wars

we knew him as
   the persians'
   god-like counsellor

he *was* a
   god-like counsellor

he led his army
   well
      e-é

our sultan
our sultan
   of old
come now
come near
come
   to the summit
   of your tomb

step high   660
   in your yellow slippers
reveal
   your royal tiara's
   crest

hurry
   father darius
   who never did us ill

come now

appear
   great king
   of our king

come and hear
 our endless
 newborn
 sorrow

for a miasma
 like the miasma
 of the styx
engulfs us now

our young men
have all been
 destroyed

hurry
 father darius
 who never did us ill

come now

aiai
aiai

we mourned you
 when you died
we reverenced you
 then

why must we mourn
 again
 a new catastrophe

how did we
 sin

why has our land
all persia
 been stripped
 of all its warships

no ships now
no
 all gone
 all gone

The ghost of **Darius** *rises from his tomb dressed in splendour, wearing sumptuous royal robes, a high headdress (or tiara) and yellow slippers. The* **Chorus** *prostrate themselves.*

Darius Of all the men I trusted, I trusted you the most. Once we were young together. Now you are Persia's elders. What is this catastrophe that overwhelms my city? The earth groans, beaten, scratched, and the sight of my wife crouched here beside my tomb fills me with trepidation. And yet, as I received her offerings, I felt compassion. And you – you – standing pressed up to my tomb, and weeping, summoning the dead and wailing so ear-piercingly – I felt such pity for you as you called on me.

It's not an easy road up from the underworld. The gods beneath the earth are always quicker to receive than to let go. Still, I do enjoy some power among them, so I've come. 690

But quickly – I don't want to be accused of wasting time. What is this new catastrophe that weighs so heavy on the Persians?

Chorus   i'm wonderstruck
                to look on you

   i'm wonderstruck
      to speak to you

   i feel the
      trepidation
   that i felt
      of old

Darius   i've risen
      from the underworld
   in answer
      to your lamentations
   so
      do not prevaricate

   be brief and
      to the point

   say
      what you have
      to say
   and finish

                forget
                    your fear
                    of me

700 **Chorus**   i fear
                    to do
                        as you command
                i fear
                    to speak
                        in front of you
                and say
                    things that are hard
                    to say
                    to one i hold
                    so dear

Darius   (*to* **Chorus**) well
             if you're paralyzed
                by atavistic fear ...

             (*to* **Atossa**) my venerable queen
             my lawful wedded wife
             my partner in my bed
                dry your tears and
                stop your weeping and
                speak to me
                    in terms that i can
                    understand

             humans are plagued by
             human problems
                all the time

             we all know that

             for any human being
                who lives
                    for any length of time
             many calamities come
                from the sea
             and many
                from the land

Atossa   you were the richest
                of all men

        yours was the most happy
           destiny

        when you still could see
           the blazing
              sun
        you led
           a blessèd life
        envied
           by persians
        worshipped
           as a god

710

        and even now
        i envy you

        you died
        before you saw
        the depth
           of all our suffering

        darius
        i'll tell you everything
           in these few words

        persia
           has been annihilated

Darius how

        some burning
           plague

        civil unrest

Atossa no
           neither of those things
        no

        near athens
        our whole army was
           wiped out

Darius which of my sons
           commanded it

| | tell me |
| **Atossa** | xerxes |

        headstrong
  xerxes

        he stripped the whole
    continent
      of men

Darius   the fool

      and this doomed
         escapade of his
    was it by land
      or sea

720 **Atossa**   by both

    a double
        expedition force
  a double
    front

Darius   how did such a massive
        army
  make the crossing

Atossa   he yoked the hellespont
      through artifice

  that's how he
  made the crossing

Darius   he managed that
    did he
  to close
    the mighty
      bosporus

Atossa   he did

  some*how*
  some *thing* from the
    spirit world

| | usurped
| | his mind

Darius   *p-heu*

    some powerful
      spirit
    came
      on him
    and stopped him
      thinking clearly

Atossa   and now we see
      how it all ended
    the whole catastrophe
      he set in motion

Darius   so then
    what
      happened

    why
      are you in mourning

Atossa   defeat
      of our navy
    led to
      the destruction
      of our army

Darius   our whole army
      to a man
    cut down

Atossa   yes   730
    which is why all susa
      emptied of her men
    is plunged
      in mourning

Darius   *o popoi*
    our
      mighty army
    our
      help and
      our defence

Atossa all of the bactrians
        to a man
            even the oldest men
        are lost

Darius the fool

        he has wiped
           the young men
              out from all our allies

Atossa but xerxes
            they say
        alone
        abandoned
        with only a few men ...

Darius how did he die

        where

        is there any hope
            that he is safe

Atossa to his relief
        he reached
            the bridge
        that yokes
            both continents

Darius he got back
            safely

        are you sure

Atossa yes

        on that
        i have received
            a most reliable report

        there is no doubt

Darius *p-heu*

        the oracles came true
            so soon

it was
   decreed by god

and zeus 740
   has poured down its
   fulfilment
      on my son

i was so confident
we had
   so much more time
before
the gods would
   bring this to fulfilment

but
when a man
   is reckless
god helps
   propel him onwards

now the well head
of catastrophe
   i think
has been unstopped
   for all i love

it was my son
who engineered it
   thanks to
   the compulsiveness
   and inexperience
      of youth
   and his ambition
   to restrain
      the sacred waters
      of the hellespont
      with chains
         as if it were
         some slave –
      the sacred waters
      of the bosporus

he engineered

>   a strange new
>   crossing
>
>   he locked it in
>   with hammered fetters
>
>   he engineered a
>   highway
>   for his mighty army
>
>   a mortal man
>   he thought
>   in his foolhardiness
>   that he could tame
>   the gods
>   even poseidon
>
>   surely some
>   mental illness
>   gripped
>   my son
>
>   i fear
>   the great wealth
>   i amassed
>   through toil and struggle
>   will prove easy pickings
>   easy booty
>   for whoever wants
>   to take it

Atossa   xerxes was
>   headstrong
>
>   he associated
>   with bad men
>   who led him
>   astray
>
>   they kept on telling him
>   that while you
>   won great riches
>   for your children
>   by your spear
>   he
>   was a coward

>   just planned wars
>   and never fought them
>   did nothing to increase
>   his patrimony
>
> time and again
> he heard these taunts
>   from bad men
> 'till he made his plans
>   to set out
>   with his expedition force
>   to conquer greece

Darius And so he undertook this great catastrophe of his – to haunt our memories forever – the greatest devastation ever to strike Susa since Lord Zeus ordained that one man should rule all Asia with its teeming flocks and wield the sceptre of authority. 760

Medos was the first to rule our people and our army. Next came his son, who kept up his good work and governed with sound judgement. Third, Cyrus took the throne, a man loved by the gods, and gave peace to all his people. He added to his empire the Lydians and Phrygians and he took all of Ionia by force. Yes, Cyrus was a gracious man, beloved by god. His son ruled next, the fourth king; and the fifth was Mardus, no credit to his country or to the ancestral throne. Brave Artaphernes and his trusted colleagues took him by surprise and killed him in the palace as was their duty. [The sixth king was Maraphis, the seventh Artapernes.] And then – by lot – I took the throne (I'd always wanted it), and I led my mighty army out on many a campaign – though I never brought catastrophe like this on Persia. But Xerxes, my son, a young man thinking young men's thoughts, does not remember my advice. 770 780

You all are my contemporaries. Be sure of this one thing: we – all of us, who ever wielded power – no-one could ever point to us and say we were responsible for such catastrophe.

Chorus What now, King Darius? Where are your words taking us? In the face of such catastrophe, what can we do in best interests of the Persians?

Darius Do not campaign against the Greeks – not even if your numbers are superior. The very land is on the side of Greece. 790

Chorus What do you mean? How is it on their side?

Darius It kills too large an army through starvation.

Chorus But we can send out an elite hand-picked detachment.

Darius No. Not even those troops still in Greece will manage to return home safely.

Chorus What do you mean? Won't all the Persian army cross the Hellespont from Europe?

800 **Darius** Only a handful out of all those who left, if we can trust the oracles of gods. And we *must* trust them when we see what has just happened. Yes, everything has been fulfilled in its entirety – not just some and not the rest. And so his optimism – leaving his elite corps still in theatre – is misplaced.

They're stationed where flatlands are watered by the River Asopus, which brings Boeotia its much-coveted fertility – and there the culmination of their suffering will meet them, payback for hubris and sacrilege.

810 Yes, when they got to Greece they felt no compunction whatsoever about looting ancient wooden statues of the gods or torching temples. Altars have been smashed. Statues of divinities have been torn down from plinths and shattered. So. Since they acted so outrageously they are suffering no less outrageously in turn.

And there is more to come. The wellspring of their suffering has not yet run dry. It gushes still. The oozing mess of blood spilled at Plataea by Greek spears will prove so prodigious that the piles of corpses will be for men a silent 820 witness – even to the third generation – that they must not think too big. When hubris flowers, it bears rich fruit – blind recklessness, a bumper harvest thick with tears.

When you observe the consequences of such deeds, remember the Athenians and Greece. Let every one of you be satisfied with what they have already. Do not drain great wealth by lusting after more. Zeus punishes whoever entertains excessive, arrogant ambitions. He makes them pay a heavy price.

So now, instruct my son – he lacks sound judgement. Give him well-reasoned 830 guidance. Teach him to desist from angering the gods through his conceit and arrogance.

(*to* **Atossa**) And you, my dear, Xerxes' revered mother, go back inside the palace. Fetch robes appropriate for royalty. And prepare to meet your son. He is tormented by the scale of the catastrophe. He has torn his robes – his rich-embroidered robes – to tatters. Soothe him with gentle words. You are the only person he will listen to, the only one he will respond to.

Me, I must go. I must descend into the darkness of the earth.

(*to* **Chorus**) Elders! Goodbye. Despite your troubles, take pleasure every 840
day from life, since, once you're dead, wealth brings no benefit.

The ghost of **Darius** *sinks back beneath the earth.*

Chorus Such ruin for the Persians already, and so much more to come! I'm torn apart.

Atossa God! All this suffering is tearing *me* apart, but most of all this one misfortune cuts me to the core – to hear the ignominy of my son dressed in rags. So. I shall go. I'll bring his regalia outside from the palace, and I'll try to intercept my son. I'll not abandon my beloved son in times of trouble. 850

Exit **Atossa**.

Chorus *o popoi*
    the life that
        we once led
    was rich and
        glorious indeed
    when our revered
        all-powerful
        peaceful
    king
        who never did us ill
    the godlike
    darius
    ruled persia
        with sound government

    we presented
        to the world
    a fighting force
        unrivalled in its
        reputation

    sound government
        a tower of strength
    made all things 860
        good

    and homecomings
        from war
    brought men back

>   trouble-free
>   unscathed
>   to well-run houses
>
>   and all the cities
>   that he captured
>   before he even crossed
>   the river halys
>   or left his hearth
>   and home
>
>   the river cities
>   on the strymon's
>   floodplain
>   near the cattlefolds
>   of thrace
>
>   and those beyond
>   the lake
>   walled cities
>   on the mainland
>   all acknowledged him
>   as king
>
>   and those rich cities
>   on each bank
>   of the wide
>   hellespont
>   and the broad bays
>   of the propontis
>   and the mouth
>   of the black sea
>
>   and sea-washed
>   islands
>   off our coast
>   lesbos and
>   samos
>   with its olive groves
>   and chios
>   paros
>   naxos
>   myconos

and teos
    nestling close to
andros

and he ruled too
the sea-splashed islands
in mid-ocean
    lemnos and   890
    icaria
        with its scattered villages
    and rhodes
    and cnidus
    and the towns of cyprus
    paphos
    soli and
    salamis
        whose founding city
        now
        is such a cause
        of lamentation

and the wealthy cities
    of ionia
    that teemed
    with greeks –   900
he ruled them
    in his wisdom

he had
    at his command
a strength that
    never tired –
a host of
    persian warriors
and allies drawn
    from every country
    on the earth

but now
    without doubt
    by the hand of god
our fortune has been
overturned

Enter **Xerxes** *in a covered carriage, dressed in the rags of his royal clothing, an empty quiver strung across his shoulder.*

Xerxes *io!* I'm overwhelmed by so much suffering. There was no inkling, no inkling at all of this catastrophe, or that some cruel, savage demon would grind all Persia under foot. And what will happen to me now, now that all this has happened? To see the city elders ... I can scarcely stand. Zeus! So many men gone! I only wish death's destiny had shrouded me with them!

Chorus *otototoi!* King! I'm overwhelmed for our great army, and for the mighty reputation of our Persian regime, and for the glory of our men scythed down now by some demon.

All Persia laments her Persian youth, slaughtered by Xerxes when he crowded Hades with our Persian dead. So many men have been wiped out, the heroes of Ecbatana, the flower of Persia, so many, such a pressing multitude of men! *aiai aiai!* We trusted in their strength. The land of Asia, the ruler of the world – brought to her knees so utterly. So comprehensively.

Xerxes look
    at me
    now
oioi
and weep

look
    at me
    born
    to bring down
    ruin
      on the persians
    destruction
      on the land of persia

Chorus to greet
    your homecoming

i'll sob
a lamentation
   fraught
      with evil omen
   fraught
      with evil destiny
a lamentation
   fraught
     with wild untamed
     despair

i'll s ob   940
a dirge
   that's drowned
   in tears

Xerxes sob
weep
   forever
     uncontrollably
the discord
   of despair

the demon
has turned and
destroyed me

Chorus i'll sob
i *shall* weep
   uncontrollably
remembering
   your fate
   and our ships
   lost at sea

i'll weep
the lamentation
   of a land
   that's lost
   her sons

i'll weep
   shrill
   piercing

            i shall weep
                shrill
                piercing

            i shall add
                my lamentations
                to my tears

Xerxes   the greeks
                    with their stockade
                    of ships
            the greeks
                stole
                all our men

            they turned the tide
                of battle
            harrowing
                the night-time
                seas
                and the death-haunted
                shore

Chorus   *oioioi!*
            shout
                loud
            discover
                everything

            where are the rest
                of all our friends and
            where are those
                who stood
                by you
            men such as
                pharandakes
                susas
                pelagon and
                dotamas and
                agdabatas
                psammis and
                susiscanes
                    who set out

	from ecbatana

Xerxes i left them all
  dead
 fallen from their
  persian ships
 battered
  on the shores
  of salamis and
  on the jagged
  rocks

Chorus *oioioi*
 shout
  loud

 and tell me
 where is
  pharnuchus and
  brave ariomardus
 where is
  the lord seualces
  noble lilaeus   970
  mephis
  tharubis and
  masistras
  artembares and
  hystaechmas

 my questions know
 no ending

Xerxes *io io*
 moi moi

 together
 they set eyes on
  ancient athens
  glowering athens
 and together
  in one
   great convulsion
 e-é
 the poor men

		gasped their lives out
		on the shore

Chorus and did you really lose
    your faithful overseer
    your eye
    who tallied all the
980   tens and
    tens of
    thousand persians
alpistus
    son of batanochus
    son of sesames
    son of megabates

did you really lose
    parthus and
    great orbares

did you
    leave them

did you
    leave them

o o o
    poor men

you tell of
    suffering
unending
    suffering
for all the greatest men
    in persia

Xerxes *io io*
you fill me with
    such longing
    for my brave
    companions
990 you stir
    such
bitter
    sorrow
    such

>   unending
>   suffering
>   with all your questioning
>
>   my heart is
>   bawling
>   bawling
>
>   i am wracked
>   with grief

Chorus and yet there are
still others
missing too

> xanthis
>   commander of
>   ten thousand mardians
> and fierce anchares
> and diaexis
> and arsakes
>   who led
>   the cavalry
> and cegdadatas
> and lythimnas
> and tolmus
>   whose thirst for war
>   was never quenched

i'm stunned   1000
i'm stunned
that they're not
   here now
   in your entourage
   behind your
   covered carriage

Xerxes those
men
those
   gods
   who led our army

all are gone

Chorus gone yes
     o-í
  and so dishonourably

Xerxes *i-é i-é*
  i-ó i-ó

Chorus *i-ó i-ó*
  you
    gods
  you
    demons
  you
    clamped us with
    catastrophe
    so unexpected yet
    so glaring
  like the glance of
  até
    goddess of infatuation

Xerxes we have been
  beaten down
  by tragedy
    that will reverberate
    throughout the years

Chorus we have been
  beaten down

  the evidence is here
    for all to see

1010 **Xerxes** by pain
    we've never
    met before

  by pain
    we've never
    met before

Chorus disastrous
    to take on
    greece's sailors

| | yes
| | persia's people
| | crushed in war

Xerxes yes
        and me too
            beaten down
        and all my
            army

Chorus is any part
        of persia
        still intact
            king

Xerxes do you see
            these rags
        all that remains
            of my regalia

Chorus i see them
        yes
        i see them

Xerxes and   1020
        this quiver

Chorus you mean that this is all
        that you have left

Xerxes my arrows'
        strongbox

Chorus so little
        left
        out of
    so very much

Xerxes so few
        left
        to defend us

Chorus the greeks
        are not afraid
            of fighting

Xerxes yes
             they love
                 conflict

             i have seen
                 catastrophe
             the like of which
             i never thought
                 to see

Chorus you mean
             our strong
             stockade of ships
                 turned
                 routed

1030 **Xerxes** i tore
                  my robes
              when i saw
                  such catastrophe

Chorus *papai papai*

Xerxes *papai papai*
            PAPAI PAPAI

Chorus disaster multiplied
                by two
                by three

Xerxes such grief
                for us
            such celebration
                for our enemies

Chorus our power
                scythed out
                from under us

Xerxes and i
                stripped
                of my retinue

Chorus by the calamities
              that met your friends
                at sea

Xerxes weep
  weep
    for all our
      sorrow

  and now
  go back
    to your homes

Chorus *aiai aiai*
    du-á du-á

Xerxes and cry   1040
    aloud
  and echo
    me

Chorus an offering
    of ruin
  given
    by the ruined
  to the ruined

Xerxes cry
    out now
  match
    your groans
    with mine

Chorus *otototoi*
  such fathomless
    catastrophe

  o-í
  i share
    your suffering

Xerxes beat
    the rhythm
    of your grief

  beat
    the rhythm
    of your grief

	and groan
	for all
	i've suffered
Chorus	my tears
	are flowing
	in my grief
Xerxes	and cry
	aloud
	and echo
	me
Chorus	i shall
	my lord
	i shall
1050 **Xerxes**	and raise
	your voices now
	in lamentation
Chorus	*otototoi*
	black bruising
	blows
	will couple
	with my
	groans
	o-á
Xerxes	and beat
	your breasts
	and raise
	a savage wail
Chorus	such
	grief
	such
	grief
Xerxes	and tear
	your white hair
	from your beard
	yes
	i command you

Chorus	fists beating
	down
	fists beating
	down
	i groan
	with all my heart
Xerxes	cry loud
	and shrill
Chorus	i shall
Xerxes	and take your robes
	in both your hands
	tear them
	to tatters
Chorus	such
	grief
	such
	grief
Xerxes	tear out
	your hair
	weep for
	our army
Chorus	fists beating
	down
	fists beating
	down
	i groan
	with all my heart
Xerxes	let tears flow
	free
Chorus	my eyes are
	wet
	with tears
Xerxes	and cry
	aloud
	and echo
	me

1060 appears at line "and take your robes"

Chorus *oi-oí oi-oí*

Xerxes go
to your homes
now
and mourn there

Chorus *i-ó i-ó*
all persia
is mourning

1070 **Xerxes** the sounds
of mourning
echo through
the city

Chorus *i-oá*
yes
we hear them

Xerxes go softly
as you mourn

Chorus *i-ó i-ó*
all persia
is mourning

Xerxes *i-é i-é*
so many men
dead
in our warships

Chorus i shall escort you in
with tears
and lamentation

Exeunt **Xerxes** *and* **Chorus** *into the palace.*

Bibliography

Alexanderson, B., 'Darius in the *Persians*', *Eranos*, 65 (1967), 1–11.
Allan, W. and Kelly, A., 'Listening to many voices: Greek tragedy as popular art', in A. Marmadoro and J. Hill (eds), *The Author's Voice in Classical and Late Antiquity*, 77–122, Oxford, 2013.
Almagor, E., 'Strabo's Barbarophonoi (14.2.28 C661–3): A note', *Scripta Classica Israelica* (2000), 133–8.
Anderson, M., 'The imagery of the *Persians*', *Greece & Rome*, 19 (1972), 166–74.
Avery, H. C., 'Dramatic devices in Aeschylus' *Persians*', *American Journal of Philology*, 85 (1964), 173–84.
Baron, A. (ed.), *The Herodotus Encyclopaedia*, 3 vols, Hoboken, NJ, 2021.
Bassi, K., 'Mimesis and mortality: Reperformance and the dead among the living in *Hecuba* and *Hamlet*', in R. L. Hunter and A. Uhlig (eds), *Imagining Reperformance in Ancient Culture: Studies in the Traditions of Drama and Lyric*, 138–59, Cambridge, 2017.
Bates, S., *The Guardian*, 22 November 2000. https://www.theguardian.com/uk/2000/nov/29/thatcher.politics (accessed 2 February 2022).
Battezzato, L., 'Lyric', in J. Gregory (ed.), *A Companion to Greek Tragedy*, 149–66, Malden, MA, 2005.
Blomfield, C. J., *Aeschyli Persae*, London, 1830.
Bowersock, G. W., Burkert and Putnam M. C. J. (eds), *Arktouros: Hellenic Studies Presented to Bernard M.W. Knox on the Occasion of his 65th Birthday*, Berlin and New York, 1979.
Bowie, A. M. (ed.), *Herodotus, Histories Book VIII*, Cambridge, 2007.
Briant, P., *From Cyrus to Alexander: A History of the Persian Empire*, 681–90, Winona Lake, IN: 2002.
Bridges, E., *Imagining Xerxes/Ancient Perspectives on a Persian King*, London, 2015.
Bridges, E., Hall, E. and Rhodes, P. J. (eds), *Cultural Responses to the Persian Wars*, Oxford, 2007.
Broadhead, H. D., *The Persae of Aeschylus*, Cambridge, 1960.
Brosius, M., *The Persian Empire from Cyrus II to Artaxerxes I*, London, 2000.
Cameron, A. and Kuhrt, A. (eds), *Images of Women in Antiquity*, Detroit, 1983.
Carlson, M., *The Haunted Stage: The Theatre as Memory Machine*, Ann Arbor, MI, 2001.
Cartledge, P., '"Deep plays": Theatre as process in Athenian civic life', in P. E. Easterling (ed.), *The Cambridge Companion to Greek Tragedy*, 3–35, Cambridge, 1997. Greek translation, 2008.
Cartledge, P., 'Greeks and "barbarians"', in A.-F. Christidis (ed.), *A History of Ancient Greek: From the Beginnings to Late Antiquity*, ch. 21, Cambridge, 2007.
Cartledge, P., *Ancient Greek Political Thought in Practice*, Cambridge, 2009.

Cioffi, R., 'Night of the waking dead: The ghost of Clytemnestra and collective vengeance in Aeschylus' *Eumenides*', Presentation at Society for Classical Studies Annual Meeting, New Orleans, 8–11 January 2015.
Conacher, D. J., 'Aeschylus' *Persae*: A literary commentary', in J. Heller (ed.), *Serta Turyniana*, 143–68, Urbana, IL, 1974.
Conacher, D. J., *Aeschylus: The Earlier Plays and Related* Studies, Toronto, Buffalo and London, 1996.
Couch, H. N., Review of O. Broneer, 'The tent of Xerxes and the Greek theatre,' *Classical Weekly*, 38 (1 Oct. 1944), 117–18.
Cropp, M., Fantham, E. and Scully, S. (eds), *Greek Tragedy and Its Legacy: Essays Presented to D.J. Conacher*, Calgary, 1986.
Csapo, E. and Slater, W. J., *The Context of Ancient Drama*, Ann Arbor, MI, 1995.
Curtis, J. and Tallis, N. (eds), *Forgotten Empire: The World of Ancient Persia*, London, 2005.
Dandamaev, M. A., *A Political History of the Achaemenid Empire*, Leiden, 1989.
Dawe, R. D., Diggle, J. and Easterling, P. E. (eds), *Dionysiaca*, Cambridge, 1978.
de Ste. Croix, G. E. M., *The Origins of the Peloponnesian War*, London, 1972.
Dodds, E. R., *The Greeks and the Irrational*, Sather Classical Lecture, vol. 25, Berkeley, CA, 1951.
Dominick, Y. H., 'Acting other: Atossa and instability in Herodotus', *Classical Quarterly*, 57 (2007), 432–44.
Dué, C., *The Captive Woman's Lament in Greek Tragedy*, Austin, TX, 2006.
Dworacki, S., 'Atossa's absence in the final scene of the *Persae* of Aeschylus', in *Arktouros: Hellenic Studies Presented to Bernard M.W. Knox on the Occasion of His 65th Birthday*, eds G. W. Bowersock, W. Burkert and M. C. J. Putnam, 101–8, Berlin and New York, 1979.
Ebbott, M., 'The list of the war dead in Aeschylus' *Persians*', *Harvard Studies in Classical Philology*, 100 (2000): 83–96.
Ewans, M., *Aischylus*, The Oresteia, London, 1995.
Fagles, R., *Aeschylus*: The Oresteia, Harmondsworth, 1977.
Fisher, N., 'Violence, masculinity and the law in classical Athens', in L. Foxhall and J. Salmon (eds), *When Men were Men: Masculinity, Power and Identity in Classical Antiquity*, 68–97, London, 1998.
Flintoff, E., 'The unity of the "Persians" trilogy', *Quaderni urbinati di cultura classica*, n.s., 40 (1992), 67–80.
Foley, H. P., *Female Acts in Greek Tragedy*, Princeton, NJ, and Oxford, 2003.
Garland, R., *Surviving Greek Tragedy*, London, 2004.
Garland, R., *Athens Burning: The Persian Invasion of Greece and the Evacuation of Attica*, Baltimore, MD, 2017.
Garvie, A. F., 'Aeschylus' simple plots', in R. D. Dawe, J. Diggle and P. E. Eastering (eds), *Dionysiaca*, 63–86, Cambridge, 1978.
Garvie, A. F. (ed.), *Aeschylus*: Persae: *With Introduction and Commentary*, Oxford, 2009.
Gera, D., *Warrior Women: The Anonymous* Tractatus De Mulieribus, Leiden, 1997.
Gillis, D., *Collaboration with the Persians*, Wiesbaden, 1979.

Goldhill, S., 'Battle narrative and politics in Aeschylus' *Persae*', *Journal of Hellenic Studies*, 108 (1988), 189–93.

Graf, D., 'Medism: The origin and significance of the term', *Journal of Hellenic Studies*, 104 (1984), 15–30.

Greaves, A. M., J. B. Knight with F. Rutland, 'Milesian élite responses to Persia: The Ionian Revolt in context'. Available online: https://livrepository.liverpool. ac.uk/3086913/1/Milesian%20Responses%20to%20Persia%20ACCEPTED. pdf (accessed 24 March 2020).

Griffith, M., *The Authenticity of the* Prometheus Bound, Cambridge, 1977.

Griffith, M., 'The king and eye: The rule of the father in Aischylos' Persians', in M. Lloyd (ed.), *Oxford Readings in Aeschylus*, 93–140, Oxford, 2007.

Grube, G. M. A., *The Greek and Roman Critics*, London, 1968.

Gruen, E., *Rethinking the Other in Antiquity*, Princeton, NJ, 2010.

Hall, E., *Inventing the Barbarian: Greek Self-Definition through Tragedy*, Oxford, 1989.

Hall, E., 'Asia Unmanned: Images of victory in classical Athens', in J. W. Rich and G. Shipley (eds), *War and Society in the Greek World*, 107–33, London, 1993.

Hall, E., 'Drowning by nomes: The Greeks, swimming, and Timotheus' Persians', in H. A. Khan (ed.), *The Birth of the European Identity*, 44–80, Nottingham, 1994.

Hall, E., *Aeschylus:* Persians, Warminster, 1996.

Hall, E., 'Aeschylus' *Persians* via the Ottoman Empire to Saddam Hussein', in E. Bridges, E., Hall and P. J. Rhodes (eds), *Cultural Responses to the Persian Wars*, ch. 9, Oxford, 2007.

Hall, E., 'Actor's song in tragedy', in S. Goldhill and R. Osborne (eds), *Performance Culture and Athenian Democracy*, 96–122, Cambridge, 1999.

Hall, E., *Greek Tragedy*, Oxford, 2010.

Hall, E. (ed., trans. and comm.), *Aeschylus*, Persians, Warminster, 1996.

Halliwell, S., *Aristotle's Poetics*, London, 1986.

Halliwell, S., *The Poetics of Aristotle, translation and commentary*, London, 1987.

Hanink, J., *Lycurgan Athens and the Making of Classical Tragedy*, Cambridge, 2014.

Hanink, J., *Did Euripides Influence the Funeral Orators? Tragic Plots and the Catalogue of Exploits*, forthcoming.

Hanink, J. and Uhlig, A., 'Aeschylus and his afterlife in the classical period: "My poetry did not die with me"', in S. Constantinidis (ed.), *The Reception of Aeschylus' Plays through Shifting Models and Frontiers*, 51–79, Leiden, 2016.

Harper, P. O., Aruz, J. and Tallon, F. (eds), *The Royal City of Susa: Ancient Near Eastern Treasures in the Louvre*, New York, 1992.

Harrison, T., *The Emptiness of Asia: Aeschylus'* Persians *and the History of the Fifth Century*, London, 2000.

Harrison, T., *Writing Ancient Persia*, London and New York, 2011.

Harrison, T. (ed.), *Greeks and Barbarians*, Edinburgh, 2002.

Heller, J. (ed.), *Serta Turyniana*, Urbana, IL, 1974.

Henkelman, W., 'Xerxes, Atossa, and the Persepolis Fortification Archive', *Annual Report of the Netherlands Institute for the Near East Leiden/The Netherlands Institute in Turkey Istanbul* (2010), 26–33.

Herington, J., *Poetry Into Drama: Early Tragedy and the Greek Poetic Tradition*, Berkeley, 1985.
Hirsch, S. W., *The Friendship of Barbarians: Xenophon and the Persian Empire*, Hanover and London, 1985.
Holland, T., *Persian Fire: The First World Empire and the Battle for the West*, London, 2005.
Hopman, M., 'Layered stories in Aeschylus' *Persians*', in J. Grethlein and A. Rengakos (eds), *Narratology and Interpretation: Reading the Content of the Form*, 357–76, Berlin, 2009.
Hopman, M. G., 'Chorus, conflict, and closure in Aeschylus' *Persians*', in R. Gagné and M. G. Hopman (eds), *Choral Mediations in Greek Tragedy*, 58–77, Cambridge, 2013.
Hornblower, S., 'Warfare in ancient literature: The paradox of war', in P. Sabin, H. van Wees and M. Whitby (eds), *The Cambridge History of Greek and Roman Warfare, Volume 1: Greece, the Hellenistic World and the Rise of Rome*, 22–53, Cambridge, 2007.
Hunter, R. L., *Critical Moments in Classical Literature: Studies in the Ancient View of Literature and Its Uses*, Cambridge, 2009.
Hunter, R. L. and Russell, D., *Plutarch: How to Study Poetry (De audiendis poetis)*, Cambridge, 2011.
Kannicht, R., Snell, B. and Radt, S. (eds), *Tragicorum Graecorum Fragmenta*, Göttingen, 1971–2004.
Kousser, R., 'Destruction and memory on the Athenian Acropolis', *The Art Bulletin*, 91 (2009), 263–82.
Kowsari, A., *Euripides: Five Plays in Persian*, Vancouver, 2016.
Kuhrt, A., *The Persian Empire: A Corpus of Sources from the Achaemenid Period*, London, 2007.
Lattimore R., 'Aeschylus on the defeat of Xerxes', in K. Abbott (ed.), *Classical Studies in Honor of William Abbott Oldfather*, 82–93, Urbana, IL, 1943.
Librán Moreno, M., '*La skené en los fragmentos tragicos anteriores a la* Oresteia', *Myrtia*, 17 (2002), 57–85.
Librán Moreno, M., *Lonjas del Banquete de Homero: Convenciones Dramáticas en la Tragedia Temprana de Esquilo*, Huelva, 2005.
Llewellyn-Jones, L. and Robson, J., *Ctesias' History of Persia: Tales of the Orient*, London, 2009.
Llewellyn-Jones, L., 'Great Kings of the Fourth Century BCE and Greek Conceptions of the Persian Past', in J. Marincola, L. Llewellyn-Jones and C. McIver (eds), *Greek Notions of the Past in the Archaic and Classical Eras*, Edinburgh Leventis Studies, 317–46, Edinburgh, 2012.
Llewellyn-Jones, L., *King and Court in Ancient Persia, 559–331 BCE*, Edinburgh, 2013.
Llewellyn-Jones, L., 'Reviewing space, context and meaning: The Eurymedon vase again', in D. Rodriguez Perez (ed.), *New Studies in Greek Art*, 97–115, Oxford: Ashgate, 2017a.

Llewellyn-Jones, L., 'The Achaemenids', in T. Darayee (ed.), *King of the Seven Climes: A History of Ancient Iran*, 50–92, Irvine, CA, 2017b.

Llewellyn-Jones, L., 'The Royal *Gaunaka: Dress, identity, status and ceremony in Achaemenid Iran', in St-J. Simpson and S. Pankova (eds), *Scythians and Other Early Eurasian Nomads*, 248–57, Oxford, 2020.

Llewellyn-Jones, L., *Persians: The Age of the Great Kings*, London and New York, 2022.

LSJ, Liddell H. G. and R. Scott (compiled), Jones, Sir H. S. with the assistance of McKenzie, R. (revised and augmented), *Greek–English Lexicon*, Oxford, 1968.

Mackie, H., *Talking Trojan: Speech and Community in the Iliad*, Washington, DC, 1996.

Manousakis, N., *Prometheus Bound – A Separate Authorial Trace in the Aeschylean Corpus*, Trends in Classics, Supp. 98, Berlin, 2020.

Martin, B., *Harmful Interaction between the Living and the Dead in Greek Tragedy*, Liverpool, 2020.

McCall, M., 'Aeschylus in the *Persae*: A bold stratagem succeeds', in M. Cropp, E. Fantham and S. Scully (eds), *Greek Tragedy and Its Legacy: Essays Presented to D.J. Conacher*, 43–9, Calgary, 1986.

McClure, L., 'Maternal authority and heroic disgrace in Aeschylus' *Persae*', *Transactions of the American Philological Association*, 136 (2006), 71–97.

MedECC (Mediterranean Experts on Climate and Environmental Change), *Climate and Environmental Change in the Mediterranean Basin – Current Situation and Risks for the* Future, First Mediterranean Assessment Report (MAR1), 2016. Available online: https://www.medecc.org/wp-content/uploads/2020/11/MedECC_MAR1_2_Drivers.pdf (accessed 9 April 2022).

Meiggs, R., 'The political implications of the Parthenon', *Parthenos and Parthenon, Greece & Rome*, Supp. 10 (1963), 36–45.

Meiggs, R., *The Athenian Empire*, Oxford, 1972.

Meiggs, R. and Lewis, D., *Greek Historical Inscriptions to the End of the Fifth Century BC*, Oxford, 1969.

Michelini, A. N., *Tradition and Dramatic Form in the Persians of Aeschylus*, Leiden, 1982.

Mikellidou, K., 'Aeschylus reading Homer: The case of the Psychagogoi', in A. Efstathiou and I. Karamanou (eds), *Homeric Receptions across Generic and Cultural Contexts*, 331–42, Berlin, 2016.

Miller, M., 'The reception of Hesiod by the early pre-Socratics', in A. C. Loney and S. Scully (eds), *The Oxford Handbook of Hesiod*, 207–23, New York, 2018.

Miller, M. C., *Athens and Persians in the Fifth Century BC: A Study in Cultural Receptivity*, Cambridge, 1997.

Miller, M. C., 'Orientalism and ornamentalism: Athenian reactions to Achaemenid Persia', *Arts: Proceedings of the Sydney University Arts Association*, 28 (2006), 117–46.

Miller, M. C., 'Persians in the Greek imagination', *Mediterranean Archaeology*, 19/20 (2006/7), 109–23.

Mills, S., *Theseus, Tragedy and the Athenian Empire*, Oxford, 1997.
Mills, S., '*Ektos Sumphoras*: Tragic Athens', *Polis*, 34 (2017), 208–25.
Mills, S., *Drama, Oratory and Thucydides in Fifth-Century Athens: Teaching Imperial Lessons*, London and New York, 2020.
Moles, J., 'Herodotus warns the Athenians', *Papers of the Leeds International Latin Seminar*, 9 (1996), 259–84.
Momigliano, A. D., *Alien Wisdom: The Limits of Hellenization*, Cambridge, 1975.
Momigliano, A. D., *The Development of Greek Biography*, Cambridge, MA, 1993.
Moreau, A., 'Le Songe d'Atossa, *Perses*, 176–214: Éléments pour une explication de textes', *Cahiers du GITA*, 7 (1992–3), 29–51.
Morgan, J., *Greek Perspectives on the Achaemenid Empire: Persia through the Looking Glass*, Edinburgh, 2016.
Mousavi, A., *Persepolis: Discovery and Afterlife of a World Wonder*, Berlin, 2012.
Murray, G., *Aeschylus the Creator of Tragedy*, Oxford, 1940.
Nevin, S., *The Idea of Marathon: Battle and Culture*, London, New York and Dublin, 2022.
O'Reilly, K., *Aeschylus's Persians*, Morda, Oswestry, 2019.
Ogden, D., *Greek and Roman Necromancy*, Princeton, NJ, 2001.
Page, D. L., *Aeschyli septem quae supersunt tragoediae*, Oxford, 1972.
Papadimitropoulos, L., 'Xerxes' "hubris" and Darius in Aeschylus' *Persae*', *Mnemosyne*, 61 (2008), 451–8.
Pearson, M., *Site-Specific Performance*, Basingstoke, 2010.
Pelling, C., 'Aeschylus' *Persae* and history', in C. Pelling (ed.), *Greek Tragedy and the Historian*, 1–19, Oxford, 1997.
Petrounias, E., *Funktion und Thematik der Bilder bei Aischylos*, Göttingen, 1976.
Prickard, A. O., *The Persae of Aeschylus*, London, 1917.
Pickard-Cambridge, A. W., *The Dramatic Festivals of Athens*, 2nd rev. edn by J. Gould and D. M. Lewis, reissued with supplements and corrections, Oxford, 1988.
Podlecki, A. J., *The Political Background of Aeschylean Tragedy*, Ann Arbor, MI, 1966.
Podlecki, A. J., The Persians: *A Translation with Commentary*, Englewood Cliffs, NJ, 1970.
Podlecki, A. J., *Aeschylus* Persians, Bristol, 1991.
Price, M., *Mountains: A Very Short Introduction*, Oxford, 2015. Available online: http://scienceline.ucsb.edu/getkey.php?key=6432 (accessed 9 April 2022).
Prickard A. O., The Persae *of Aeschylus: Edited with Introduction, Notes, and a Map*, London, 1879.
Rabel, R. J., 'Suffering and learning in the *Oresteia*', in H. M. Roisman (ed.), *Encyclopedia of Greek Tragedy*, vol. 3, 1374–5, Chichester, 2014.
Radt, S., *Tragicorum Graecorum Fragmenta*, Vol. 3: *Aeschylus*, Göttingen, 1985.
Rehm, R., *The Play of Space: Spatial Transformation in Greek Tragedy*, Princeton, NJ, 2002.
Rehm, R., 'Aeschylus in the balance', in S. Constantinidis (ed.), *The Reception of Aeschylus' Plays through Shifting Models and Frontiers*, 131–46, Leiden, 2016.

Rich, J. and Shipley, G. (eds), *War and Society in the Greek World*, London and New York, 1993.
Roberts, J. T., *Accountability in Athenian Government*, Madison, WI, 1982.
Robertson, N., 'Aristeides' "brother"', *Zeitschrift für Papyrologie und Epigraphik*, 127 (1999), 172–9.
Roisman, H. M. (ed.), *Encyclopedia of Greek Tragedy*, 3 vols, Chichester, 2014.
Romm, J. S., 'Introduction and translation', in *The Greek Plays: Sixteen Plays by Aeschylus, Sophocles and Euripides*, 5–43, New York, 2016.
Rosenbloom, D., *Aeschylus: Persians*, London, 2006.
Rosenbloom, D., 'Aeschylus *Persians*', in H. M. Roisman (ed.), *The Encyclopedia of Greek Tragedy*, vol. 1, 46–54, Chichester, 2014.
Rosenmeyer, T. G., *The Art of Aeschylus*, Berkeley, CA, 1982.
Rouhani, F., *Persians*, Bethesda, MD, 1998.
Ruffy, M. V., 'Deixis am Phantasma in Aeschylus' Persae', *Quaderni Urbinati di Cultura Classics*, 78.3 (2004), 11–28.
Rung, E., 'The language of the Achaemenid imperial diplomacy towards the Greeks: The meaning of earth and water', *Klio*, 97 (2015), 503–15.
Russell, D. A. and Winterbottom, M., eds, *Classical Literary Criticism*, Oxford, 1989.
Sage, M. M., *Warfare in Ancient Greece: A Sourcebook*, London and New York, 1996.
Saïd, E., *Orientalism*, London, 1995.
Saïd, S., 'Darius et Xerxès dans les *Perses* d'Eschyle', *Ktema*, 6 (1981), 17–38.
Saïd, S., 'Tragedy and reversal: The example of the *Persians*', in M. Lloyd (ed.), *Oxford Readings in Classical Studies: Aeschylus*, 71–92, Oxford, 2007. Originally published in 1988 as 'Tragédie et renversement: L'exemple des *Perses*', *Mètis*, 3: 321–41.
Sampson, C. M., 'Aeschylus on Darius and Persian memory', *Phoenix*, 69, 1/2 (Spring–Summer 2015), 24–42.
Sancisi-Weerdenburg, H., 'Exit Atossa: Images of women in Greek historiography of Persia', in A. Cameron and A. Kuhrt (eds), *Images of Women in Antiquity*, 20–33, Detroit, MI, 1983.
Sancisi-Weerdenburg, H., 'Yauna by the sea and across the sea', in I. Malkin (ed.), *Ancient Perceptions of Greek Ethnicity*, 323–46, Cambridge, MA, 2001.
Sansone, D., 'The size of the tragic chorus', *Phoenix*, 70 (2016), 233–54.
Schenker, D., 'The Queen and the Chorus in Aeschylus' *Persae*', *Phoenix*, 48 (1994), 283–93.
Seaford, R., *Cosmology and the Polis: The Social Construction of Space and Time in the Tragedies of Aeschylus*, Cambridge, 2012.
Shepherd, W., *The Persian War: In Herodotus and Other Ancient Voices*, Oxford, 2020.
Sidgwick, A., *Aeschylus' Persae with Introduction and Notes*, Oxford, 1903.
Sier, K., 'Vorschläge zum Aischylos-Text', *Hermes*, 133 (2005): 409–23.
Skinner, J., *The Invention of Greek Ethnography: From Homer to Herodotus*, Oxford, 2012.
Smethurst, M. J., *The Artistry of Aeschylus and Zeami: A Comparative Study of Greek Tragedy and Nō*, Princeton, NJ, 1989.

Sommerstein, A. H., *Aeschylus*, 3 vols, Cambridge, MA, 2008.
Sommerstein, A. H., *Aeschylean Tragedy*, 2nd edn, London, 2010.
Sommerstein, A. H., 'The Persian War tetralogy of Aeschylus', in D. Rosenbloom and J. Davidson (eds), *Greek Drama IV: Texts, Contexts, Performance*, 95–107, Oxford, 2012.
Stevenson, R., *Persica: Greek Writing about Persia in the Fourth Century BC*, Edinburgh, 1997.
Stoneman, R., *Xerxes: A Persian Life*, New Haven, CT, and London, 2015.
Story, I., *Eupolis, Poet of Old Comedy*, Oxford, 2003.
Strasburger, H., 'Thucydides and the political self-portrait of the Athenians', trans. J. Rusten, in Rusten, *Thucydides: Oxford Readings in Classical Studies*, 191–219, Oxford, 2009. Originally published as, 'Thukydides und die Politische Selbstdarstellung der Athener', *Hermes*, 86 (1958), 17–40.
Stuttard, D., *Phoenix: A Father, a Son and the Rise of Athens*, Cambridge, MA, and London, 2021.
Taplin, O., *The Stagecraft of Aeschylus: The Dramatic Use of Exits and Entrances in Greek Tragedy*, Oxford, 1977.
Thalmann, W. G., 'Xerxes rags: Some problems in Aeschylus' *Persians*', *American Journal of Philology*, 101 (1980), 260–82.
Torrance, I., *Metapoetry in Euripides*, Oxford, 2013.
Tuplin, C., *Achaemenid Studies*, Stuttgart, 1996.
Uhlig, A., *Theatrical Reenactment in Pindar and Aeschylus*, Cambridge, 2019.
van Wees, H., *Greek Warfare: Myths and Realities*, London, 2004.
van Wees, H., 'War and society', in P. Sabin, H. van Wees and M. Whitby (eds), *The Cambridge History of Greek and Roman Warfare, Part I: Archaic and Classical Greece*, 273–300, Cambridge, 2007.
Vlassopoulos, K., 'The barbarian repertoire in Greek culture', *Ariadne*, 18 (2012), 53–88.
Vlassopoulos, K., *Greeks and Barbarians*, Cambridge, 2013.
West, M. L., *Introduction to Greek Metre*, Oxford, 1987.
West, M. L., *Iambi et elegi Graeci ante Alexandrum cantati: Callinus. Mimnermus. Semonides. Solon. Tyrtaeus. Minora adespota*, Oxford, 1972.
Wiesehöfer, J., *Ancient Persia*, trans. A. Azodi, London, 1978.
Wilamowitz-Moellendorff, U. von, 'Die Perser des Aischylos', *Hermes*, 32 (1897), 382–98.
Wilamowitz-Moellendorff, U. von, *Aischylos: Interpretationen*, Berlin, 1914.
Wiles, D., *Tragedy in Athens: Performance Space and Theatrical Meaning*, Cambridge, 1997.
Wilson, J. R., 'Territoriality and its violation in *The Persians* of Aeschylus', in M. Cropp, E. Fantham and S. Scully (eds), *Greek Tragedy and Its Legacy: Essays Presented to D.J. Conacher*, 51–7, Calgary, 1986.
Winnington-Ingram, R. P., *Studies in Aeschylus*, Cambridge, 1983a.
Winnington-Ingram, R. P., 'Zeus in *Persae*', in *Studies in Aeschylus*, 1–15, Cambridge, 1983b.

Wintjes, J., '"Keep the women out of the camp!": Women and military institutions in the classical world', in B. Hacker and M. Vining (eds), *A Companion to Women's Military History*, 15–59, Leiden, 2012.
Worman, N., *Tragic Bodies*, London, 2021.
Wright, M., *The Lost Plays of Greek Tragedy, Volume 1: Neglected Authors*, London and New York, 2016.
Wright, M., *The Lost Plays of Greek Tragedy, Volume 2: Aeschylus, Sophocles and Euripides*, London and New York, 2019.
Ziolkowski, J., *Thucydides and the Tradition of Funeral Speeches at Athens*, New York, 1981.

Index

[Aeschylus], *Prometheus Bound*,
   11, 15, 22
Abydos, 62
Achaemenes, 36
Achaemenids, 15–16, 21, 29, 32, 36,
   38, 41, 47
Achilles, 56, 73, 76, 79–83, 119, 158–9
Acropolis (Athenian), 2, 8, 17, 20, 27,
   59, 75, 100, 109
Aegisthus, 175
Aeschylus, *Agamemnon*, 6–7, 100,
   119, 121, 133, 138, 140, 157, 173,
   175
Aeschylus, *Choephoroi*, 5–6, 157, 175
Aeschylus, *Eumenides*, 6, 9, 100, 157
Aeschylus, *Glaucus*, 4–5
Aeschylus, *Libation Bearers* (*see*
   Aeschyus, *Choephoroi*)
Aeschylus, *Necromancers* (*see*
   Aeschylus, *Psychagogoi*)
Aeschylus, *Oresteia*, 4–6, 19, 47, 100,
   157, 173
Aeschylus, *Phineus*, 4–5
Aeschylus, *Prometheus*, 4–5
Aeschylus, *Proteus*, 100
Aeschylus, *Psychagogoi*, 158
Aeschylus, *Psychostasia*, 158
Aeschylus, *Suppliants*, 9
Aeschylus, *Weighing of the Spirits*
   (*see* Aeschylus, *Psychostasia*)
Aeschylus, *Women of Aetna*, 10
Afghanistan, 33, 177
Agamemnon, 6–7, 78, 80, 83, 100,
   119, 133, 157, 173–5
Ahura Mazda (*see* Ahuramazda)
Ahuramazda, 20, 33, 36
Alcaeus, 163
Alexander the Great, 10
Alexander historians, 33
Ameinias, 3

Amistres, 77, 87
Amphistreus, 95
Andromache, 83
Apadana, 15, 21
Apollo, 100, 137, 174
Ares, 80, 171
Argo, 5
Argonauts, 4
Argos, 132, 145, 173, 175
Aristophanes, 11, 21, 59, 163–4,
   166
Aristophanes, *Frogs*, 11, 59, 160, 163
Aristotle, 29, 85, 160, 164
Aristotle, *Poetics*, 85, 160, 164–5
Aristotle, *Rhetoric*, 165
Artabanus, 129
Artaphernes, 35, 77
Artaxerxes, 44
Artaxshaça (*see* Artaxerxes)
Artembares, 95, 155
Artemis, 1, 174
Artemision, 2
Asia, 1, 3–7, 16, 30–4, 48, 77, 79,
   87–9, 91–2, 95, 101–2, 104–6,
   109, 120, 122, 124, 151, 153, 169,
   171, 174
Asia Minor (*see* Asia)
Astaspes, 87
Ate,
Até, 6, 48, 80, 117
Athena, 6, 20, 80, 100, 110
Atossa, daughter of Aryaspes, 37–8
Atossa, mother of Xerxes (*see also*
   Queen), 2, 7, 9–10, 12, 37–8,
   49–50, 52–3, 55, 85–6, 93–4, 96,
   129–46, 151–2, 166–70,
   173
Attica, 2, 15, 45, 50, 106
Augustus, 118
Auletta, Robert, 11

Babylon, 32, 48
Bactria, 32
Banham, Simon, 183, 188
Bardiya, 37
Battle of Eurymedon, 56
Battle of Himera, 5, 10, 115
Battle of Lade, 17–18
Battle of Marathon, 2, 16, 18–19, 27, 30–1, 53–4, 63–4, 68, 117, 142, 165, 167
Battle of Mycale, 129
Battle of Plataea, 2, 5, 9, 53, 55, 65, 67, 75, 85, 103–4, 107–8, 120–1, 170
Battle of Salamis, 2–3, 5, 7, 9, 12, 16, 18–19, 21–2, 27, 34, 45, 47, 49–50, 52, 54, 56, 59, 65, 74, 78, 86–7, 90, 94, 101, 104–5, 108, 115–7, 120–1, 129–30, 139, 142, 145, 152, 167, 172, 180, 185
Battle of Stirling Bridge, 110
Boeotia, 104, 107
Bonaparte, Napoleon, 110
Bosporus, 4, 53, 101, 106, 143
Brecon Beacons National Park, 177
Broadhead, H. D., 110, 144
Brookes, Mike, 183, 188
Bush, George W., 11

Cambyses, 34, 37
Carlson, Marvin, 160
Carthage, 5
Carthaginians, 5
Cassandra, 157, 174–5
Catania, 10
Charon of Lampsacus, 35
Cilieni, 177–81, 183, 187
Cioffi, Robert, 157
City Dionysia, 4–5, 9, 15, 17–19, 21, 45, 66, 100, 109, 129, 165
Cleisthenes, 17, 19
Clytemnestra, 130, 132–3, 138, 146, 157–8, 160, 173–5
Crete, 67
Croesus, 16

Cyrus (II *aka* The Great), 16, 32, 35–7, 40, 53, 118, 131

Dadaces, 78, 95
daimon, 6, 39, 53, 62, 109–10,
Dārayavaush (*see* Darius)
Darius, 1–4, 9–11, 16–18, 20, 28–37, 39–40, 47–9, 53–5, 61–2, 65–7, 82, 85, 93–4, 96, 100–4, 106–7, 109–10, 117–19, 121, 123–4, 129, 131–46, 152–7, 159–60, 165–7, 169–70, 172–4, 179–84, 186–7
Darius Painter, 48
Datis, 118
Death (Kēr), 73
Delian League, 4, 19, 60, 65–6, 68
Delos, 118
Demaratus, 37
Democedes, 37
Diomedes, 80
Dionysus, 4, 9, 11, 21, 54, 163–4
Dionysus of Miletus, 34
Dodds, E. R., 110
Dorians, 39, 104, 107
dream (Atossa's), 7, 49, 62, 65, 82, 85, 94, 102, 119–20, 123, 131–8, 145, 152, 166–8, 185
Durrell, Lawrence, 100

earth and water, gifts of, 1, 17, 30,
Ecbatana, 32, 154
Edonians, 104
Egypt, 32, 100, 120
El Din, Hamza, 11
Elam, 32
Eleusis, 15, 106
Eos, 159
Epidaurus (*see* Epidavros)
Epidavros Festival, 5, 12
Eris (*see* Strife)
Eupolis, *Marikas*, 21
Euripides, 8, 17, 22, 40, 46, 163–5
Euripides, *Children of Heracles*, 68
Euripides, *Hecuba*, 159
Euripides, *Ion*, 46

Euripides, *Iphigenia Among the Taurians*, 40
Euripides, *Iphigenia at Aulis*, 133
Euripides, *Orestes*, 40
Euripides, *Suppliants*, 68

Falklands War, 5
First War of Scottish Independence, 110
Furies, 9, 157

Garvie, Alex, 86, 96, 121
Gelon, 10
ghost scene (in *Persians*), 6, 35–6, 53–5, 67, 85–6, 93, 100–3, 106–7, 109, 121, 132–3, 138, 140–1, 143, 152–3, 156, 170, 173, 186
Gulf of Oman, 33

Halicarnassus, 16
Hall, Edith, 20, 22, 35, 64, 79
Hamadan, 32
Hamlet, 8
Handel, *Serse*, 22
Hardy, John, 184, 188
Haxāmanish (*see* Achaemenes)
Haxāmanishiya (*see* Achaemenids)
Hector, 56, 74, 77, 80–3
Hecuba, 8, 83
Helen, 76, 174
Hellanicus of Lesbos, 34, 37
Hellespont, 2, 6, 53, 62, 88–9, 90–3, 101, 104–6, 119, 129, 143, 166, 170
Hephaestus, 73
Heracles, 34
Herodotus, 8, 15–20, 28, 31, 34–5, 37–9, 41, 61–3, 65–6, 81, 104, 120, 129, 145
Hesiod, *Theogony*, 90
Hieron, 10, 46
Hippias, 17
Hipponax, 163
Hitler, Adolf, 110
Homer, 8, 56, 62, 73–4, 76–83, 153, 158, 164–5, 173

Homer, *Iliad*, 73
Homer, *Iliadic Catalogue of Ships*, 77, 155
Homer, *Odyssey*, 158
Hornblower, Simon, 74
hubris, 4, 8, 36, 52–3, 55, 61–2, 67, 102, 111, 118, 132, 170, 174, 179
Hussein, Saddam, 179
hybris (*see* hubris)
Hyperbolus, 21

India, 28, 31, 33
Ionian Revolt, 1, 17, 28, 31, 35
Ionians, 28, 30, 39, 65–6
Iphigenia, 133
Isocrates, 29
Isthmus of Corinth, 3

Karadzic, Radovan, 182
Kēr (*see* Death)
Khshayathra (*see* Xerxes)
Kissia, 166, 172
Koniordou, Lydia, 12
Kowsari, Abdollah, 17, 22
Kudoimos (*see* Turmoil)
Kuh-e Rahmat, 33
Kūrush (*see* Cyrus)

Laurium, 2, 116
Libya, 33
Ligdanis, Dimitrios, 12
Lycurgus, 46
Lydia, 16–17, 92

Macedonia, 3
Magnesia, 104
Malian Gulf, 104
Mardonius, 129
Mardus, 35, 118
Matallus, 78, 95
McGrath, John, 177
McLaughlin, Ellen, 11
McSweeny, Ethan, 11
Mede(s), 1, 9, 15–16, 19, 27, 33, 35, 65, 116

Media, 82
Medos, 35, 53
Megabates, 77, 87
Memnon, 158–9
Menelaus, 174
Meskoub, Shahrokh, 22
Mesopotamia, 31
messenger speech, 2–3, 6, 50–3, 55, 64, 78–9, 81, 85, 87, 94–6, 100, 105–8, 116, 120–1, 123, 130, 132–3, 138–43, 145–6, 153–5, 167–9, 180, 185–6
Miletus, 1, 17–18
Miller, Margaret, 21, 40
Mimnermus, 163
Minotaur, 67
Moray, Andrew de, 110
Mount Aigaleos, 81
Mount Kithairon, 100
Mount Olympus, 99
Mount Tmolus, 92
Mussolini, Benito, 182

Naqsh-i Rustam, 33
National Actors Theater, 11
National Theatre Wales (NTW), 12, 177
necromancy scene (*see* ghost scene)
nemesis, 28, 179
Nineveh, 34
Ninus, 34
North Korea, 181

O'Reilly, Kaite, 177, 179
Odeion, 17, 21
Odeum (*see* Odeion)
Odysseus, 158, 173
omen of hawk and eagle, 134–5, 137, 167–8
Orestes, 100, 175
Otanes, 20

Page, D., 121
Pale, Kosovo, 182

Pan, 3
Paris, 174
Parthenon, 20
Pasargade, 32
Patroclus, 79, 81
Pearson, Mike, 12
Peloponnese, 31, 129
Pericles, 9, 19–20, 27, 45, 47, 75
Persepolis, 15, 21, 32–3, 37–8
Perses, 35, 120
Perseus, 35, 120
Persian War(s), 4–5, 7, 11, 15, 29, 34–5, 59, 61, 63–8, 166
Phineus, 4
Phrynichus, 1, 7–8, 17–19,
Phrynichus, *Capture of Miletus*, 2, 7–8, 17–18
Phrynichus, *Miletou Halôsis* (*see* Phrynichus, *Capture of Miletus*)
Phrynichus, *Phoenician Women*, 7–8, 18–19, 47
Phrynichus, *Phoenissae* (*see* Phrynichus, *Phoenician Women*)
phthonos, 50, 117
Plataea, 5, 100–1, 104
Plato, 29, 165
Plato, *Ion*, 165
Pollux, 159
Poseidon, 53, 93, 101, 118
Priam, 56, 81–2, 174
Proteus, 100
proskynesis, 10, 40, 109
Psyttaleia, 3, 52, 65, 101, 104, 107, 168, 172
Punjab, 33

Queen (*see also* Atossa), 6, 37, 40, 49, 52, 62, 64–5, 78, 82, 85, 94, 100, 102–3, 106, 109–10, 116–7, 119–20, 123–4, 129–30, 132, 134, 139, 145–6, 166–71, 179, 184–7
queens, 36–8, 55

River Asopos, 101, 104
River Indus, 33

River Scamander, 79
River Spercheios, 101, 104, 107
River Strymon, 62, 100–1, 108, 110, 169
Rouhani, Fuad, 22
Runcie, Robert, 5
Russia, 33, 110

Said, Edward, 20
Sappho, 163
Sardis, 1–3, 17, 28, 30, 48, 77, 129
Saronic Gulf, 52, 100–1, 104, 109
Sancisi-Weerdenburg, H., 145
Scythia, 4, 28
Sellars, Peter, 11
Semiramis, 37
Sennybridge, 180
Sennybridge Training Area (SENTA), 177
Shakespeare, William, 8
Sicilian Expedition, 120
Sidgwick, 131
Simonides, *Plataea Elegy*, 75
skene, 9, 47, 173, 183
Skills House, 182–3, 186, 188
Socrates, 165
Solon, 61, 65, 163
Sommer, Elysse, 11
Sommerstein, Alan, 109, 136
Sophocles, 46, 164
Sophocles, *Polyxena*, 159
Sparta, 4, 19, 21, 30, 65, 107, 164
Strife, 73
Susa, 3, 32–3, 47–8, 77, 109, 121, 129–30, 134, 151, 153
Syracuse, 46, 115

Taplin, Oliver,
Tarybis, 152
Temple of Cybele, Sardis, 1
Theatre of Dionysus, Athens, 8, 20, 27, 46, 75, 158, 163

Themistocles, 3, 18–19, 50, 63, 104, 115
Thermopylae, 2
Theseid, 66
Theseus, 66–7
Thessaly, 101, 107
Thrace, 100–1, 104, 108, 139, 169
Thucydides, 63, 74, 120
Timotheus of Miletus, 21
Tiresias, 158
Trojan War, 7, 73, 77–8, 82, 120, 158
Troy, 6, 8, 75, 77, 80, 82, 138, 173–4
Trozen, 66
Turmoil, 73
Tyre, 5

Udusana (*see* Atossa)

van Wees, Hans, 74
Vietnam, 110
Vincentelli, Elisabeth, 12

Wallace, William, 110
Wilamowitz-Moellendorff, U. von, 85, 138
Wiles, David, 88
Winnington-Ingram, R. P., 110

Xenophon, 29
Xerxes, 1–3, 6–7, 9–10, 16, 18–19, 21, 27, 29, 31–2, 34–7, 40, 45, 48–55, 60, 62–5, 58, 74, 77, 79–83, 85–96, 100–10, 115–21, 123–4, 129–46, 152–6, 165–75, 179–80, 182, 185–7
Xshayarashā (*see* Xerxes)

yoke metaphors, 48, 62, 65–6, 82, 89, 92–4, 101–3, 166

Zeus, 68, 78, 80, 99, 104, 110–11, 137, 153, 159, 170

www.ingramcontent.com/pod-product-compliance
Lightning Source LLC
Chambersburg PA
CBHW062127300426
44115CB00012BA/1844